D1441944

THE DUKE,
THE LONGHORNS,
AND CHAIRMAN MAO

THE DUKE, THE LONGHORNS, AND CHAIRMAN MAO

JOHN WAYNE'S POLITICAL ODYSSEY

Steven Travers

TAYLOR TRADE PUBLISHING
Lanham • Boulder • New York • Toronto • Plymouth, UK

Published by Taylor Trade Publishing
An imprint of Rowman & Littlefield
4501 Forbes Boulevard, Suite 200, Lanham, Maryland 20706
www.rowman.com

10 Thornbury Road, Plymouth PL6 7PP, United Kingdom

Distributed by NATIONAL BOOK NETWORK

British Library Cataloguing in Publication Information Available
Library of Congress Cataloging-in-Publication Data
Travers, Steven.
  The Duke, the Longhorns, and Chairman Mao : John Wayne's
political odyssey / Steven Travers.
     pages cm
  Includes bibliographical references, filmography and index.
  ISBN 978-1-58979-897-7 (cloth : alk. paper) — ISBN 978-1-58979-898-4
(electronic) 1. Wayne, John, 1907–1979. 2. Motion picture actors and
actresses—United States—Biography. 3. Southern California Trojans
(Football team) 4. Texas Longhorns (Football team) I. Title.
  PN2287.W454T73 2014
  791.4302'8092—dc23
  [B]

                                        20130485

∞™The paper used in this publication meets the minimum
requirements of American National Standard for Information
Sciences—Permanence of Paper for Printed Library Materials,
ANSI/NISO Z39.48-1992.

Printed in the United States of America

To two great Trojans, Bruce and Heath Seltzer

CONTENTS

ACKNOWLEDGMENTS

I CAME UP WITH THE IDEA OF WRITING THIS BOOK IN 2005 WHEN I WAS researching *One Night, Two Teams: Alabama vs. USC and the Game That Changed a Nation.* In particular when I interviewed former University of Southern California football broadcasters Tom Kelly and Mike Walden, as well as ex-Trojans quarterback and assistant coach Craig Fertig, they kept referring to John "Duke" Wayne's amazing weekend at Austin, Texas, in 1966. So, right off the bat I must thank Tom, Mike, and Craig. Unfortunately Craig Fertig is no longer with us.

I suppose I had known John Wayne was a Trojan, perhaps from reading Don Pierson's *The Trojans: Southern California Football,* a gift from my wonderful dad on Christmas Day 1974, but it was a high school baseball teammate of mine, prep all-American and straight-A student Jim Connor, who further brought Wayne's persona home to me.

Jim may have been leaning toward Stanford, where his older brother played football, when he made his recruiting visit to USC, attending a celebrity softball game at Dedeaux Field. Jim found himself sandwiched in between *The Odd Couple,* Jack Lemmon and Walter Matthau (promoting *The Bad News Bears*), who, perhaps urged on by coach Rod Dedeaux, gave a sell job for USC.

"How could you go anyplace else?" he recalled them asking him. All the while, the most famous cowboy in America, John Wayne, was riding its most famous steed, Traveler, around the baseball field. Indeed, Jim agreed to go to USC. Enthralled not only by USC's academic pedigree, tradition, and national champion baseball program, he was equally mesmerized, as so many before and since have been, by the mystique of USC, which I always equated with an early scene in *Patton*. A Moroccan monarch asks General George Patton, played by George C. Scott, for his impressions of his country.

"I love it Your Excellency," he replies. "It's a combination of the Bible . . . and Hollywood!"

To me, this always described USC; on the one hand, a traditional, high-character institution that once offered Methodist religious instruction, yet, on the other, home to numerous celebrities and children of movie producers, directors, agents, and screen stars. Indeed, when I arrived on campus, there was a rumor that Tom Cruise was enrolling but never did because *Risky Business* suddenly made him a star. I recall another old high school teammate-turned-Trojan baseball player named Mickey Meister, who greeted me at an off-campus watering hole dubbed "The 502 Club" in the company of a pretty girl he introduced as Jennifer. He then leaned into my ear and further declared, "As in Jennie Nicholson, Jack's daughter." That was how it was all the time at the University of Southern California. With very few exceptions, this is a unique aspect of USC's appeal and perhaps a siren song attracting Jim Connor, as it attracted so many others.

I can recall years later attending a meeting at the famed William Morris Agency in Beverly Hills with Magic Johnson's agent, Lon Rosen, to discuss the film potential of *One Night, Two Teams: Alabama vs. USC and the Game That Changed a Nation*. There were eight people seated around a large desk. Every one of us was a Trojan. This is the way it still is; production companies, talent agencies, and studios often seem to be an extension of the USC campus.

But it was John Wayne's Trojan persona that really came alive for me when I enrolled at the school. I went to the bookstore to purchase my class books and supplies when I saw Ken Rappoport's *The Trojans: A Story of Southern California Football* on a prominent table. I bought it and well recall reading it cover to cover in my student apartment during hot, smoggy, late August days before the fall semester began. I was struck by two chapters, "Time Out: John Wayne" and "Hooray for Hollywood," both delving into Wayne's involvement with the school as well as the larger role of the film industry, which, along with USC and the city of Los Angeles, grew, magnificently and monumentally, side by side in the twentieth century.

The Wayne chapter had an awesome photo of young Marion Morrison, his given name before taking on the stage character John Wayne (his nickname "the Duke" actually came from his childhood), as a young lineman playing for the legendary Howard "Head Man" Jones in the 1920s. I was struck by great pride that this legendary American hero had once been an undergraduate at the same university I was now attending. I particularly enjoyed Rappoport's interview with Nick Pappas, an ex-Trojans football player as well as good friend and fraternity brother of the Duke. In his chapter on Wayne, Rappoport details through Pappas the actor's speech to coach John McKay's football team prior to the opener of the 1966 season at the University of Texas. Little did I know then that this speech would be the centerpiece of my twentieth published book. Little did I know then that I would even become a professional writer.

Surely, looking with admiration at the place Rappoport's book held on a table of distinction near the entrance to the USC Bookstore, had somebody then told me someday I too would have my own table of distinction in that same store, displaying with the publication of this my sixth book on USC history and Trojans football; that I would make speeches to Trojan alumni, parents, and students; that I would sign autographs at the Los Angeles Memorial Coliseum; that football coach Pete Carroll would call me "the next great USC historian"; and that the Annenberg School for Communication and Journalism (where I have been a guest speaker for seven years) would describe me as "USC's athletic department biographer"—well, as you could imagine, I would have taken that, then and there.

I knew when I set foot on the USC campus and began my journey as a student that this school of such mystique and prestige would lead me on a magical journey. I could not predict in my wildest dreams what that journey would be. I met my wife on that campus and today show my daughter, Elizabeth, landmarks of my time there.

My "John Wayne connection" did not begin or end with Jim Connor's story or Ken Rappoport's book. My good friend and fellow USC alum Jeff Cole once lived in a beautiful home with a dock on Balboa Bay in Newport Beach. Once visiting there, I was told that Jeff's home once belonged to Jimmy Cagney's brother and that the house some three doors down had belonged to Wayne, who would take Cagney and others out on the bay for ribald parties better left to the imagination.

My love of USC also led me beyond Rappoport's book to the writings of Braven Dyer, John Hall, Mal Florence, Jim Murray, and others who told colorful tales of the Duke and Trojan lore of yesteryear. In particular, I found that Loel Schrader and Steve Bisheff often wrote of Wayne's USC loyalty, and their fabulous book *Fight On! The Colorful Story of USC Football* (2006) is one of the best ever written on the subject. These works proved invaluable in research I have already conducted, particularly on John Wayne stories from my books *The USC Trojans: College Football's All-Time Greatest Dynasty, What It Means to Be a Trojan: Southern Cal's Greatest Players Talk about Trojans Football,* and *The Poet: The Life and* Los Angeles Times *of Jim Murray.*

Many of the people I met at USC, then and over the years, are due much in the way of thanks, for this book as well as the upward mobility of my career. Once upon a time, things looked low for me, my dreams seemingly unattainable, but always I adhered to the long-held Trojan motto "Fight on!" So I did.

Early on, I met Jim Perry, who brought me in as a volunteer in the school's sports information office and is due thanks for helping me with *One Night, Two Teams: Alabama vs. USC and the Game That Changed a Nation.* In 1983, I also met Tim Tessalone, who succeeded Jim and with his staff has granted me every possible request for assistance over the years. Thanks also to the great Dr. Andrew Casper, whose class on film history and appreciation I scored an A in at USC, providing the first fertile seeds of creative inspiration that later became a journalism career. Thanks also to Rosemary DiSano, Veronica Callejas, and Cecil Brown of the USC Bookstore; to former head coach Pete Carroll; to assistant athletic director John K.

McKay; to Murray Scholars counselor Jabari Brown and Mrs. Linda McCoy-Murray; and especially to my good friend Professor Dan Durbin, who has invited me to address his class "Sports, Culture and Society" since 2006 while beginning an entire sports media division at Annenberg. Dan's class has been a major source of all-around support for my research and endeavors.

I want to thank many people for their generous sharing of time and memories, the seeds of this particular story. Further thanks are due the Trojan Football Alumni Club, Ambrose Schindler, Frank Gifford, C. R. Roberts, Adrian Young, Willie Brown, Trudi Fertig, Todd Marinovich, Rod Sherman, Bill Fisk, Mike Battle, Tim Rossovich, Steve Sogge, Bill "Spaceman" Lee, Tom Seaver, George Lucas, John Milius, Tom Selleck, Ron Yary, John Papadakis, Manfred Moore, Charles "Tree" Young, Pat Haden, Allan Graf, John Robinson, Paul Hackett, Dave Levy, Patricia Goux, Scott Schrader, Art Spander, Bruce Jenkins, Cherie Kerr, Dwight Chapin, Garry Paskewitz, Pete Arbogast, Don Andersen, Jason Pommier, Kerry McCluggage, Matt McCluggage, Barry Kemp, Paul Goldberg, the John Wayne Birthplace, the Western Heritage Museum, and the University of Texas sports information office.

Thanks also to Amanda Tinkham Boltax, George Ambrose, Chuck Arrobio, Nick Arrobio, Ron Schwary, Pua McGinness, Betty McCartt, Ethan Wayne, Patrick Wayne, Aissa Wayne, Jeff Bitetti, Justin Dedeaux, Mike Garrett, Bill McCoy, Sam Tsagalakis, Robert Klein, Scott Ostler, Bill Dwyre, Fred Wallin, Ross Newhan, Claude Zachary, Steve Hanson, Shirley Ito, Elizabeth Daley, Dr. Richard Jewell, Professor Dave Edwards, Professor David Prindle, Stephen Harrigan, Brian Downes, Steve Grady, Fred Dryer, Dick Cook, Joe Jares, Bob Case, Bill Little, John Bianco, Francis Ford Coppola, the late Jeff Prugh, and late coach John McKay.

I would be most remiss indeed if I did not mention two of my mentors, the late, great Bud Furillo and Maury Allen. Thanks to two great Trojans and friends, Kevin McCormack and Terry Marks; to my pal Mike McDowd (who originally suggested some years ago I write a book about the Duke's relationship with his alma mater); and to the awesome Jake Downey, who may root for the Bruins but has the nobility of a Trojan. He also played a major role in selecting this book's title. This could not have been possible without my publisher (of five books now, not including paperback reprints) and friend Rick Rinehart. Thanks to Karie Simpson, Bruce Owens, and Jehanne Schweitzer of Taylor Trade.

Thanks as always to my agent in Hollywood, Lloyd Robinson (USC, 1964) of Suite A Management in Beverly Hills, and to my literary representative (and big USC fan) Ian Kleinert of Objective Entertainment in New York City.

Thanks to my great mom, Ingeborg Travers, and my fabulous daughter, Elizabeth Travers Lee, as well as the memory of the best father in all of human history, Donald Travers, along with my Lord and Savior, Jesus Christ.

I love hearing from readers with all opinions and observations, so reach out to me at my Web page at www.redroom.com/member /steven-robert-travers or e-mail me at USCSTEVE1@aol.com.

AMERICA,
WHY I LOVE HER

AMERICA, IN THE FIRST HALF OF THE TWENTIETH CENTURY, INDEED, FOR
sixteen more years right on up to September 17, 1966, the date of
the college football season opener pitting the University of Southern California Trojans on the road against the Texas Longhorns,
was John Wayne's America. It was his country in spirit, in action,
in politics, in war, and in peace. It was a nation Wayne loved, and
she loved him right back, unconditionally on both ends of the spec-
trum. It was a nation that offered Wayne a free lunch, a parade, a
tribute, a debt of thanks, gratitude, and honor from one end of the
Fruited Plain to another.

Today, we live in an entirely different world and nation. Seemingly all that John Wayne once stood for has been refuted by a large
segment of society, certainly by most of the media, by his beloved
Hollywood, and by political elements. Those who believe in Wayne's
America are viewed as "bitter clingers" or other pejoratives.

The question is, How did this happen? When did this happen?
Using September 17, 1966, as the date certain of a "turning point"
is futile on the one hand but, on further inspection, commonsensi-
cal. Man can trace many events that have shaped modern society,
often via direct turnabout away from previous status quos. The Greek

philosophers advocated a pursuit of truth as the bedrock of democracy. The Romans appeared to have formed a republic in the Greek model until a leader assumed dictatorial powers, a cult of personality. They subsequently turned from the values that made them great, becoming beyond immoral: depraved. Yet their wives espoused the values of the man the empire killed, Jesus Christ, forcing their husbands to abandon orgies and child sex, to instead treat them with respect. Thus did an empire crumble and a religion grow.

The Spanish Inquisition began 500 years of brutal colonization. Out of this grew the slave trade and a forced Christianity that, while growing billions of believers, also turned millions away from traditionalism. The British Empire ruled over the dark-skinned peoples of the earth. The French became the face of white brutality. Then America was forged into being.

Thus a conundrum. On the one hand, America was the picture of anticolonization. Their language of "all people being created equal" resonated among all races. They were the country where slavery came to die, a thriving institution as old as man itself, unable to survive the words of the U.S. Constitution. Hundreds of thousands of white American citizens freely volunteered to fight—and die—so that blacks of African origin could be free. If anybody had predicted four score and seven years prior to this event or even four years and seven days prior to it, they would have been considered daft. It was an impossible concept, and yet it happened as surely as the sun will come up tomorrow. There are many who believe that only the hand of God involving Himself in the affairs of man could make such a thing happen, but as Jesus says in the Gospel according to Matthew, "With men this is impossible, but with God all things are possible."

The union secure, a nation then took its place among global powers. An industrial revolution was forged, and out of this a strange "competition" to determine who would "win" this revolution. Germany, long united by a common language but divided by tribal affiliation, became unified and joined forces with the political winners of post-Napoleonic Europe, the Austro-Hungarian Empire. Seeing the future—oil—they aligned with the Ottoman Empire and embarked on world domination, a quest in which their main competition came from the United States and Great Britain, old rivals now allied by common purpose. Waiting in the wings: Russia and Japan. Two world wars followed.

John Wayne and patriotic American citizens like him view these events in much the same way. They saw a small group of agrarian colonies, separated by an ocean from the salons of political power, commerce, and military might. They saw her grow, a promised land of opportunity and prosperity dotted with biblical names like Bethel, New Canaan, and Bethlehem. They saw her meet the challenge of ending slavery, then tip the scale in favor of democracy in World War I. They saw her enter a decade of isolationism and pacifism, followed by a Great Depression in which her military was reduced to training using brooms instead of guns, so weak that dictators decided this was that key moment in world history in which to strike and ultimately "win" the long struggle for industry, technology, oil, and, with it, global conquest.

They saw her dragged into a Satanic conflagration of good versus evil by a sneak attack, her unprepared soldiers vulnerable to devastation, her coastlines unprotected, the prospect of one enemy driving to Chicago before he could be realistically stopped, a stronger enemy poised to devour all before her from the east.

Then, at least in the worldview of John Wayne and millions like him, a miracle. A miracle in the form of God Himself, favoring this promised land, this beautiful nation, this "shining city on a hill," just as surely as He once favored the Israelites. Yes, and just in the nick of time, too, did God strengthen America, making her powerful enough, moral enough, to rise up in what President Franklin D. Roosevelt called her "righteous anger" to assume the role of "Christian soldiers," to oppose and defeat evil—Satan's armies in the form of Nazi Germany and Hideki Tojo's Japan. The dropping of atomic bombs was viewed as proper retribution by a favored people given, as if in the hands of Zeus, God-like power.

But these patriots were taught by a thousand Sunday sermons that evil never dies, it just changes form, and to always be on the lookout, vigilant of its presence and form. For John Wayne's America, it was obvious what that form now looked like: international communism. For Wayne himself, this was his war. He had opted out of service in World War II for reasons that have been disputed by his supporters and detractors but, for whatever reason, justified in his mind perhaps that he could do more good by uplifting morale through the making of patriotic war films. Most loved the films and credited them for doing just that. A minority then, growing now, felt otherwise.

But communism was on his front, Hollywood. It became his cause, his quest, his Holy Grail. The 1950s were a jingoistic, patriotic period of American history, at least for white people, Republicans, and John Wayne types. A Cold War became hot, Korea its proxy, and, after that, escalation and more proxies in the so-called Third World, an unaligned global battleground of mostly dark-skinned peoples, often in colonized countries.

The great deliverer of the twentieth century, the man who led the Crusade in Europe, to quote the name of President Dwight Eisenhower's book, identified Vietnam as the next "hot spot," tacitly endorsing the view that if one nation fell to atheistic communism, others would similarly fall in a "domino theory." Cold Warriors Richard Nixon, John F. Kennedy, and Lyndon B. Johnson bought this theory, propelling America into this conflict, a "final effort" to destroy communism—lost in the wake of General Douglas MacArthur's firing after Inchon and the Chinese incursion of Korea— once and for all.

But John Wayne heard voices. He had heard these voices in the past. They were easily identified, vilified: "Red Emma" Goldman, Tokyo Rose, Ezra Pound, and Alger Hiss. Marginalized, convicted, and imprisoned. Yet now he heard a chorus rising in opposition to the Vietnam War. To him and those of like mind, such a chorus was no less traitorous, no less shameful, no less cowardly. Thus did John Wayne confront these voices as 1966 came and, amid consequential international events, pushed inexorably toward 1967.

The people Wayne identified as traitorous, shameful, and cowardly heard voices, too. They had been hearing those voices for a long time. They started as whispers but were growing louder. The voices they heard were called world history. Increasingly, the most educated, spoiled generation in American history, freed by the "greatest generation" to prosper economically and gain postwar college educations in numbers previously unimagined, were listening to professors and political figures telling them world history, John Wayne's history, was a lie.

Christianity, particularly Catholicism, was painted as an archaic religion meant to keep women and the poor in their place. It was sadistic, violent and racist, embodied by the Spanish Inquisition. Fyodor Dostoevsky's *The Brothers Karamazov* was dusted off, new meaning given Dostoevsky's words, and with it accusation of Catholicism.

Discredited revolutions were glorified. The French Revolution, given voice first by Jean-Jacques Rousseau's *The Social Contract*, was now viewed as a call to arms by the left, the oppressed proletariat of centuries. One hundred twenty years of European revolution followed, with virtually all post-Napoleonic countries rising up in one form or another in 1848. Out of this, new thinking: Karl Marx's *Communist Manifesto*. In 1917, Russia's communist revolution.

"Red Emma" Goldman and John Reed found favor in communism and anarchism. The director of the Federal Bureau of Investigation, their nemesis J. Edgar Hoover, was considered an anticommunist hero but increasingly an oppressor by the left. The writings of Upton Sinclair propelled socialism and the union movement, giving rise to these concepts in the Great Depression. To the left, it was only the "distraction" of World War II that diverted the egalitarianism of these movements, replaced by John Wayne jingoism. They felt further that only the violence and terror of global war had divided America from its "ally," the Soviet Union, causing unnecessary hatred and suspicion that could finally be abated when "reasonable" people eventually took over on both sides.

But it was the Cold War that sowed the seeds of American domestic division, increasingly leading to the cataclysmic 1960s. First, there was Alger Hiss. He was a hero of the Democratic Party, an urbane, sophisticated Harvard lawyer, New Dealer, and high-ranking aide to President Roosevelt whose influence was keenly felt during formation of the United Nations, which abandoned Eastern Europe to Joseph Stalin. Hiss was a paid, true-believer communist spy, exposed by a rumpled ex-communist, Whittaker Chambers, who identified him as his handler. Even more infuriatingly, Hiss's conviction empowered the Red-baiting, overripe California conservative

Richard Nixon. The left wept and gnashed their teeth as Nixon's star rose against all their protestations, from Congress to the Senate to the White House. Priority one: destroy Nixon and, in so doing, all he stood for.

This became the great quest of liberal America, an overriding obsession that, like all obsessions, comes with blinders. Those blinders required that a lie be lived as if a truth. The best way to propel a lie is to create an alternate past. Their tools: the media, academia, and Hollywood. Goal one was to rehabilitate Hiss.

This is a telling tale of the human condition. When a person or a collective people places all their faith, all their hopes, and all their effort into a cause, when they invest every ounce of their energy into something they fervently believe in only to have such a thing exposed as a fraud, what do they do?

When confronted by guilt, by facts, and by truth, does one confess in shame, turn from past sins, ask forgiveness, and seek a righteous path? This is the essence of Christian salvation, the great balm of Jesus Christ. Millions have found the Way through centuries of bondage to sinfulness.

The *New York Times* chose another path. They were Alger Hiss's greatest cheerleaders. A decision was made. They had backed this horse. It was calculated that to divest themselves of all they so fervently had stood for would be too great a fall from grace. A long march was embarked on, articles spanning years, then decades, explaining Hiss's innocence, the lies of the rumpled Chambers, and the deviousness of "Tricky Dick" Nixon. Chambers became a conservative hero, his best-selling *Witness* (1952) and Nixon's ascent grating on the very souls of these Ahabs.

Then a Great White Whale even greater than Chambers and Nixon: Senator Joe McCarthy. Built on the back of Nixon's House Un-American Activities Committee and Hiss's conviction, then Democratic President Harry Truman's "failure" to save China from the Reds and prevent the Soviets from exploding their own atomic bomb and the firing of MacArthur that led to stalemate in Korea, McCarthy rose as a real-life accuser so hated and horrible on a grand scale that only literature did him justice: Javert of *Les Misérables* and the Grand Inquisitor of *The Brothers Karamazov*.

McCarthy's premise was that communist spies and "fellow travelers" had infiltrated America. They had subverted our way of life. They were in politics, the administration, the military, the diplomatic corps, the spy services, the schools, the movies, and our very homes, a monstrous "conspiracy so immense" as to dwarf all previous enemies ranging from Hitler to Hirohito. It was portrayed as a kind of malevolence so all-encompassing that only Original Sin could explain or be compared to it.

Some of the most hated organs of this so-called conspiracy—the media, Hollywood, and the universities—began to rebut McCarthy. By the late 1950s and early 1960s, this campaign was under way: for the *New York Times*, the Hiss template; for Hollywood, backlash against the Blacklist beginning with *The Sweet Smell of Success* (a diatribe against the anticommunist columnist Walter Winchell, a stand-in painted as an incestuous monster) and *Advise and Consent* (fictionalized, with Burgess Meredith as a daft, unbelievable Chambers and Henry Fonda as the heroic Hiss); and, in 1962, with *The Manchurian Candidate*, which is arguably anticommunist yet depicts a McCarthyite character as utterly drunk, stupid, and reprehensible. These were accompanied by films glorifying left-leaning sensibilities. In *Spartacus* (1960), the Roman Empire is viewed as a metaphor for an oppressive United States. In *Seven Days in May* (1964), right-wing militarists threaten a coup against a peace-loving liberal president. *Dr. Strangelove* (1964) depicts war-loving generals leading us into nuclear Armageddon.

A few select universities, most notably the University of California, Berkeley, in the West; Columbia University in the East; and, to a much lesser extent, the University of Michigan in the Midwest, began to radicalize in the form of rejecting sports dominance (California) while embracing alternative life choices manifesting themselves in certain nearby city centers: New York's Greenwich Village and San Francisco's North Beach.

In the late 1950s and early 1960s, poets, pacifists, artists, musicians, homosexuals, radicals, and communists rejected bourgeois capitalism, forming a movement that started as the beats, then the beatniks, and then the hippies and eventually would combine forces with rock-and-roll music to form the antiwar movement, which,

while still small, was a growing chorus of great concern to the John
Waynes of the world by 1966.

Beyond all of this, beyond the shores of the United States, was
the Third World, and perhaps this was the most simmering of pent-
up hatreds, for here was the entire history of mankind rolled up
into one festering twentieth-century resentment. Here was the great
conflict, the clash of civilizations and cultures marking all of human
experience. Since the Greeks defeated the Persians and the Romans
consolidated Asia Minor, European Christianity had on the backs of
these events ascended as the dominant religious, political, cultural,
and militarized power on earth. The British Empire was built on
trade. The industrial revolution required the plundering of natural
resources in order to fuel the commerce of a new, gilded age. The
United States stood in the most advantageous position; it had greater
size, unlimited economic potential, and its own natural resources
in order to fuel itself. Other global powers had to colonize in order
to get at the natural resources of countries populated with Africans,
Asians, Indians, and islanders. By the 1960s, with the French having lost in Vietnam and the Middle East; England's empire having
disintegrated, its political will a thing of the past; and the Arab con-
solidation of World War I increasingly becoming nationalized, these
plundered regions were proxies of the Soviet Union and hotbeds of
radical, racial animosity toward white Europeans. Since they represented the dominant world power, the United States found herself,
despite her anticolonial policies and flowery constitutional language,
a greater target of this radicalism, which was increasingly spilling onto
her shores. The communists had long endeavored to use race as a
stepping-stone against the West. By the 1960s, this strategy was in full
force.

In 1962, the Cuban missile crisis fueled liberal sentiment
against traditional notions of militaristic valor. Those days were
long gone. A push-button age was upon us and with it a monstrous
immorality. In 1964, President Lyndon Johnson's Great Society consolidated the left into the Democratic Party. The Republicans, marginalized by McCarthyism, were viewed as extremist. Johnson won in
a landslide, but he embarked on an escalation of the Vietnam War,

from a "police action" requiring only advisers and select Special Forces into a full-scale ground war by 1965–1966.

Also building was the increasing notion, embodied by Roosevelt's New Deal and Johnson's Great Society, already fully embraced by Europe, that only government could solve the problems of the world. Perhaps this view most thoroughly began to manifest itself after World War I, when British economist John Maynard Keynes crafted the economic model of European reconstruction. At the heart of Keynesianism was the view that in a new industrial age of mechanized war, in which destruction dwarfed the effects of all previous conflicts, only something as monolithic as government, albeit even world government, had the capacity to handle such tasks. Any kickback against this philosophy was dealt a severe blow by a second world war some twenty years later, followed by the Marshall Plan and Soviet expansion. The old days of private competition fueling something like the transcontinental railroad were replaced by government projects ranging from highways to bridges to the space race. Once-aristocratic countries like France had already completely turned their back on their old traditions, choosing instead existential thought, radical socialism, and immorality on a grand scale.

Thus was the stage set for confrontation by 1966. There was the world of John Wayne, taken so for granted by a generation or more of God-fearing American traditionalists comfortable in their Tocquevillean wombs, versus this strange new brew of protestors, radicals, and "others" representing something very alien to the traditionalists.

In 1966, the war was beginning to go badly. General William Westmoreland was telling the American public and President Johnson that we were winning. We were not, and while a majority—including Wayne—still believed we were winning, the numbers who believed otherwise were growing exponentially, their voices gaining strength.

Wayne supported the Vietnam War all the way. He believed it was a test of American honor to stand up to and defeat Godless communism. He made a recording called *America, Why I Love Her* in response to that chorus of unrelenting voices he viewed as unpatriotic. He believed in their right to dissent, that the war had been fought for and won with blood, and expressed such sentiments along with a series of highly patriotic, emotional, and loving tributes to all aspects of traditional Americana, some militaristic.

"My hope and prayer is that everyone know and love our country for what she really stands for," Wayne wrote on the album's cover. Many did, but many just believed then and now that such sentiments were merely covering up immoralities such as racism, greed, and hegemonistic violence. The idea Wayne expressed—that there is such a thing as American exceptionalism and that in so stating this he endorses the notion not only that we have done greater things than any other nation but also that God has favored us in this endeavor—perhaps infuriates the left more than any proposition.

1

LITTLE DUKE

JOHN WAYNE WAS A PRODUCT NOT ONLY OF HIS ENVIRONMENT AND HIS background but also a reaction to it.

"The Scotch-Irish, we're tribal people," said former University of Alabama all-American and New England Patriots Hall of Fame football star John Hannah. "Scotch-Irish aren't feudal; they don't like government interfering with their rights," adding that while the "liberal media never believes this," such people do the "right thing on our own given the chance to do it our way." The Scotch-Irish were the dominant ethnic heritage of most southerners, who thought themselves misunderstood in their civil rights stance during the 1960s, as well as for midwesterners like the Wayne clan.

"I'm just a Scotch-Irish little boy," Wayne told a Hollywood reporter in the 1950s.

Like many Scotch-Irish, John Wayne always tried to do the "right thing." He too found himself the target of the "liberal media," who sometimes ascribed in his actions and opinions an accusation, implying his way was not the right way during the Vietnam War, also in the 1960s. Wayne believed in doing the right thing on his own, without prompting, spurred only by his benevolent desire to do so. He felt misunderstood and always had. He stubbornly persisted without complaint. It had always been that way.

Wayne's mother Molly did not like him. She apparently never liked him. There does not appear to be any explanation for this odd psychosis, for he was lovable, ambitious, smart, handsome, athletic, and dutiful and a very good son. His reaction to this lifelong rejection by his own mother was not unlike his reaction to the liberal media: he suffered it. Like those independent cowboys forging a new life in the Old West of his movies, he just trudged onward, absorbing the slings and arrows of outrageous fortune with quiet dignity.

For reasons that equally make no sense, Molly immediately loved his younger brother Bobby more than him. Bobby was born on December 18, 1912, when Wayne was five. Wayne rode by train from Keokuk, Iowa, to Earlham, with his father Clyde, to meet his new little brother. He was excited and proud. Upon arrival, he ran toward the bed, where Molly held her infant baby. His shoes were wet from the snow. When he reached the bed, he grabbed the metal headboard. This caused a slight electric shock, which irritated Molly.

Improbable as this sounds, this could have "sparked" her lifelong dislike of her elder son, but apparently she already decided to hurt him by stealing something precious from him. She took his name, giving it to Bobby. John Wayne was not born John Wayne. He was born Marion Robert Morrison on May 26, 1907, in Winterset, Iowa, after his grandfathers, Marion Mitchell Morrison and Robert Emmett Brown. Molly decided to name her new baby after her father, Robert. Upon hearing this, five-year-old Marion was confused because he thought he had been named after him.

All still could have been copacetic, however. Robert was only his middle name, but Molly decided that in naming the newborn Robert, Marion needed to have all vestiges of her beloved father's legacy removed from his name. It was as if only this new baby was worthy of her father's memory. She insisted that Marion's name be changed from Marion Robert Morrison to Marion Mitchell Morrison, the same as his paternal grandfather.

For sixty years, she showered love and affection on Bobby, all but ignoring Marion—long after he had become John Wayne, long after he became rich and famous, loved by all of America from coast to coast and internationally as well. Quietly, without fanfare or asking for anything in return really, John Wayne showered his mother with love and affection but received little if any back.

By 1962, Molly lived with her second husband, Sidney Preen, in Long Beach, California. All the neighbors were well aware that she was the great John Wayne's mother. He came around often. All their neighbors knew how well he treated her. Preen was full of thanks for the good fortune of having married John Wayne's mother.

Wayne sent the two of them on an all-expense-paid round-the-world trip to the great tourist destinations, aboard luxury cruisers with first-class air accommodations, complete with top-of-the-line hotels, restaurants, and shows. Upon their return, Preen thanked him with enthusiasm. Molly found only complaint in the service, the long flight, and whatever else. Wayne just absorbed her complaints, graciously saying good-bye and leaving. Mary St. John, his private secretary, had enough. She told Molly she should be "nicer" to him.

"I don't give a damn about him," she replied.

John Wayne, aka Marion Robert Morrison, aka Marion Mitchell Morrison, was of Scottish and Irish ancestry, Presbyterians. The family settled in Ireland. Someday Wayne would make a celebrated film, *The Quiet Man*, about an American returning to his Irish roots. The title and reserved dignity of its lead character, Sean Thornton, embodied John Wayne personally, a gentleman who reacted to his mother's lack of love with love. It was Sean's way as it was Wayne's.

His great-great-grandfather, Robert Morrison, came to America in 1799, some sixteen years after the revolutionaries saw the last defeated British troops—who had dominated Morrison's people in Scotland and Ireland—leave once and for all. Not unsurprisingly, politics and religion created the conflict in Ireland, propelling Robert and his mother to leave for America in 1799. They did not stay in New York, choosing to migrate to the South, so dominated by the Scotch-Irish, whose fierce independent streak would be a major impetus for the Civil War some sixty-two years later.

But they did not stay in South Carolina, moving first to Kentucky, then to Ohio, the great western outpost before Manifest

Destiny. The Morrisons were among that pioneer stock who, like Wayne's numerous cavalry characters, fought the Indians. Morrison's grandson, Marion Mitchell Morrison, was sixteen years old when the family resettled in the "land of Lincoln," Illinois. Marion joined the Union army and served during the great Civil War, which, until Vietnam, split the United States like no other event. Surviving, he returned to Monmouth, Illinois, and wed Weltha Chase Parsons in 1869. Her family were New England Presbyterians, a bit more "blue blood" than the Scotch-Irish Morrisons. They moved to Indianola, Iowa, which had been major staging grounds of covered wagon settlers. Council Bluffs, overlooking the river separating Iowa from Nebraska, was the last gathering place of families, supplies, and courage before embarking on the grand, dangerous journey to California, which included the trek over both the Rocky and Sierra mountain ranges. The transcontinental railroad was nearing its final stages of completion before realizing the late President Abraham Lincoln's dream of connecting the nation.

Marion became a pillar of the community, politically active, raising four children: George, Guy, Clyde, and Pearl. He succeeded in real estate, was elected county treasurer, was deacon of the Presbyterian church, and joined the Masons.

Clyde Leonard Morrison was born on August 20, 1884, in Monmouth, Illinois, but was three when the family arrived in Indianola. He attended Indianola High School and the Middle Academy prep school, then played football at Iowa State and Simpson College. He excelled in music and sports, was handsome, and was popular with girls. Clyde then studied to be a pharmacist at what later came to be Drake University in Des Moines. He passed his examinations and became a licensed, professional man.

Clyde met Mary Alberta Brown, a short, red-haired, green-eyed telephone operator in Des Moines who attended the same Methodist church he did. Her folks called her Mary, but she went by Molly. Her father, Robert Emmett Brown, was born in Pennsylvania, also of Scotch-Irish descent. He moved to Kansas and served in the Union army before moving to Lincoln, Nebraska. He married an Irish woman named Margaret, an immigrant from County Cork who, like so many Irish, came to America to escape the potato famines.

Molly was their third child, born in Lincoln in 1885. Robert was a Presbyterian, Maggie a teetotaling Irish Catholic. They raised their children as Protestants.

They moved to 1716 High Street in Des Moines, a comfortable middle-class family. Robert was a printer, Maggie a seamstress. Molly was independent and strong willed, smoking cigarettes at a time in which such a thing was considered shocking for girls. She was ambitious in her dating habits, preferring college boys. When she was nineteen, she met Clyde Morrison, one year her senior. Attracted by his good looks, she fell in love with his kind ways. With Clyde about to take a new job in Waterloo, they eschewed the traditions of wedding preparation, instead eloping to Marion County. The justice of the peace married them on September 29, 1905. They settled in Waterloo. They were "complete opposites," remarked John Wayne.

Clyde was a dreamer but could not get ahead financially. Molly was impatient and chided him over his inability to get past his station in life, which was stable but lacked a great future. He was extremely handsome and attracted women but, according to reports, very moral, not a philanderer. Nevertheless, the way women looked at him irritated Molly. He was kind and outgoing in discussing medications with his women customers at the store, which further irritated his wife. Furthermore, Molly was the daughter of a teetotaling mother, while Clyde liked to drink. It did not affect his career, but to her it was a waste of money, took from time better spent on more productive pursuits, and deprived him of the drive to make more of himself.

"Mrs. Morrison was tough as nails," a neighbor said. "But Mr. Morrison was just the opposite, as soft and sweet as a marshmallow."

Both young newlyweds missed their parents and endeavored to move closer to them. Clyde was able to land a job as a registered pharmacist at a drugstore in Winterset, Iowa, the county seat of Madison County, only thirty-five miles from Des Moines. They rented a home on South Second Street. It was, as described by Wayne biographers Randy Roberts and James Olson, "the prototype for Norman Rockwell paintings," like the fictional Carvel of Andy Hardy fame, a town in which evil was seemingly "foiled," according to film critic Charles Champlin.

On May 26, 1907, firstborn son Marion Robert Morrison was born. Roberts and Olson's biography, *John Wayne: American*, described small-town American pride best embodied by Alexis de Tocqueville's *Democracy in America* (1835, 1840), which only people born before 1960 can truly relate to, maybe only people born before 1950. Of those born later, only people with vivid imaginations, love of old movies, and a thirst for reading can grasp the nature of American patriotism during this post–Civil War period, in which love of country was a sacred duty, an honor bestowed. Only by grasping this dynamic can one truly engage in the political nature of John Wayne's life and his reaction to World War II, communism and Soviet subversion, and Vietnam and the protests. In understanding this, one understands also that men and women of this era, upbringing, and way of thinking are almost programmed, so propagandized that it is not natural to expect such people to act "rationally" toward, say, flag burning at Berkeley.

Clyde's father had fought hand to hand against the Confederates in the Battle of Pine Bluff, Tennessee. Molly's father had not seen action in the Civil War but battled the Arapahoe and the Cheyenne during the Indian wars in Kansas. Both children were inculcated with militaristic traditionalism. Nothing in Winterset dissuaded them or anybody from a wholehearted belief in the righteousness of the American way.

The Morrisons were literate, devoted readers who absorbed *Democracy in America, Uncle Tom's Cabin* by Harriet Beecher Stowe, and Mark Twain. They were absolute Republicans who looked upon the Democrats as a treasonous party aligned with the rebellious Confederacy and, therefore, slavery. Their politics were fully in line with their county's politics. Roberts and Olson's biography points out that there were virtually no minorities of any kind, whether they be blacks, Hispanics, Indians, Catholics, Jews, Europeans, or known homosexuals. For this reason, there was, in line with love of Abe Lincoln and the Union cause of freeing slaves, a semiliberal attitude propelled by the fact that none of these "others" were even around to find fault with. It was Pollyanna. In pure Tocquevillean manner, every possible service organization thrived in Winterset. Membership was not mandatory, but everybody was in something.

Clyde Morrison made a reasonable living working at the M. E. Smith Drugstore, but in a small town, opportunity extended only so far. Real entrepreneurial spirit, so much the cornerstone of the American Dream, required mobility that often required moving from a place like Winterset. Molly Morrison complained about money.

"Mom was just not a happy woman," recalled Wayne. "No matter what I did, or what Dad did, it was never enough."

In a strange way, her nagging and complaining helped form the impetus leading to the events making John Wayne an international film star: the move to California. But it was only part of the story.

Clyde moved the family to Brooklyn, Iowa, closer to his dad. He worked in another drugstore, but the pay was no better, and he yearned to own his own business. His mother passed away, and Marion Mitchell Morrison, lonely yet filled with wanderlust late in life, decided to pursue real estate opportunities in California. He loaned Clyde money to buy a drugstore in Earlham, but it failed.

Clyde "couldn't pay his bills because he hated to press his customers to pay their bills," said John Wayne. On December 30, 1911, the Morrisons declared bankruptcy. Molly became pregnant, and the financial hardships created separation in which young Marion lived with and became quite close to his father Clyde. Marion was a "daddy's boy," inseparable from Clyde, who read books to him every night. This may well have been the genesis of Molly's resentment of young Marion, as she was jealous of her son's unerring devotion to a man she regarded as a failure who drank too much.

After Bobby, Marion's younger brother, was born in 1912 and Marion's middle name was switched to Mitchell, Clyde, perhaps out of depression, had developed a three-pack-a-day smoking habit. This caused lung problems and a doctor's admonition that he live in a warmer, drier climate. His dad was remarried to a widow in Los Angeles. Clyde was twenty-nine, broke, and living off his in-laws with a wife and two small kids. He was a college graduate and not very proud of himself. He needed change. Marion found them cheap land in the Mojave Desert that he bought for Clyde to farm.

In 1914, Clyde moved his family to the Mojave Desert. If he thought "southern California" was akin to "Hollywood," just beginning to reach the national imagination for the silent films produced there, or the Los Angeles described in Otis Chandler's *L.A. Times*, which sent a yearly advertisement to midwestern farmers as boosterism building up the population—finally able to grow with the building of the Owens Valley Aqueduct—then he found something much different. However, while not glamorous, he and his family indeed found themselves in a real-life adventure, a place that had already assumed mythic dimensions in the national imagination. It was the American West. Indeed, events and people marking the winning of the West—the gold rush, Indian wars, westward settlement, gunslingers, Wyatt Earp, Billy the Kid, "Buffalo Bill" Cody, Kit Carson, Jim Bridger, and many, many more—did not mark life in the Mojave; these were part of the past, not the present. But the physical dimensions and sheer awesomeness of the surroundings made it seem, especially to young Marion Morrison, as if these legends were hiding behind every rock or around the next turn in the road. The Mojave was the high desert, a plateau marking a gradual lowering of the elevation of the northernmost Sierra, which included the magnificent Yosemite Valley and peaked at Mount Whitney, the highest elevation in the lower forty-eight states. The Mojave was between the natural cathedrals of the Sierra range and the low-lying Nevada desert to the east, some of the most barren territory anywhere. This would later be where post–World War II test pilots would fly new jet aircraft, their frequent crashes posing little danger to civilians in such a sparsely populated area. In 1948, Chuck Yeager would break the sound barrier in the skies over the Mojave.

"There was a sharp bend in the road where it made a turn around a cliff, and he would pretend a gang of outlaws was waiting to ambush him," wrote John Wayne biographer Mike Tomkies. "The boy would manage to scare himself half to death, imagining that he'd been 'pumped full of lead.' Then he would dig his heels into [his horse] Jenny, and she'd gallop home."

It was the last vestige of a time and place soon to be no more. Democratic President Woodrow Wilson was elected in 1912 after Theodore Roosevelt split the Republican ticket after years of GOP dominance. In 1913, he instituted the first American income tax, a tiny chink in the unique, ruggedly individualistic nature of America, especially in the West. It would be decades before this fact would truly hit home, but 1913–1914 most likely marks the last real year of the British Empire in full power, its post–World War I and especially post–World War II positions propped up by the United States, the new global power.

In 1914, World War I began, and with it the end of horse cavalry charges, medieval valor, or warfare as a knight's adventure. It was replaced by mechanized mass death on a scale dwarfing even that of the Civil War. This war would mark the great chasm of world history. It would give rise to communism, Nazism, socialism, Keynesianism, and modernism, turning America into a great power, largely in opposition to all these "isms." It would at once make for the America of John Wayne.

While Mark Twain dominated nineteenth-century literature, a new American ethos was now embodied by the western adventure writers, among them Frank Norris, Hamlin Garland, Jack London, Stewart White, Owen Wister, and, later, Zane Grey, Max Brand, and Louis L'Amour, and series and titles like *The Pony Rider Boys*, *The Lone Ranger*, *The Black Stallion*, and *Black Beauty*.

Hollywood would take notice. The geographical location of the burgeoning film industry was not an accident. San Francisco had a fairly thriving film industry, but it centered in Los Angeles quickly because the year-round weather was better (less fog, rain, and wind). The broad expanse of the L.A. Basin was mostly flat and easy to get around by car, with no bay absent any bridges and fewer winding hills to deal with. The topography was key. Within fifty miles of downtown Los Angeles, virtually every kind of scenery existed: beach and ocean, mountain, desert, rural, farm, forest, woods, city, and more. The union movement, picking up steam, was trampled down in Los Angeles, largely due to the efforts of the Chandler family and their *Los Angeles Times*. Movie crews were easy to organize and not laden with labor costs.

Of all the movie genres, the western was most appealing from the beginning. The Mojave scenery the Morrisons first encountered drew many movie sets looking to replicate the O.K. Corral, dusty gunslinger showdowns, Apache raids, cavalry charges, and the like.

But unlike self-contained movie sets, the Morrisons were on their own. Life was hard. The arid desert land did not yield much.

Water was sparse, the well running dry, rain often spare. Rattle-snakes abounded, causing Marion to have nightmares imagining the slithering creatures everywhere, as in those St. Patrick con-fronted in Ireland. Clyde Morrison was not a farmer anyway, but this land was God-forsaken. Jackrabbits ate what little corn or peas he could sprout. Oil was being discovered all throughout southern California—the deserts, the coast, and in Los Angeles itself—but none was found under Clyde Morrison's property. They were broke, and they lived near the hottest place in all of America, the appro-priately named Death Valley. It was unbearable, sometimes as high as 118 degrees. It was too much for Molly, who already disrespected her husband, in her mind a loser. Her hopes for him were dashed.

"Like any married couple, they were going through a tough time," recalled Wayne. "But that broke them. They never made the adjustments where they could get together again."

For some reason, she vented her wrath not just at Clyde but also at little Marion, who she somehow felt was in league with his father in some strange conspiracy, depriving her of her right to be happy. She favored the second boy, Bobby.

Despite the snakes, Marion loved it in the Mojave. It fed his sense of adventure. The Morrisons were readers, and he was absorb-ing some of the boys' adventure novels of the era, often describing surroundings like his own. He roamed the country imagining him-self a cowboy, a hired gun, a cavalry soldier, and an Indian fighter.

But the stay in the Mojave Desert, much to the relief of Molly, would be a short-lived one. One of the reasons opportunity pre-sented itself to Clyde in Los Angeles was something running right through the Mojave. The Los Angeles Aqueduct, also known as the Owens Valley or Owens River Aqueduct, took five years to complete (1908–1913). Beginning between Big Pine and Independence in eastern California, north of the Mojave, it ran freshwater all the way to the San Fernando Valley, a rural swath of land near Los Angeles that, as mythologized in the movie *Chinatown*, would become incor-porated into the city itself, creating a metropolis.

Los Angeles was topographically not unlike the Mojave in that it was a desert with little freshwater in the way of lakes, streams, or rivers. It had a beautiful ocean and a Mediterranean climate and seemed a Shangri-la, an Eden of sorts, but without freshwater the land could support only a limited population. San Francisco, 400 miles to the north, also sat on the same beautiful Pacific Ocean, featuring a bay sixty-seven miles long from Vallejo to San Jose, with delta straits extending an incredible ninety miles to Stockton, the most inland saltwater port in the world. But above all other considerations, it could support its big-city population through numerous freshwater sources emanating from nearby mountains, producing lakes and rivers. Some were dammed to divert water to the population. Eventually, they built an aqueduct of their own, from the Hetch Hetchy Reservoir in Yosemite, but originally the city survived on the same natural resources the Indians and Spanish had.

The Los Angeles Aqueduct was an engineering marvel on par with the transcontinental railroad. It is the single biggest factor in the growth of Los Angeles, above movies, politics, wars, or baseball. It was promoted by the Chandler *Times* and overseen by the brilliant engineer William Mulholland, one of the "city fathers" who decided Los Angeles would indeed be a major metropolis to equal and even surpass San Francisco. The aqueduct immediately created a population boom in Los Angeles, the greatest expansion of people and regional growth in human history over the next decades.

This boom meant opportunity for Clyde Morrison, who found it specifically at the Glendale Pharmacy on West Broadway in Glendale. He moved his family to 421 South Isabel, abandoning the Mojave homestead to the snakes.

To the young man of destiny, upon reflection such a move made much sense. While Clyde, a small-town midwesterner, thought of Glendale as the "big city," close enough to downtown Los Angeles as it was, with its well-traveled roads, its railroad, its hospital, and its real estate and construction boom, all growing the population daily, in fact the Glendale of Marion Morrison's youth was still very rural, not the suburban "bedroom community" it became. It featured much topography perfectly suited for a western movie shoot: big rocks, wide expanse, and chaparral landscape amid a still open valley. It was nestled equal parts in between downtown Los Angeles proper a few short miles to the south, halfway between the Hollywood section of town to its west, and Pasadena, already famous for its Rose Bowl football game, to the east. It was afforded magnificent mountain vistas: the San Gabriel range beyond Pasadena, the Hollywood hills sloping toward the Santa Monica Mountains, and the Pacific Ocean some twenty-fives miles due west. In the distance, the summit peak of Mount Wilson overlooked the L.A. Basin.

"I understand my fans because I had idols," John Wayne said. "They were Harry Carey and Tom Mix. Glendale was a popular location for picture makers, and I got to see a lot of scenes being filmed. I remember seeing Douglas Fairbanks filming a woodland scene from *Robin Hood*."

It was hot but not overwhelming, like the Mojave. There was no smog yet. Orange blossoms sweetened the clean air. Manzanita, scrub oak, lotus, Jacaranda, and many other colorful, incredibly beautiful plants, flowers, and natural fauna flourished, adding to the image of a promised land. This imagery was already used by propagandists describing the place with its year-round warmth. Chandler boosterism drew many new citizens every year.

The Chandlers and the political power structure was settled in downtown Los Angeles, where the University of Southern California campus had been built two miles from the city center in 1880, and in the Pasadena–San Marino area. There was little beyond Western Avenue. Santa Monica featured beach cottages where the wealthy owned vacation homes, but there was a small population. In 1919, the University of California, Los Angeles, would open for business on a wide-open expanse of virgin land called Westwood. At first, many scoffed, claiming nobody would go all the way out there for school.

Los Angeles was slightly southern, embodied by the horsey set and family of General George S. Patton, a scion of Confederate military aristocracy. These were people who chose Los Angeles after the transcontinental railroad was built, with a coastal route connecting San Francisco to Los Angeles, because San Francisco was dominated by Boston Yankees of Union sympathy. Los Angeles was on the way to becoming the most conservative Republican city and region in the United States, surely reflecting Chandler politics and antiunion antipathy. It was not paradise for blacks and Spanish-speaking people but was probably friendlier, offering more opportunity than any other region of America.

Oil played a role in the political division between northern and southern California. There has not been a lot of oil discovered, as yet, north of Santa Barbara. From central California to Mexico, however, lie some of the most abundant oil fields in the world. To this day, high school nicknames reflect this: Oilers, Drillers, and Tars. As reflected in the 2007 film *There Will Be Blood*, greed for oil money overshadowed any consideration for the environment. The city of Signal Hill, located near Long Beach, was so overflowing with oil that wells and drills were built up and down residential blocks, even in private backyards. As films like *Volcano* (1997) and the existence of the La Brea Tar Pits demonstrate, the city of Los Angeles—some of its tallest skyscrapers and most prestigious Wilshire Boulevard business addresses—are built directly atop oil fields. The business of oil overshadowed concerns over health, spills, and disaster. This created a Republican, business-friendly city, all fostered by the Chandler *Times*. Unquestionably, oil wealth built southern California every bit as much, if not more, as the film industry. A direct offshoot of the technology and politics of oil exploration first led to a car culture, then an aviation culture, and eventually the military-industrial complex, which played such a huge role in defeating the communist monolith John Wayne would come to despise so much. All of this helped create prosperity and opportunity, drawing the Clyde Morrisons of the world to this vast new promised land. Indeed, people really did think of it as the promised land, a sort of Eden where humanity could start anew, putting aside failures and prejudices of the East Coast in a place that really was one of "milk and honey," not to mention palm trees, orange groves, towering mountaintops, endless strands of surf, lush foliage, and deserts resembling those Christ Himself walked upon. It was all offered in year-round warm sunshine. Paradise found.

The Chandlers could not have shaped the citizenry through a targeted recruitment of certain types of citizens more assiduously had they been given the benefit of Google algorithms even then. They wanted "midwestern farmers," not necessarily actual farmers (like Clyde Morrison) but hardworking, conservative, Protestant Republicans, many of these being the fiercely independent Scotch-Irish, who resisted government interfering with their lives.

Southerners had been flooding their population since Reconstruction. They did not want Jews, Catholics, northern rabble-rousers, unionists, or immoralists. They got what they wanted and, despite enormous growth over the course of several decades and two world wars bringing countless numbers to their fair city, largely continued to get a population reflecting this vision of America until the 1960s.

For young Marion, it was destiny also in the proximity to Hollywood, like the Rose Bowl, the other great international attraction already putting Los Angeles on the world map. The film industry was a separate inducement. This was where Jews found their first real opportunities in America, a freewheeling gamble, unregulated, because there was no template for success, not unlike the Internet in the 1990s. The movers and shakers of Hollywood settled in the hills above Sunset Boulevard, away from the white Anglo-Saxon Protestant (WASP) aristocrats of San Marino, beginning the expanse of wealth toward Beverly Hills and what would come to be known as the Westside.

As the movie business grew, Los Angeles began to identify itself as an "industry town." Many handsome young men and small-town beauty queens began to trek west in search of fame on the silver screen, but much of the work was available in the form of stagehands, grips, technicians, and all the myriad ancillaries of moviemaking then and now. Marion Morrison would grow up in this environment, in which his classmates would be the sons and daughters of employees at the Fox studios, the Charlie Chaplin film lot, and other large campuses filled with workers. If a budding actor did not make it, he could often find work behind the scenes.

As a child, Marion had a horse named Jenny. "The nosy biddies of the town called the Humane Society and accused me, a seven-year-old, of not feeding the horse," he recalled. "This was proven to be a lie."

As Marion grew, he developed a strong body like his father, the former college football player. Clyde taught him how to throw, kick, run, and tackle. Marion played with a neighbor friend named Frank Hoyt. They took trips to the beach, where Marion learned how to bodysurf, a favorite pastime that would ultimately have profound consequences on his life. Life in Glendale was pleasant enough to end the acrimony between Molly and Clyde, at least temporarily. While much of the original Los Angeles had a southern aristocracy to it, by 1916 Glendale and Los Angeles were more midwestern in nature.

Marion did not like his name. Kids teased him, saying it was a "girl's name." "I got into a lot of fights at school because my classmates laughed at my midwestern accent and especially at my God——n name," he later said.

He tried to get people to address him as "Morrison," but some local firemen came up with the perfect solution. Marion would traipse by the firehouse with the family dog, a huge Airedale named Duke. Duke would stay at the station, located at 315 East Broadway, sleeping while Marion went to school. The firemen did not even known Marion's name, so they called him "Little Duke." He loved the name and started asking his friends to "just call me Duke." It stuck, and he became Duke to all who knew him. As he grew in height and stature, the firemen surely stopped calling him "Little Duke." He was Duke Morrison now.

The family moved to different houses. While Clyde worked steady, there were bills, which caused anxiety. Duke took a paper route, delivering the *Los Angeles Examiner*, sometimes with his father driving him in the family Nash.

"You won't believe this," Molly told an inquirer years later, "but sometimes I had to take Duke's paper route money to pay bills." Duke was happy to contribute, but it fostered further antipathy by Molly toward her husband.

Duke grew to be smart, talented, and popular. Girls loved him. He engaged in every imaginable wholesome activity for boys. He traipsed about the rural areas of Glendale, where rocks and trees looked like the Old West, imagining himself a cowboy or a soldier. The family attended a Methodist church, and Christianity was a major part of his upbringing. Aside from the beach trips, he also had the opportunity to sail a boat off Long Beach, sponsored by the YMCA. He developed a lifelong love of the sea.

America entered World War I in 1917. In searching for times in U.S. history that point toward the societal, political chasms that by 1966 would so divide the nation, one can do worse than start with World

War I. Obviously, the Civil War and the industrial revolution created huge changes in the fabric of American life, but World War I ushered in communism and the seeds of Nazism. These two political-military ideologies would lead to some 170 million to 200 million deaths in less than a century. Although eventually the United States would ascend to unmatched global power largely because of her triumph over these murderous forces, she would not escape its cancer.

Ancient hatreds, prejudices, forms of racism, and class envy, always present, were allowed to bubble to the surface as never before. What had started in the French Revolution of 1789, expanded in Europe throughout the nineteenth century, and now come to fruition, even touching American shores, was the Red Scare. At its heart was the anarchist movement, a reaction to the "militarist" and "imperialist" decision to enter World War I, which the United States did three years after it started. American forces turned the tide, defeating the Kaiser's Germany and rendering the world "safe for democracy" by 1918. But "Red Emma" Goldman, an anarchist-communist, embodied a strange new underclass. It may have started with Henry David Thoreau, who resisted America's war with Mexico; been continued by Mark Twain, a fervent anticolonialist; and been furthered by the writings of Upton Sinclair, whose novel *The Jungle* was a unionist call to arms.

Goldman and John Reed, the latter an American journalist who experienced the Russian Revolution firsthand and wrote *Ten Days That Shook the World*, were the face of early American communism. Attorney General A. Mitchell Palmer made it priority number one to eradicate it after the war. The anarchists were violent. The Ferdinando Sacco–Bartolomeo Vanzetti case shocked the nation. Palmer himself was the target of a bombing that nearly killed him. Young J. Edgar Hoover, who made the destruction of communism his Holy Grail, succeeded him. For millions of Americans just like young Duke Morrison, this was God's work as surely as he was alive. All of Morrison's neighbors supported Palmer and Hoover in opposing communism. Duke was an avid reader and learned much about history, all of which confirmed in his young mind that America was given a Godly duty: to destroy the evils of communism.

He also went to the movies regularly. "My folks always let me go to the movies every Saturday," he recalled of hours spent at the new Glendale Theater at 124 South Grand. They cost about ten cents, some of the least expensive entertainment in the country. He handed out handbills for the theater. His pay? Watching Rudolph Valentino star in *The Four Horsemen of the Apocalypse* fourteen times in a single week, all for free.

The movies of his youth tended toward patriotic war films and westerns, with Tom Mix emerging as a big cowboy star. His father was a semifailure, and through the heroic characters Duke saw on-screen, he began to formulate his idea of what a hero was. He began to see himself in that light. His younger brother Bobby was begin-ning to act out, drinking and missing school, yet oddly Molly contin-ued to love him more than Duke, who was honest and industrious to a fault. Perhaps his faithful love of Clyde, for whom she had no respect, still motivated this odd attitude.

At Glendale High School, Duke was instantly popular. His fans have an image mostly of the older John Wayne; rough-hewn, wrin-kled from the sun, a drinker, and a bit paunchy. Young Duke Mor-rison more resembled Rudolph Valentino, only manlier. He was six feet tall, muscular, with a shock of dark hair, a classically handsome face, and a smile that twisted "his mouth up in one corner," recalled classmate Ruth Conrad, an early admirer. Another was Mildred Power, who called him the "most handsome thing you ever saw. I was in awe." Dorothy Hacker called him "stunningly handsome," adding he could "stop traffic."

Still, he was bashful and not comfortable with girls. Randy Rob-erts and James Olson theorized it was because of Molly. He enjoyed the company of men, as he preferred the company of Clyde as a kid. This would endure throughout his life. He certainly was attracted to girls, but despite many at Glendale actually praying to go out with him, he did not date much. He was an excellent student, engaged in all school activities, including student politics, but avoided con-flict and argument, probably also because he disliked hearing Molly bicker with Clyde. All who knew him recalled his maturity.

He had a role in the school play *Dulcy* and participated in Shakespearean contests at Glendale High. "I delivered Cardinal Wolsey's speech from *Henry VIII*," Wayne recalled. Duke was an honors student, president of the Letterman Society, and senior class president and debated and helped chair the school dance.

But it was on the football field where Duke shone the brightest. He was aware that many talked of his father, his unpaid bills, and public arguments with Molly. Glendale High was an upper-class school, and most of his classmates were from successful families. Duke felt football was a great equalizer. Years later, he asked a telling, rhetorical question: "Do you think the color of your skin or the amount of your father's property or your social position help you there?"

He had little engagement with black people, but to the extent that he considered their obvious plight in America at that time, his own position on the low rung of the social ladder may already have allowed him to empathize, as others have said childhood poverty allowed Alabama football coach Paul "Bear" Bryant to do. But he definitely embraced egalitarianism as an American attribute, seizing upon football as his first real chance to make his mark, which would allow him to move beyond his father's place in the social order.

"Duke was uncomfortable talking about his childhood long after he attained success, fame, and wealth beyond his parents' wildest dreams," wrote his wife Pilar in *John Wayne: My Life with the Duke* (1987), with Alex Thorleifson.

Clyde's advice was succinct: "1) Always keep your word. 2) A gentleman never insults anyone intentionally. 3) Don't go around looking for trouble but if you get in a fight make sure you can win it." This was similar to the philosophy of the famed frontiersman Davy Crockett. Duke became fascinated with the Alamo from high school friends Bill and Bob Bradbury. Their dad, Robert Bradbury, made a 1926 film called *Davy Crockett at the Fall of the Alamo*. His son Bob was in it.

"To me it represented the fight for freedom, not just in America, but in all countries," recalled Wayne.

2

THE DUKE OF TROY

CLYDE DESPERATELY WANTED HIM TO ATTEND COLLEGE. HE HAD THE GRADES and the aptitude but not the money. The only way he could attend college and hope to see his way to a degree was via a scholarship of some kind. His first hope was the U.S. Naval Academy. He was a perfect officer candidate who would have likely made a great navy man. He also would have been sailing the world throughout the late 1920s and early 1930s; if he re-upped, likely he would have seen duty in World War II. He would not have been in Los Angeles pursuing the movie career that was his destiny. However, his application was rejected.

In 1924, Duke Morrison also became one of the finest high school football players in Los Angeles County. His talents did not escape the attention of Howard Jones, recently hired head football coach at the University of Southern California, the oldest private university in the West, having begun operations in 1880.

"Duke was a good guard," recalled Norman C. Hayhurst, his coach at Glendale High. "He played a big part in our winning the Central League and the southern California championship. He was one of the seven players selected for a football scholarship at USC. Our 1924 team was a good one." Wayne joked that Glendale High was so tough that half went on to become the USC Trojans, the other half the Dillinger gang.

Originally offering religious instruction, USC sports teams were called the Methodists until *Los Angeles Times* sportswriter Owen Bird wrote of a 1912 track meet that they "fought like Trojans."

They started playing football in 1888, but it was a small-time operation, even morphing into rugby for a few years. On the West Coast, the University of California, Berkeley, and Stanford University were major national powers. They built their reputations on their great natural Bay Area rivalry and membership in the Pacific Coast Conference (PCC), which annually sent its champion to the "granddaddy of 'em all," the Rose Bowl game.

USC was not in the PCC and had no rival. The University of California, Los Angeles (UCLA), begun in 1919, was a commuter school, a glorified junior college, and not yet a worthy sports opponent. USC occasionally played games against Stanford and California without embarrassing themselves, but they normally had to settle for local opponents, like Cal Tech, Whittier, and Pomona. Nobody was mistaking them for Notre Dame or California or Stanford. But school president Rufus von KleinSmid decided after World War I to make USC into a national football power. He hired Elmer "Gloomy Gus" Henderson, who from 1919 to 1924 achieved just that. During his tenure, the Rose Bowl in Pasadena and the Los Angeles Memorial Coliseum, two of the great, enduring sports palaces of American lore, were built. USC joined the PCC, and in 1923 the Trojans defeated Penn State in the first Rose Bowl game played in the new stadium.

Henderson won some 90 percent of his games but could not defeat California's "Wonder Teams." Neither did anybody else. Coach Andy Smith's Golden Bears were undefeated from 1920 to 1924, one the great dynasties in college gridiron history. Stanford under legendary Coach Pop Warner was almost as strong.

Charles Darwin's theory of evolution had created revolutionary new social ideas. Among these was the eugenics movement, a racist concept promoted by Margaret Sanger advocating the abortion of black and other "inferior" babies in order to promote white supremacy. Social scientists were trying to determine whether racial genetics did indeed produce superior versus inferior species of man, one of the major components of Nazism. Adolf Hitler himself studied American sports of the 1920s. He was alarmed to discover a disproportionate number of German American football stars, particularly at the University of Michigan, or big-league stars like Lou Gehrig. He openly worried that most of the "good Germans" had left for America in the nineteenth century and about the flower of modern German youth lost in World War I.

In the United States, sportswriters began to theorize that California produced the best athletes for a number of reasons. The sunshine was said to invigorate growth or to give the fruits and vegetables extra vitamin enrichment. Others said that handsome men and pretty girls coming to Hollywood seeking fame met, married, and produced more athletic children. For whatever reason, the rise of California, Stanford, and now USC as sports powerhouses of the 1920s spurred this debate.

Duke Morrison was pushing six feet four inches, was over 200 pounds, and had the body and looks of a Greek god. USC was and now is legendary for its beautiful coeds, who no doubt swooned at the first sight of this young stud. He was intelligent, a great student, very worthy of admittance to USC, with a bright football future ahead of him, but he was intimidated.

USC was then, as it is now, an extremely expensive, elite private institution. It was a "rich kid's" school, and Greek fraternity life, the elitist of the elites, dominated its social environment. It had always provided scholarships for worthy students without financial means to attend. As early as the turn of the century, the first black lawyers and doctors in Los Angeles were graduated by USC, but true "acceptance" meant wealth, the right family.

It was already an institution of class envy on a political scale. Upton Sinclair's 1927 novel *Oil!* set the tone for twentieth- and now twenty-first-century liberalism. Its main character was based on Edward Doheny, a huge USC contributor and oil tycoon caught up in the infamous Teapot Dome scandal that brought down President Warren Harding. Its Southern Pacific University was an obvious stand-in for USC. Sinclair lambastes its snobbery and class distinctions, using a variety of characters, such as a radical Jewish student who falls in love with the oil tycoon's son. Together, they abandon the father's ambitious greed in favor of a Bohemian lifestyle embodied by nudity, free love, and experimentation. This novel foreshadows the 1950s beats and the 1960s hippies, but its use of sexual "liberation" was also adopted by communism, particularly as a means of recruitment in the bourgeois West.

While popular and initially successful in both football and academics at USC, Duke Morrison felt out of place. One of Wayne's campus jobs was to "sling hash" at sorority houses. He joined a fraternity, Sigma Chi, along with several of his high school friends. One of them, Ralf "Pexy" Eckles, recalled in a newspaper interview that Wayne once got out of a college fight by putting ketchup in his mouth and letting it leak out.

"The guys let him go because they thought he was bleeding," recalled Eckles. "He would have got away with it, if he hadn't started to laugh."

The invitation to rush the Sigma Chi house was a very heady honor indeed, but Randy Roberts and James Olson pointed out in *John Wayne: American* a scene in which Gary Cooper as Lou Gehrig is made fun of by snooty frat bothers he was forced to wait tables for in order to pay his way through Columbia in *Pride of the Yankees* (1942). This scene hit home with Duke.

Chet Dolly, a player of the era, recalled a "big, rough and tough" guy who walked around campus "with patches on the seat of his pants. . . . He could play football, no doubt about that, even though he wasn't the best-dressed on campus."

Morrison's scholarship was not the "full ride" of modern standards, which in many cases is "enhanced" by ancillary and, by National Collegiate Athletic Association (NCAA) standards, illegal, extra alumni inducements. Morrison's deal covered the $130-per-semester tuition and a meal on weekdays. Other meals and meals on weekends were not included,

"The training table was a five-days-a-week thing," recalled Eugene Clarke, a former USC trustee who was a boyhood, high school, and college friend of Wayne's, in a 1979 *Trojan Family* article. "We sort of had to scratch around for our other meals and for all of our meals on weekends. We were always pretty hungry by Monday morning."

Another key component of the scholarship was that it covered players on the "regular squad." While interpretation of this was relatively flexible based on Coach Jones's needs, it would ultimately play a major role in Duke Morrison's life and John Wayne's career. Duke scalped the tickets he received as a player for the heady price of $25 at the Hollywood Athletic Club. He also worked at the telephone company.

His lifelong friend, actress Loretta Young, said that "he did well academically during his freshman year, and he learned from his fraternity brothers how to drink and play cards. Not that he didn't like girls. He found himself the center of attention from a number of college girls who warmed to his natural naive charm and good looks." She added that he treated women "with good old-fashioned respect" and never swore in their presence.

But first, Duke starred on the 1925 freshman team, which outscored opponents 261–20 in fashioning a 7–0 record. This was the nucleus of the "Thundering Herd," a period of Trojan glory rivaling over the next fifteen years California's Wonder Teams, Pop Warner's Stanford Indians, and Knute Rockne's "Four Horsemen of Notre Dame."

USC was in the middle of the most Republican city in the most Republican state in the country at a time—the Roaring Twenties—that was dominated by the Grand Old Party. It was a period of tremendous postwar economic prosperity and isolationism from the problems of Europe. Prohibition was the law of the land, but USC, despite being a school of midwestern Republican temperance, was still dominated by frat boys looking for a party. Alcohol was not hard to find and come by. The Southern California Masons erected the Shrine Auditorium, future home of the Academy Awards, across the street from the campus. They were a perfect partner in the civic sense, the Greek system at USC a veritable "minor league" of future Los Angeles society—judges, politicians, doctors, movie producers, and business tycoons—not unlike Yale's Skull and Bones. USC, as much as the Chandlers, the *Los Angeles Times*, the Los Angeles Aqueduct, and the film industry, built and molded southern California.

They were "the biggest, richest, most popular school," according to future UCLA football star Woody Strode, the tall, Nubian physical specimen well known for his role as Draba, the gladiator who sacrifices his life so that Kirk Douglas can live in *Spartacus* (1960). If they were already the "biggest, richest, most popular school" when Duke Morrison arrived, the Howard Jones era would increase that times ten.

A combination of events, some socioreligious in nature, would conspire to create a football rivalry that defines the college game to this day, expanding the romantic imagination of American sports fans forever in the 1920s. It started in Lincoln, Nebraska, when Notre Dame and its coach, Knute Rockne, boarded a train. The Fighting Irish had lost to Nebraska in freezing-cold conditions. It was miserable, and they were not in a good mood, but the weather and score were only half the problem.

After World War I, a tremendous Christian revival took place in America, a search for meaning after the carnage. Tent revivals sprung up throughout the land. Charismatic preachers like Aimee Semple McPherson rallied the faithful. While spiritually uplifting, it was Protestant and Pentecostal in nature. Out of this a strange, alarming dynamic emerged: the rise of the Ku Klux Klan and anti-Catholicism. Some of its strongest sanctuaries were in the Midwest. In Lincoln, Rockne's Irish heard vicious taunts. Notre Dame had not yet built its stadium, so it was a kind of barnstorming team in those days, playing many road games. Rockne began to formulate the notion that, instead of playing at Lincoln or Ames, Iowa, or some such rural, Protestant setting, he should showcase his team in big cities with large Catholic populations, such as games at Chicago's Soldier Field and New York's Yankee Stadium.

Enter USC student manager Gwynn Wilson. He was sent by Coach Jones to speak to Coach Rockne on the train about setting a series of home-and-home games with Notre Dame. At first, Rockne resisted. Los Angeles was too far away, and the administration was already on him about road games and time out of school. But Wilson's wife was meeting with Rockne's wife in a separate compartment. She told her of the great weather in Los Angeles in late November, when the game would be played. She described marvelous fashions from Paris lining the trendy new shops of Rodeo Drive. Mrs. Rockne told her husband she was excited about the game.

When he said no, that he was not going for the plan, she basically told him that, yes, he was. Rockne further realized that his strategy of playing before large big-city crowds would be realized at the new Los Angeles Coliseum. Thus was born the USC–Notre Dame rivalry, today the kingpin of collegiate grid annals. When this happened, it elevated USC to a place equal with the legendary Fighting Irish, probably the two greatest traditions. It gave them just a slight edge, allowing the Trojans to push past California and Stanford. This led to much jealousy, which would eventually manifest itself in a certain amount of social conflict regarding the politics and comparable wealth of the schools. In time, it would allow UCLA to grow into USC's greatest rival on the West Coast, surpassing the two Bay Area schools.

The USC–Notre Dame rivalry also symbolized the new popularity of sports in America. There was a reason the city of Los Angeles named its stadium the Coliseum. Not since the ancient Greeks and Romans had crowds gathered to watch such spectacles of sport. It was the age of new, magnificent stadiums: in addition to the Rose Bowl and Coliseum, Stanford Stadium, Memorial Stadium (Berkeley), "the Horseshoe" (Ohio State), "the Swamp" (Florida), Michigan Stadium, Yankee Stadium, soon Notre Dame Stadium, the Orange Bowl, the Sugar Bowl, and the Cotton Bowl. Never, at least since the height of the Roman Empire, had the citizenry risen to such economic heights as America in the 1920s. Never had average people had such money to spend on leisure activities. It was the rise of radio, built on the national strength of sports appeal, with golden-throated announcers like Graham McNamee and Ted Husing breathlessly describing the feats of Jack Dempsey and Babe Ruth. Red Grange was the "Galloping Ghost" of the new National Football League. Sportswriters like Grantland Rice and Ring Lardner wrote romantically of "Four Horsemen" performing glorious feats on the "green plains" below. Charles Lindbergh crossed the Atlantic solo, and Rudy Valentino made women swoon. It was a golden age of golden heroes, an American Renaissance.

Coach Jones already envisioned the USC–Notre Dame legend. He had been hired to make USC a national power and was determined to achieve this goal. It meant the players under his charge would be subject to discipline and hard work that college football players, for the most part gentlemen of the Ivy League, not recruited scholarship "blue chippers," had never experienced. When Andy Smith employed these hard-core methods at California, his players rebelled. Only after he convinced them of the payoff did they cooperate and become champions. Now Jones was doing the same thing at USC.

In between his freshman and sophomore seasons, Duke Morrison settled into an enjoyable life at the Sigma Chi house. He also dated girls, who were plentiful on campus and especially to handsome young USC fraternity brothers. Duke was invited on a blind date with Polly Ann Belzer, older sister of Gretchen Belzer, later known as the actress Loretta Young. Romance did not bloom, but it led to a second date, this time with Polly's friend Carmen Saenz. Romance did not bloom between Duke and Carmen either, but it led to Duke's meeting Carmen's younger sister Josephine. This time Duke was infatuated.

She was a devout Catholic girl of Spanish blue-blood origin, social register types. Her father was a prominent businessman, and the family had long roots in southern California, obviously a Spanish pueblo long before the Chandlers and Anglo-Americans came to dominate its populace. While the Saenzes did not consider Duke their equal, coming from a rather poor family with no "breeding," his position as a football player and fraternity brother at USC helped to elevate him in their eyes.

In 1926, the Trojans were among the favorites to compete for a national championship, which in recent years had been won by California, Stanford, and Notre Dame, their last-game opponent in Los Angeles. Troy had never won one. Cowboy star Tom Mix was a big fan, and Coach Jones made a deal with him. If he arranged for USC players to get summer jobs over at the Fox lots in the summer of 1926, he could have his own personal cluster of box seats. Mix agreed, and thus was born a marriage made in Hollywood. Duke Morrison went to work at Fox for $35 a week. According to the original story, Duke and a star player named Don Williams ran three miles every morning with Mix to help him get ready for his role in *The Great K & A Train Robbery*. They also worked as set dressers, moving furniture. It was an enormous recruiting tool, which in the days before the NCAA was available to southern California and, really, nobody else. UCLA was still not a speck on the athletic horizon.

"Tom Mix gave me my first movie job," Duke recalled. "I was attending the University of Southern California, playing tackle on the football team. My father, who lived in Glendale, was having a tough time. The Depression had started and he simply was not a good businessman, although a fine man and a wonderful father. He had opened a new drugstore in Glendale, and it failed. An ice cream company also failed." Wayne's recollection that the "Depression had started" was inaccurate; it was three years away.

"Howard Jones, the Trojan football coach, heard that I needed a job. It seems that Jones had arranged for Mix, a football enthusiast, to get some choice seats, and the grateful actor had promised the coach he'd get some of his players jobs that summer.

"I was given a job with a 'swing gang,' a sort of utility work outfit. My wages were $35 a week. My job was to lug furniture and props around to arrange them on the set."

Mix promised Jones that he would find work for any of his players who needed summer jobs. "So in the summer of 1926 me and my buddy Don Williams were sent to Fox."

Much of John Wayne's football career at USC and early years in Hollywood are shrouded in hyperbole, courtesy of ripe press agents. Longtime friend and legendary director Henry Hathaway, who was working in silent films under Victor Fleming and Joszef von Sternberg at the time, disputed the original Mix connection to some degree.

"I'm not sure that Tom Mix actually took Duke on as a trainer," recalled Hathaway. "I think it's one of those stories that the studio put into his biographies because it made for a good story. And once it was in print, Wayne couldn't actually ever turn it around and say that it wasn't true, so he went along with it."

"I arrived at the studio and they put me straight to work carrying props," said Wayne. "I got to meet Tom Mix at Fox. That was a real thrill for me. He used to like talking football more than movies . . . I was also a grip. Around the rest of the country, they call that a janitor."

One of Wayne's biographers, Michael Munn, also mentioned that Mix, Wayne, and Williams would drink together. Mix "took Duke to his favorite speakeasy and proceeded to pump him for inside information about the team," wrote Pilar Wayne. "In the course of what proved to be a long, drunken night, Mix promised to put Duke on his own payroll, as his personal trainer. It sounded like a dream job.

"When Duke reported to the studio the next morning, he learned that Tom Mix's promise had been nothing more than 'drunk talk.'" Wayne's "fragile sense of dignity had been badly bruised," and he "never forgave Mix for disillusioning him."

"Mix promised my father *two* jobs—one as his personal trainer, one as an extra in the star's next movie," wrote Wayne's daughter Aissa in *John Wayne: My Father.* Later, Wayne confronted Mix about how he lied to him, but Mix just turned away.

"There's some real SOBs in this business," John Wayne later said.

Work on a movie lot was not particularly strenuous. The pay was good, and there were beautiful actresses roaming about. It was a tremendous inducement to a young football stud, certainly enough to convince one that USC might just be a little more attractive than California or Stanford, both of which competed fiercely with Jones for star players at the many high schools in both northern and southern California. In addition, the work had the potential to be something more. A young fellow might be selected as an extra in one of the many epics of that film era: perhaps a French Legionnaire, one of Pharaoh's soldiers, or a horse cavalryman in the Union army. Beyond that, there was the outside chance, which to so many with stars in their eyes seemed not such an outside chance, of being "discovered." To Duke Morrison, who had acted in Glendale High School stage productions and no doubt knew exactly how beautiful a physical specimen he was at that time, such a prospect had to cross his mind.

In 1926, Hollywood had reached the golden era of silent films. Europe finally settled into an uneasy peace after World War I. Germany had a thriving film industry and loved American movies. England also was mad for movies, with many Shakespearean performers and playwrights journeying to Hollywood to try their hands. Paris, spared carnage in the war, was a place of creative myth and lore, hosting the "Lost Generation" of American expatriate writers and poets. The Jewish entrepreneurs who gambled on Hollywood were now moguls of great wealth and power, with status never reached in their 2,000-year European Diaspora. The big movie studios were built and in business, finely honed machines of the new American art form.

There was in the Roaring Twenties a natural symbiosis between the movie industry and "Hollywood's school," USC. The Trojans were a fan favorite in Los Angeles long before the Dodgers, Angels, Lakers, or UCLA Bruins. Wayne and his USC teammates appeared as themselves in the film *The Drop Kick*. Trojan football players routinely appeared as extras in the epics of Cecil B. DeMille and others known for extravagant productions.

Coach Jones began to receive fan mail from the likes of Oliver Hardy of the Laurel and Hardy comedy team, Gary Cooper, Vilma Banky, Mary Pickford, Douglas Fairbanks Sr., Harold Lloyd, Norma Talmadge, Richard Dix, Hoot Gibson, Ronald Coleman, Nancy Carroll, and Reginald Denny.

"Is the quarterback's value greater today than it used to be?" asked Hardy.

"Yes," was Jones's written reply, "because the introduction of the forward pass broadened the field for the employment of strategy."

Gary Cooper was interested in what constituted a penalty and why some were more severe than others. Vilma Banky wanted to know who the best football player ever was. Jones's surprising answer was Tom Shevlin, Yale's captain in 1905, because he was "powerful physically" with "great mental characteristics."

Jones's reply to Miss Banky's query may have hearkened back to a quaint time and place that still reverberated sentimentally in Jones's Yalie dreams. However, the idea that Shevlin or any Ivy Leaguer from the Teddy Roosevelt era could compete at the level of Morley Drury, Ernie Nevers, or Red Grange was preposterous. The two decades that separate football from the 1900s to the 1920s is a period of great growth. Possibly in later years, the separation between the 1940s, when the players were mostly white and the equipment still archaic, and the 1960s, when integration was taking full force and the game had become one of gladiators, was a more shocking contrast.

While Duke Morrison was a student-athlete, the Hollywood–USC connection also led to one of the great scandals in movie annals. Scandal was already the order of the day, with the Fatty Arbuckle murder case only a few years old. Charlie Chaplin's radical politics led to scrutiny over his sexual immoralities. Movie actresses totally changed the image of what women were supposed to be. During the Roaring Twenties, hemlines shortened, flapper dresses accentuated sexuality, and an entirely new age was upon the world. Nowhere was this reflected more so than in the movies, and no actress embodied it more than the "it girl," Clara Bow. Her on-screen persona was that of a sexually liberated "party girl," the kind of fantasy always held out as taboo but secretly desired by men on the make.

Clara liked football, or at least she liked football players. She had a beautiful home and reportedly threw wild parties on Saturday nights. Young Hollywood would be there, single men and women looking to score with each other. Actresses Joan Crawford and Linda Basquette were regulars. So were the USC Trojans, of which Duke Morrison was one. There was a lot of drinking (which lasted all night), sunrise swims in her pool, and perhaps couples paired off in the home's bedrooms. Coach Jones, who was really quite a prude, a Christian gentleman who did not drink or smoke, most likely took pains *not to know* what really went on at Bow's parties. He also knew that the stories of wild fun with sexy Hollywood actresses, passed around by the players, often embellished, were in the long run excellent for recruiting. If they helped him field champions, so be it, but he left the details to others.

The Clara Bow rumors and obvious advantages of using Hollywood as a place to find employment for players, amid the inducements of movie glamour and maybe even sex, created a certain amount of criticism for Coach Jones. He was an unlikely target since he was the most rigid, un-Hollywood man imaginable. He was like a later coach, UCLA's John Wooden, who ran his program like the "book of Leviticus," according to *Los Angeles Times* sports columnist

Jim Murray. Amid an atmosphere he called "Gomorrah by the Sea," a place where half-naked coeds looked like Barbi Benton (who was one of those coeds when Wooden coached there), sorority parties were sometimes junior varsity tune-ups for the real things at Hugh Hefner's mansion a mile or so away, and rumors of a cheerleader sex fest ran rampant, "Wooden quietly went his winning ways with the Bible in one hand and a basketball in the other."

Ever since Jones, dubbed by the writers the Head Man, this has been a conundrum rather unique to Los Angeles, a professional sports town in which sex literally sells yet collegiate values of amateurism and even purity struggle against the pressures of a very different society placing little worth on such concepts.

The Clara Bow details *did* emerge into a scandal. The "details," however, were not true. How they started is anybody's guess: a player, an exaggerated storyteller, a snooping reporter, or somebody out to hurt Clara Bow, which is likely. She had enemies. Her form of sexuality was threatening. Years later, Natalie Wood portrayed an actress seemingly modeled after Clara Bow in *Inside Daisy Clover.* It was the story of a pretty young girl who grew up not so much on the wrong side of the tracks as on the wrong side of everything, in virtual squalor with no social manners or pedigree whatsoever. She is discovered, made into a star, and sexualized, becoming the pawn of handsome men and Hollywood power brokers. Daisy is never accepted because she is "low class." Rumors spread about her help bring her down.

The rumor about Clara Bow is that one Saturday night she took on the entire Trojans football team in a wild "gang bang." One by one, the players waited their turn while she serviced them in a pornographic scene, two or three at a time. Duke Morrison was said to have been one of those players who, after waiting his turn, had at her until satiated. Only after the "Trojan army" had achieved the ultimate "conquest" of Clara Bow did the sex end, presumably with the "it girl" ridden hard and put away wet.

GraphicC, a quasi-pornographic New York City tabloid, first reported the "gang bang" of Clara Bow. One cartoonist depicted her dressed like a cross between Helen of Troy and a song girl, the Trojans lined up behind her. It was further rumored that Clara presented each player with gold cigarette cases, gold cuff links, and bootleg booze as thanks for the—effort.

The story became the stuff of legend and, as in *Inside Daisy Clover*, was used to bring down the career of a talented, beautiful actress in over her head in the shark-infested waters of Hollywood. The "it girl" did not achieve long-term success; she certainly did not survive the transition to "talkies" and faded into oblivion, perhaps even tragic oblivion. The rumor persisted and was furthered by Kenneth Anger's *Hollywood Babylon* (1975). *Los Angeles* magazine printed as fact the "gang bang" story in 1999.

Clara may or may not have had sex with USC football players, maybe with more than one, or maybe with more than one at a time, but there is no actual evidence of it, and all the eyewitnesses denied it. She certainly did not have sex with the whole team in a single night. There is no evidence she had sex with Duke Morrison.

"We had a good time," said Duke's teammate Lowry McCaslin. "But it wasn't *that* exciting."

"Her escapades with the USC football team were not the stuff of legend," wrote her biographer David Stenn, author of the aptly named *Clara Bow: Runnin' Wild.* Star quarterback Morley Drury did date Clara but claimed "nothing happened," which could be true, or he might have just been a gentleman about it.

As the old expression goes, where there's smoke, there's fire. Clara Bow was reputed to be a sexual libertine at least to some extent, certainly beyond the normal confines of so-called good girls, although the morals of the 1920s were drastically looser than any previous period in American history. What is true is that her father heard the rumors and put his foot down, causing her to move the parties to the infamous Garden of Allah Hotel on Sunset Boulevard. Dad then insisted this too come to a stop. After that, she hosted the team only once a year, a more formal dinner held at her house.

When the Internet came to be, the rumor found a place to flourish. The "Clara Bow gang bang" rumor found entirely new life, with much speculation one way or the other. Snopes.com/movies/actors /clarabow.asp certainly appears to refute the rumor once and for all.

"The wild rumors about crazed orgies where Clara Bow provided personal 'entertainment' for the entire 'beer-swilling, gangbanging' Trojan squad grew over the ensuing decades," the website reads, even though "the facts reveal a group of well-behaved boys who were, in Morley Drury's own words, 'too damn innocent' to be anything else."

The story was repeated in *The USC Trojans: College Football's All-Time Greatest Dynasty, Trojans Essential: Everything You Need to Know to Be a Real Fan!,* and *Fight On! The Colorful Story of USC Football* (2006), the latter written by well-respected Trojan historians Loel Schrader and Steve Bisheff.

"Bow had a reputation for high living, and the film industry wasn't averse to using anything it could to capture attention for its stars," wrote Schrader and Bisheff in *Fight On!* "Given Hollywood's penchant for invention and its lust for publicity, it wasn't surprising that rumors began circulating that Bow, known as the 'it' girl, had serviced the entire USC football team. When the situation was investigated, it turned out Miss Bow, closely supervised by her father, held a post-game party at her home for some of the Trojans." The book added that Morley Drury, the "noblest Trojan of them all," dispelled the "silly rumors."

In an odd case of life imitating rumor, a real-life gang bang actually did take place when in 2001 Anabolic Video filmed *The Gangbang Girl 32* on the turf of the Los Angeles Coliseum. It was filmed at night, with the city-run stadium's lights turned on. There is no evidence any USC officials had anything to do with permitting this (Pete Carroll was head coach at the time), but it must have required the cooperation of somebody in the City of Los Angeles to allow the cast and crew into the stadium with the lights on. The scene features a brunette porn star named Kimberly playing a cheerleader servicing an entire football team in a wild display of hard-core sex. While the film was distributed in 2002 and obviously was filmed at the Coliseum, it was not until 2012 that it caused any sort of public consternation, which amounted to a certain amount of embarrassment for USC.

At six feet four inches tall, the "Greek god" Duke Morrison was slated to start at tackle for the 1926 USC Trojans. Had there been an Associated Press preseason poll (its rankings did not start until

1936), Troy most likely would have been ranked first or second in the nation. Other powerhouses of the time included Notre Dame, Pop Warner's Stanford Indians, and the defending national champions, the University of Alabama.

Morrison's parents were divorced by then. Clyde moved to Beverly Hills, and Molly took Bobby to live with her folks in Los Angeles. In the summer of 1926, Duke had to sleep in a bedroom above a friend's garage. He worked at Fox and met famed director John Ford. He stayed in shape as best he could, getting ready for preseason practice in August. He loved the beach and on weekends regularly trekked, in a friend's car or hitchhiking, to the Redondo strand, Santa Monica Pier, "Tin Can Beach" between Huntington Beach and Seal Beach, and Newport's Balboa Beach.

Newport's waves are notorious. This is the home of the infamous "Wedge," an anomaly in which the ocean floor is steeply shaped, a shore break with a very strong backwash. It is unpredictable and dangerous. The waves can get enormous, causing human bodies to be violently slammed to the ocean floor. Paralyzed surfers are sometimes found gazing out upon the ocean wearing T-shirts declaring, "Victim of the Wedge."

"When we moved to California, I discovered the ocean, and I loved it," Wayne recalled. "My ambition was to become an officer in the United States Navy. I applied to the Naval Academy but was turned down." After that, he decided to study law and become an attorney after his collegiate football career.

"I had a hand in making him a picture star, I always say," joked Eugene Clarke, a lineman, in *The Trojans: A Story of Southern California Football* by Ken Rappoport.

"In Wayne's sophomore year he was slated for first string right tackle at Southern Cal, but he had a bad accident the summer before the season started. I was with him when it happened. Duke and I used to go down to Balboa Beach and ride those big ocean waves. One day we're on the sand with pretty coeds all around. You know how everyone likes to show off, particularly Duke and me.

"These big waves started to come in. We called them, 'buttbusters.' I mean, they were BIG! They were washing the bottom of the pier. Duke says, 'Come on, let's go ride them.' I said, 'You gotta be nuts, they'll kill us.' He said, 'Come on, you've got no guts!' And I said, 'Dammit, if you're crazy enough, I'll go.'

"It took us fifteen minutes to get past the breaker lines because when these waves hit they pound so hard on the sand that you have to dive down and hang on. So we finally get out to where they were breaking, and I warned Duke that the breakers cup hard and will drop you straight down. I told Duke if they start cupping to back out of them. 'Okay,' he said.

"By this time there were a lot of people on the pier nearby wondering who these damn fools were in the water. The last thing I saw was this wave coming, and I mean it was a big one. It started to cup, and I screamed, 'Get out of it, Duke.' And I tucked my butt back in the wave as it came over, see. But when I last saw Duke, he was going straight down. He hit the sand, and if he hadn't pulled his head to one side he probably would have busted his neck. As it was it dislocated his shoulder . . .

"Now this is three weeks before football practice starts, and he was playing right tackle in the old Howard Jones power plays and in this system you used right shoulder blocking all the time.

"Duke wouldn't block, and he was afraid to tell the old man he'd hurt his shoulder swimming. The old man would give him hell for it. With Jones you slept, ate, and drank football 365 days a year. He wouldn't understand anyone getting hurt in a foolish accident like that."

Clarke's story seems to be legitimate. He was a teammate and eyewitness, not a studio publicist. However, this is where the John Wayne legend first starts to take a few turns or, as Wayne himself said in *The Man Who Shot Liberty Valance*, "when the legend becomes fact, print the legend."

Daughter Aissa Wayne recalled the bodysurfing incident to be in November 1926, "the season practically over," adding, "With his right shoulder muscle ripped, he kept going to practice all week, traumatizing the tissue even more. Though my father stayed on the roster and received his varsity letter, his shoulder would not allow him to play football."

The 1926 Trojans played—and won—three games in November of that season before losing 13–12 before 74,378 fans in the first-ever game against Notre Dame at the Los Angeles Memorial Coliseum, en route to an 8–2 record in a season in which Pop Warner's Stanford Indians and the Alabama Crimson Tide played to a 7–7 tie in the Rose Bowl, sharing a co–national championship. If Duke Morrison injured his shoulder in November, missing these games—in particular the epic one-point loss to the Fighting Irish—it would have engendered great ire in the coach everybody called "the Head Man." The loss to Rockne's team could have cost the Trojans a shot at the national title shared by archrival Stanford. Any tiny disadvantage could have made the difference in such a narrow defeat.

Morrison's injury also underscores his crossing paths with a groundbreaking figure not only in USC but also college football history. Morrison came out of Glendale High a guard, but at USC there was already an all-American guard named Brice Taylor. Head Man Jones moved Duke to right tackle. Morrison's injury was obviously serious, but just how serious is only speculation. Had he stayed at tackle, perhaps he could have withstood the pain (at least enough to stay in the starting lineup), fulfill his duties, and, if indeed the injury occurred in the summer and not in the fall, perhaps heal a few games into the season. But as Clarke pointed out, the switch to right tackle and with it the emphasis on right-shoulder blocking (his dislocated shoulder) meant he could not handle the job.

In part, this may have been because of Taylor. Duke never spoke disparagingly of Taylor, as in "Had it not been for that darn Brice Taylor playing my position I'd been a star." Instead, Morrison accepted his fate, a lesson learned. Taylor was the better player and earned his spurs. It was one of those things that formed for Duke his meritorious philosophy—that things happen for a reason, that the best man should get the job no matter what.

In the case of Brice Taylor, he was African American. According to *Turning of the Tide* (2006) by Don Yaeger with Trojan football players Sam "Bam" Cunningham and John Papadakis, Brice Union Taylor was so named by his parents when he was born on July 4, 1902.

He was not only African American but also a descendant of the Indian chief Tecumseh, who was killed by Kentucky militiamen at the battle of Fort Malden, Ontario, during the War of 1812. Tecumseh and his Shawnee tribe were allies of the British. After the battle, Tecumseh's infant son was found abandoned by the escaping Indian squaws and leaders. A rich Irish immigrant who owned a tobacco plantation in Kentucky took the baby back to his home. He was raised Bob Taylor, named after the plantation owner, and married a slave girl who had been kidnapped in Basutoland, then brought to America on a slave ship.

"That Indian was my great-grandfather—my progenitor," recalled Taylor. "After the Civil War, when they were free, my family ancestors moved west, settling for a time in Emporia, Kansas, where my great-grandmother became the first Negro schoolteacher in that city. Much later, my family moved to Seattle, where all my brothers and sisters—and I—were born."

He was born with no left hand, but that did not deter Taylor from starring at Franklin High School. In 1924, he was awarded a scholarship to USC by Elmer Henderson, a legendary former Seattle high school coach who built the early Trojans dynasty largely with recruits from the Pacific Northwest. Washington State produced the best high school football stars in America in the 1900s and 1910s. The reason? The Alaska gold rush, a subject of one of Wayne's best movies, *North to Alaska*. The gold rush drew so many to Washington, the last gathering place before the treacherous journey, that it grew the population. Taylor was among those brought to USC by Henderson from Seattle. He never let any of his "handicaps"—being black, part Indian, or without use of a hand—handicap him.

Taylor was switched from fullback to guard. There is no evidence that Duke harbored any resentment over playing with or possibly losing his job to a black man. He had little experience with blacks growing up: in the Mojave, in Glendale, at Glendale High, and certainly not at the Sigma Chi house. Duke Morrison probably had the same attitude toward blacks that most reasonable white men of his region and era did. Taylor may well have represented the first one who was his equal and, in fact, his superior. Nobody ever heard John Wayne express openly racist views toward blacks or, in reality, anybody. In later years, he was accused of not having enough black representation among the cowboys in his movies, of not glorifying them. He called Indians of the nineteenth century "savages" and expressed animosity toward the Vietnamese during the Vietnam War. These are explainable positions based on standards of the time and identifying enemies of America during wars, as Indians and Vietnamese at various times in history were.

Los Angeles was not the Harlem renaissance. Few if any places in America with predominantly white populations, outside of Harlem, parts of New Orleans, Kansas City, and a few other locations, had large black populations. Life for blacks in Los Angeles, however, was about as pleasant as could be expected. Taylor navigated his share of land mines at USC, but he was given the opportunity to fulfill his dreams and goals.

There were Negro League baseball stars, but Taylor was one of the very first African American college sports stars. Fritz Pollard had been an all-American football player at Brown University in 1916. Some of the early sports teams at crosstown UCLA featured an African American athlete named Ralph Bunche, who would later win the Nobel Peace Prize for helping to negotiate an agreement between Israel and Palestine, but such examples were very rare indeed.

In 1924, Taylor played on Henderson's last team, which beat Missouri in the Christmas Festival on December 25 at the Los Angeles Coliseum, to finish 9–2. In 1925 under Coach Jones, Taylor set a national record, playing 656 minutes and earning the very first all-American honors in USC football history. The 11–2 Trojans "threw" five shutouts, while Taylor was the blocker most responsible for opening the holes that Mort Kaer ran through, when USC outscored the opposition, 456–55. Kaer earned his all-American honors in 1926.

A 17–12 upset by Washington State sent the Cougars to the Rose Bowl, where they lost to Alabama, propelling the Crimson Tide to their first national title. While Jones would coach four national champs, his first team may have beaten any one of them. Certainly Taylor making all-American at guard with his senior year coming up in 1926 meant no other player would threaten his position and may have propelled Jones to switch Morrison to right tackle. Having a black man who was not only a teammate but also the biggest star on his team was, if not an enlightening lesson absorbed by Duke Morrison, certainly a unique experience most white men of the era did not share.

Taylor, also a member of USC's world record–setting mile relay team, won several national meets under legendary coach Dean Cromwell. Forgoing a chance in the fledgling National Football League, he enrolled in a seminary, earning his doctorate of divinity before accepting a pastoral position with the First African Methodist Episcopal Church as well as being a teacher in the Los Angeles public schools and a coach at black colleges in the South.

"Don't tell me America isn't the land of opportunity," Taylor told audiences. "Where else could a crippled colored kid receive the help, the encouragement, and inspiration to go as far as his ability could carry him?"

There are differing reports over Morrison's injury: a broken collarbone, a broken leg, an injury suffered before the season, or, according to his own daughter, an injury that occurred during the season. Exactly what prompted Morrison to leave school is not entirely clear. His motivations and the memories (or opinions) of others vary from teammates to family to teammates to public relations mavens to biographers.

The injury of the 1926 campaign certainly affected Morrison's football career, with implications far beyond that. Many believe he was a great player ticketed for stardom.

"He had all the football ability in the world," said teammate Leo Calland. "He had savvy, a great build and the equipment."

"He was a tough guy," all-American tackle Jesse Hibbs was quoted saying in *Fight On! The Colorful Story of USC Football* by Loel Schrader and Steve Bisheff. "The one thing that I remember is that just as he was about to be paddled at the fraternity house, he would wince perceptibly. But that didn't mean he was a softie. No way."

Others have a different view.

"Wayne was great guy, and he hasn't changed any," recalled one unnamed source in *The Trojans: A Story of Southern California Football*. "But he wasn't really a top-notch player."

Another told Ken Rappoport in confidence, "I'm not criticizing Duke, but some guys have more desire than others. He had too many distractions. He was a big, good-looking guy with black, curly hair and a great build, and had to fight the girls off.

"Now Ward Bond, the actor and Wayne's close friend, was just the opposite. He had all the desire in the world, but he didn't have the same equipment. Both were tackles in college, and I always said that if you took Ward Bond's desire and John Wayne's equipment you'd have an All-American."

Either way, the only opinion that counted was Coach Jones's, and according to Clarke, "Well, what happened was the old man thought Wayne didn't have any guts. He didn't know about the shoulder injury. So he put him down on the fourth or fifth team."

Duke tried to play with a shoulder harness, "but Jesus, how it hurt," he recalled.

"That took Wayne off the training table, and he had to scrounge for his own meals," added Clarke.

Clarke remembered this as a hard time for Wayne. "Duke was in bad shape, financially. He owed money to the fraternity for his dues, room and board, and he didn't have a dime. The fraternity was urging him to pay up; he felt his football playing days were over because of his bad shoulder. So he did what he felt he had to do. He quit school and went to work at the studios."

His friend Eckles found him a place to live. "He had no place to go and he knew my folks, so I brought him home and he lived upstairs over our garage for a while."

"His glory days shockingly over, he sulked and received poor grades," wrote Aissa Wayne in *John Wayne: My Father* (1998). "That summer he asked John Ford for a full-time job."

Woody Strode would clash with John Wayne on set in the 1960s. "Wayne was never a great football player, but somehow he got into USC's Hall of Fame," said Strode in 1976. "I guess becoming the greatest movie star in the world will do that for you."

As a star player for the Bruins, where he was a teammate of all-time greats Jackie Robinson and Kenny Washington, Strode had key insight into the goings-on of collegiate football.

"It's unlikely, almost unthinkable, that a good coach would drop a promising All-American because of one injury," he said. "Duke was just not good enough to stay on the team."

The "all-American" moniker was one the studios attributed to Wayne in trying to make him into a star, along with nefarious reports that he was not nicknamed after his dog but was instead descended from European royalty or some other lofty untruth. To his credit, Wayne never retold this about himself, instead jokingly—for the most part—refuting the more lavish descriptions. Wayne joked he was the only guy named all-American "by the Hollywood Women's Publicist's Guild" but also said, "If it hadn't been for football and the fact my leg broke [with the loss of an athletic scholarship] and I had to go into the movies to eat, why who knows, I might have turned out to be a liberal Democrat" (*The Quotable John Wayne* by Carol Lea Mueller).

This statement certainly refutes his all-American status—he was never even first string—but sheds strange questions. He herein describes not a shoulder injury but a broken leg (not to mention the troubling-for-many notion that such a fragile turn of events might have produced John Wayne: Democrat).

"I don't know if Duke ever had a shoulder injury," said George Sherman, who knew Wayne for decades and directed him in *Big Jake* (1971). "All I can tell you is that when we first worked together, he never showed any sign of a weakened shoulder. But by 1939 he was already becoming less agile. For one thing, he suffered with back pain. My feeling is that if Duke said he hurt his shoulder, then it was true, but I don't believe that was the reason he was dropped from the college football team. He never could run particularly fast, and if you look at pictures of Wayne up to the time he made *The Big Trail* [1930], you can see that he was tall but not well built, which means he was never going to be a star football player. But it looked good to the fans in those early days to say he was, and it was something Duke was never going to dispute."

(Photos of Marion Morrison in uniform seem to thoroughly discredit Sherman's description of a football player who was "not well built.")

The 1926 football season was another year of triumph for the rest of the Trojans. Featuring Taylor, quarterback Morley Drury, tackle Jesse Hibbs, Don Williams, and their second all-American, Mort "the Red Bluff Terror" Kaer, Jones's team was just beginning to pick up the moniker Thundering Herd. They electrified Los Angeles, but little if any glory washed over Duke.

His great academic plans began to fray. Duke, a member of the USC debate team, hoped to become an attorney, but the lessons of being a poor kid with no money at a rich school surrounded by those who did weighed on him.

"If I keep studying law, I'm gonna wind up writing briefs in somebody's back room for people who aren't as smart as I am," he reasoned. Perhaps, but his 1926 summer of wanderlust "training" Tom Mix for *The Great K & A Train Robbery*, combined with his experience in the Glendale school play and some limited Shakespearean training, planted the seed of Hollywood in his mind. It is a powerful seed that has made many a man and woman scrape and claw and fight with all they have to become an actor. This seed was beginning to grow in Duke Morrison.

"He owed the fraternity house so much dough that they had to ask him to move out until he could pay," added Eugene Clarke. "He dropped out of school and went to Fox studios."

"It was as natural a transformation as anyone could make, really," wrote Rappoport. "He always played cowboy games as a youth and eventually hungered to be an actor."

"It was a case of my having to work, and then they began paying me good money to be in front of the camera so I stayed with it," John Wayne would say.

Clyde did not like the idea of his son working in the movies. He urged him to stay in school. He worked in the spring and summer of 1927 to pay off his fraternity debts. He propped for directors Raoul Walsh and John Ford, the latter of whom told him he would find a place for him with Fox. But Clyde still wanted him to stick it out at USC.

Duke showed up for football practice in August 1927. Technically, he was still on scholarship, but Jones wrote him off, discouraging him from staying on the team, which promised to compete for a national title.

"So when my shoulder didn't feel any better at the start of my junior year, I decided to drop out for a year and let it heal," he recalled. "I never got back."

Duke took Ford up on his offer and found employment at Fox studios. He moved into an apartment in Beverly Hills and even brought his younger brother Bobby along as a roommate. An affable loser, Bobby had dropped out of school. Molly somehow blamed Duke. Under Duke's guidance, he managed to graduate from high school and after attending junior college even enrolled at USC in 1931 and was a member of their 1932 unbeaten national champions, one of the best college teams ever. Jones by this time was firmly established among the all-time greats in the coaching profession, as this was his third national champion. His 1928 champions were one of the great powerhouses, and his 1931 Trojans rallied to score sixteen fourth-quarter points, upsetting Notre Dame at South Bend, 16–14, to propel themselves to another title.

Knute Rockne was gone, having perished in a tragic plane crash. In the 1939 Rose Bowl, a reserve quarterback named Doyle Knave hit a reserve end named Al Kreuger for a touchdown to beat unbeaten, untied, and unscored-upon Duke, 7–3. The next season, Jones added his fourth and last championship with a win over Bob Neyland's Tennessee Volunteers in the 1940 Rose Bowl game.

USC football was not merely a Hollywood favorite and juggernaut of the green plains. UCLA started playing football. With their ascendance, along with the Notre Dame rivalry, California and Stanford were no longer USC's main opponents. Jealousy pervaded their attitude, which began to take on a negative tone that would continue, coming to a head in the volatile 1960s and 1970s.

By the late 1930s, when Robinson, Washington, and Strode—all African Americans—starred for the Bruins, games against integrated Trojan squads before 90,000 fans became veritable social statements a decade before Robinson broke baseball's "color barrier," some two decades before *Brown v. Board of Education* and Little Rock, and almost three decades before the Great Society. By this time known as John Wayne, the actor saw the success of his teammate Brice Taylor and the smooth integration of Robinson and others at crosstown UCLA. Certainly, the city of Los Angeles seemed to be a place that was getting it right, but Wayne made a mental note that this progress was not the result of protests, lawsuits, or legislation. It was essentially a profound accomplishment of the American private sector, one that he most certainly admired.

USC in the 1920s and 1930s, years in which Duke Morrison was intimately involved in Trojan football, remains one of the great dynasties. It produced, among numerous others, USC Hall of Famers of the Morrison vintage, among them Morley Drury, Jesse Hibbs, Gus Shaver, Jess Mortenson, Mort Kaer, Nick Pappas, and Aaron Rosenberg.

As for the Saenz family, the combination of Clyde and Molly's divorce with Duke dropping out of school, then choosing the immoral world of Hollywood, convinced them that Josephine must never see Duke again.

All his life, Duke Morrison had lived to please other people. These included Clyde and Molly, his Sigma Chi fraternity brothers, Los Angeles high society, the Saenz family, and Coach Howard Jones. He had chosen a structured, ordered world of hard work, academic excellence, and the rigors of football discipline. He was dutiful and did as he was told. Now he was about to enter a freewheeling world, a world known as showbiz, which many would tell you is not a business. It was his destiny.

3

THE DUKE OF HOLLYWOOD

"MORRISON WAS TALL, WELL BUILT, AND HAD THE WASPISH GOOD LOOKS OF A leading man, but in high school and college he had been a debater, a chess player, and a diligent, accomplished student," wrote Randy Roberts and James Olson in *John Wayne: American.* "He was always quick to please, though those efforts stopped short of obsequiousness."

"His good looks inspired someone in the casting department to give him a job as an extra and even as a stuntman in a number of films," wrote Michael Munn in *John Wayne: The Man behind the Myth.*

Indeed, old photos of Duke Morrison in a three-point stance at USC, as an extra in old silent movies, or as a cowboy of the silver screen reveal a tousle-haired stud of such profound physical handsomeness as to rival any screen idol of that or perhaps any era: Rudolph Valentino, Clark Gable, Robert Redford, Tom Cruise, or Matt Damon. For one, he was a massively built, muscled powerhouse, while most male screen legends over the years are disappointingly short in stature when observed in person. This has always been a huge selling point with his fans and over time took on the persona of Duke Wayne: "larger than life," literally and philosophically. His critics and competitors were pipsqueaks in comparison, throwing barbs he was too big to notice.

But as Roberts and Olson noted, despite earning a scholarship to USC courtesy of his football prowess, he was a man of the mind. Andrew McLaglen, who directed him in several pictures, said Duke "was an intellectual. He read avidly and could hold a discussion about many subjects. He made himself aware of politics both nationally and internationally."

"He knew what the 1917 revolution in Russia was all about," George Sherman recalled. "He knew he didn't like Communists."

"When I was a sophomore at USC, I was a Socialist, pretty much to the Left," said Wayne, again negating the later vision of a totally rigid lifelong right-winger. "But not when I left the university. I quickly got wise. I'd read about what had happened to Russia in 1917 when the Communists took over."

If Duke Morrison "read about what had happened to Russia in 1917," he did not read it in the *New York Times*, the nation's "paper of record." Even then, a left-wing element pervaded the news media. First, John Reed "witnessed" the communist takeover, then breathlessly reported in *Ten Days That Shook the World* that it was nothing less than the hope of a desperate world.

Then Walter Duranty of the *Times* went to the Soviet Union, reporting that harvests were good, trains ran on time, and a proletariat class of peasants had created, after a millennium of human suffering and greed, a "workers' paradise."

Both men were shown only what V. I. Lenin and Joseph Stalin wanted them to see, reporting back in unquestioning fashion, all to the tune of great praise from the Soviet despots who recognized two "useful idiots" of the first order. In the meantime, the Jewish exodus from starving Russia to Jerusalem, freed for the first time in 2,000 years from the Ottoman Turks by T. E. Lawrence and the British army, was so great that it would eventually create the modern state of Israel.

Reed, Duranty, and their ilk failed to report that Russia's harvest, bountiful for centuries under the czars, dried up under communist rule; that only emergency food shipments from the United States prevented worse starvation than occurred; or that their vaunted "five-year plans" always failed, replaced the next year or so by another failed five-year plan.

Morrison may have been hearing from early Russian expatriates, many the "Whites" with ties to the Romanovs (restaurateur Mike Romanoff claimed, apparently falsely, he was related) who flocked to Hollywood in the 1920s and 1930s. One was Ayn Rand, a Jewish émigré and aspiring screenwriter whose novel *Atlas Shrugged* would infuse the conservative movement as few before or after. But Duke's information probably came from conservative classmates, even professors at USC, and from the totally Republican *Los Angeles Times*, which in the 1920s was controlled by the ultraconservative Harry Chandler.

One of the reasons it was so easy for Duke Morrison to land work so fast was the lack of union graft and corruption. He started as a set dresser, work he had done with quarterback Don Williams, bathed in glory leading the 1928 Trojans to their first victory over Notre Dame and with it the first of their eleven national championships. But the real reason he made it so quickly was the man who gave him his first chance, who would also help make him a star (indeed, a leading man), and who would also be one of his greatest influences: a father figure and mentor in a relationship with few if any equals throughout Hollywood annals. Fellow director Frank Capra called John Ford "half-tyrant, half-revolutionary; half-saint, half-Satan; half-possible, half-impossible; half-genius, blah-blah; half-Irish, half-man—but all director and all American."

Friends called him "Jack."

"Duke Wayne was just a stick of wood when he came away from USC," director Allan Dwan commented. "Jack gave him character."

"The first picture I worked on was *Mother Machree* which John Ford was directing," recalled Duke Wayne, adding that he "studied" and "loved" John Ford ever since he was a "goose-herder" for him in 1927.

Working as prop man for Ford, Morrison allowed a gaggle of geese to fly all over the place instead of into the camera shot. Ford yelled at him. Morrison did not take kindly to it.

"You're a football player, aren't you?" Ford asked him.

"Yes," Wayne replied.

"What position did you play?"

"Guard."

"Do you think you can block me?" asked Ford, an out-of-shape, thirty-one-year-old former gridder with an inflated ego.

"Yes."

"I used to be a fullback. Think you can take me out?" asked Ford.

"Yeah, I know I could."

"Get down on your three-point stance."

They lined up, a few feet apart.

"See if you can stop me." Ford kicked his hand away, and Morrison fell. Ford, having caught him by surprise, rushed past. Morrison got a partial grip, kneed him in the chest, and brought him down to the dirt.

He asked to try again. Morrison did not wait for Ford but drove straight into him, scattering tables and chairs. The man Wayne would know as "Pappy" laughed.

"You'll do all right, now get those f——g geese back in the pen and we'll try again."

Morrison and Ford became as close as any friends can get, but their values and views, sometimes infused by Ford's jealous streak, occasionally clashed. This clash of values again came to the fore when in 1929, Ford made *Salute*. It was directly inspired by the Trojans' stunning 1928 national title, capped by a 27–14 trouncing of Notre Dame before a packed house at the Los Angeles Coliseum. USC–Notre Dame games at Chicago's Soldier Field drew well over 100,000 fans. The Trojans were the darlings of Los Angeles at a time in which college football and American sports were at their all-time height. Their success was partly attributable to the Olympics coming to the Coliseum in 1932. They were a golden team. Ford wanted to take full advantage of that. His first lieutenant was Duke Morrison.

The film was actually based on the U.S. Naval Academy, but Ford decided to use all USC players for the football scenes, letting the box office public know full well they were really seeing the national champions on the screen. In some ways, it was the first visual football broadcast. The shooting was scheduled for the spring of 1929 in Annapolis, Maryland, before the midshipmen were let out for the summer. Ford wanted to train the USC players in Maryland, putting them up at the Naval Academy for the duration of the shoot. School was not yet out at USC, either. Critics labeled it "professionalization" and "commercialization," which is of course exactly what it was. It was also a tremendous publicity boost for USC, sure to boost alumni donations, draw more freshman applications, and lead to increased tuition, all while bringing in capacity crowds for the 1929 football season. They were causes célèbres.

But before any of that, Ford's first request for twenty-five USC players in *Salute* was turned down, so he asked for Morrison's help. Duke approached George von KleinSmid, one of his Sigma Chi fraternity brothers and the son of President Rufus von KleinSmid, who arranged a meeting. Duke smartly framed the trip as a patriotic venture replete with a full tour of nearby Washington—a kind of D.C. semester, a popular aspect of political science education today. He proposed that they be given their final exams a few weeks early, freeing them up. Von KleinSmid agreed. It was a tremendous coup for Duke Morrison, elevating him to great heights in Ford's eyes. While he would go on to tremendous fame, it cannot be understated how important an event this was in promoting the career of the man who would be John Wayne. Had he failed to deliver, it would have been a setback, if not worse. It was also huge redemption; the injured football player, called gutless by Coach Jones and all but run off campus, returning bathed in glory and Hollywood imprimatur.

Morrison overcame major administrative hurdles in securing permission from school officials, which impressed Ford. He led a delegation that trained east in May 1929 amid much fanfare. The players included Clark Galloway, Russ Saunders, Jack Butler, Tony Steponovich, Jess Shaw, Frank Anthony, Al Schaub, Marshall Duffield, and Nate Barragar. The professionalism issue did cause some concern since the work involved players benefiting financially by virtue of the fact that they played football at USC.

When it comes to the legacy and mythology of John Wayne, Henry Hathaway was something of a curmudgeon. "Wayne had no pull with the university," he stated. "He was probably totally forgotten by the university. There was no way he had any authority to cast the film. Only a studio executive could do that, and that's what really happened. No one was handpicked by Duke; Ford chose his team from photographs the studio collected."

"Duke couldn't help laughing at the irony of the situation," wrote Pilar Wayne. "He was finally going to the Naval Academy—as an actor rather than a cadet!"

Ford picked twenty-five players, most of whom were Wayne's Sigma Chi brothers, plus a few Sigma Chi nonplayers. Ford also picked a 220-pound tackle named Wardell Bond, a man with large ears, thick lips, and an "ugly" face Ford found interesting. Duke disliked Bond and tried to talk Ford out of it.

Bond was an "interloper," according to Pilar Wayne, who tried to sneak on the train at the Santa Fe railroad station in Los Angeles.

"You're not getting on this train, Bond," Morrison told the lineman sternly. "You're too ugly to be in the movies."

"Screw you, Duke," Bond retorted, shoving his way on the train (this was a "scene" that played itself out in many films over the years).

"Who the hell is this?" asked Ford.

"His name is Ward Bond. He's just a big loudmouth who thinks he can play football."

"He sure is ugly."

"He's a lousy football player, too," Duke added.

"Leave him be," Ford said. "I'm going to use him," adding, "You're right, Duke. He is ugly. But I like his style."

Hathaway insisted Ford "never invented a part for Ward Bond. That was already in the script. I tell you, that Jack Ford really knew how to blarney! And I can tell you, Wayne thought the world of Ward Bond."

"When the train pulled out of the station, Duke and Wardell were enemies," wrote Pilar Wayne. "When they returned to California several months later, they'd become the best of friends, and both were calling John Ford 'Pappy' or 'Coach.'"

Ford assigned Bond and Morrison the same sleeping compartment on the train. Naturally, they became lifelong friends, a sort of John Wayne trait both on- and off-screen, assuredly one repeated numerous times in humorous scenes, often involving barroom fights followed by drunken, bloody-lipped camaraderie.

During one on-field squabble, Ford approached demanding, "What is this bull——t, anyway?" He called Bond the "big ugly guy. The one with the liver lips and the big mouth."

Ward was "all ego and gall," recalled John Wayne. He once "stole" $20 from Ford in plain sight for a night on the town, swiftly asking the director if he wanted to come along, then departing before the stunned Ford could finish shaving and answer. Ford loved that sort of thing. Bond never paid attention to the amount of meal money he was given. He ordered expensive items, then signed the name of Ford's older brother, the "paymaster" Eddie O'Fearna. Morrison was mortified, but again Ford appreciated his brazen attitude. Instead of causing trouble for Duke, Ford began to see the two as a pair, formulating in his creative mind future film scenes they could do together. Ward Bond was doing for John Wayne's career something few, if any, other people could do. It was all serendipity and destiny, literally a Hollywood story with a Trojan twist.

But Bond's bold ways did create friction. Ford took up with a groupie who wanted to be an actress. Bond came up from behind her, putting on a "full-court press" and resulting in her immediately French-kissing him before jumping into his bed. When Ford wanted some action, he could not find her. He asked Duke to look around. He discovered her stumbling out of Bond's room in the morning and confronted the player. Unaware she was "Ford's girl," Ward decided to lay low in Baltimore, but Ford forgave him. He was back on set in short order.

Also on the set of *Salute* was the famed black actor Stepin Fetchit. Duke acted as his "dresser" so he would not have to room separately from the rest.

Salute was a big hit—for Ford, the studio, the Naval Academy, college football, and USC. *Variety* called it "the best picture of its kind to date." Publicity informed a fawning movie public that the realistic football scenes could be attributed to actual Trojan stars performing on the field.

Duke made a small appearance, unnoticed by critics, but Bond was identified as a comer. The success of *Salute* did cement Duke as a full-time employee of a Hollywood movie studio. Once and for all, he decided not to return to USC. He was making $35 a week plus additional cash for stunt work and small roles.

USC was not the only school that produced football players in *Salute*. Loyola, a small Catholic college in Los Angeles, also provided a few players. A few years later, the outmanned Loyola Lions gave mighty USC their toughest game of the season before losing by only 6–0. The Loyola players credited their time on the same Annapolis field with USC players filming *Salute*, when they came to realize the men of Troy were just that: men.

By 1929, talkies were changing the economics of Hollywood. Duke Morrison's good looks and physical stature were his prime attributes. Famed director Raoul Walsh was casting for the role of a trail scout in a talking feature called *The Big Trail*. New York stage actors were brought in, as they had experience speaking their parts, but none could ride a horse. He wanted Gary Cooper, but he was too busy. Walsh felt Duke Morrison might fit the role's needs. His "voice training" consisted of shouting until hoarse in the canyons around Mulholland Drive and reading newspaper editorials out loud, enunciating each word. When Walsh decided to cast him, for some reason he felt Duke Morrison was not American enough. The name Anthony Wayne, a Revolutionary War figure known as "Mad Anthony," was one possible moniker, but somebody said it was "too Italian."

Walsh liked neither Anthony nor Tony Wayne and apparently felt Marion sounded like a girl. Somebody suggested "John Wayne." Walsh said "fine." Then and there, without even being in the room or having a part in the discussion, Duke Morrison was now John Wayne.

Supposedly.

Wayne's son Michael Wayne said Morrison's agent's name was Morrison, and, not wanting confusion, he just suggested "John Wayne."

Wayne did not like it. He never cared to be called Marion, but Duke was a great, manly name, and "Morrison," while nominally Irish, was certainly not un-American. But he was John Wayne on the big screen, the industry and his fans saw John Wayne, and John Wayne it was. His friends, however, would always call him Duke Wayne, and over time he would be known as the Duke.

The Big Trail typified Wayne's career: the story of America's Manifest Destiny, today vilified by the left as a violent conquest of Indians. He plays Breck Coleman, a frontier trailblazer who utters in his lines political statements of a sort, urging the settlers that they were "building a nation" and that, in so doing, "you gotta fight!" It was an epic saga, not a small story. The "villains" include southern politicians blocking expansion to the West, the Mexican government, and, of course, the Indians. Wayne's face was still young and pretty, a matinee idol, beautiful to women but manly enough to be believable.

The $2 million extravaganza premiered at the lavish Grauman's Chinese Theatre in 1930. Wayne called Molly's bluff when she insisted she and Bobby be given his two passes, not Clyde. Wayne refused, and Clyde attended with his second wife, Florence. Huge crowds spilled onto Sunset Boulevard. It was the essence of movie fanaticism, which, despite the Great Depression now descending on the nation after the 1929 stock market crash, found solace in the talkies. Reviews were very strong. John Wayne was immediately a movie star. He was sent on a nationwide publicity tour but was embarrassed by a fake biography released by Fox. He was said to have been a Texas Ranger, raised on the frontier, then an all-American football star at USC. He took every opportunity to set the record straight, but in response to one query by a female reporter asking if he always wore the frontier clothes of Breck Coleman, he replied with a trademark phrase: "What do *you* think, sister?" In *True Grit* some thirty-nine years later, he refers to Kim Darby throughout as "little sister."

Now a big movie star, he visited his friend Gene Clarke at the Sigma Chi fraternity house. He noticed a derby that had been given Clarke as a member of USC's 1931 team. After rallying to beat the Fighting Irish at South Bend, the "men of Troy, conquering football heroes," wrote the *Los Angeles Examiner,* were met by 300,000 fans at Union Station. Each player wore a bowler gifted them by a Chicago haberdashery. The city of Los Angeles seemed to have determined not to participate in the Great Depression, giving the Trojans a ticker-tape parade through downtown all the way to campus, two miles away.

"There seemed to be half a million people lining the streets," recalled all-American Ernie Smith. USC sports information director Al Wesson called it "the wildest sports demonstration that the city of

Los Angeles ever had." The *Examiner* added, "Bankers and laborers . . . industrial kings and clerks . . . merchants and typists" were all Trojans for a day, USC their adopted alma mater.

But Clarke did not wear his bowler.

"Don't you wear it?" asked Wayne.

Clarke thought it was silly, but Wayne was so taken with the memento from USC's stirring victory over the Irish that he "wore that derby for the longest time, hardly ever took it off," said Clarke.

4

THE DUKE OF WAR

By 1939, Duke Wayne was married to Josephine and had a large young family. The year 1939 is viewed as the greatest in the history of film, with movies like *Gone with the Wind* and *Mr. Smith Goes to Washington* among classics. Wayne starred in one of those classics, John Ford's epic western *Stagecoach*. It cemented Wayne as an actor of substance and a box office hit.

During the Christmas holiday season of 1939, Ford took John Wayne, Ward Bond, Preston Foster, Wingate Smith, and George Schneiderman on his boat, the *Araner*, south off the Baja California coast. Ford was still a lieutenant commander in the U.S. Naval Reserves. Before the trip, Captain Elias Zacharias, chief intelligence officer for the Eleventh Naval District, asked Ford to write a detailed, unofficial report on any Japanese maritime activity he might see. Indeed, Ford discovered a Japanese photographer who eluded his attempt to contact him, a Japanese shrimp boat anchored at Guaymas, and a Franco-American fishing boat—with a Japanese crew.

According to Wayne, it was on the *Salute* set where U.S. Navy Rear Admiral William Sims officially first contacted Ford about conducting surveillance of Japanese "tourists" during his coastal and Baja excursions. Ford also conducted surveillance while filming *Men Without Women*, a submarine feature.

Ford had seen fishing crews all his life: grimy, drunken men on shore leave looking for female action. Not so with the men of this "trawler," who he noted were young, ramrod straight, and neatly dressed and who he was "positive" were "navy men." On the train back to Los Angeles, the group noticed Japanese men "sublimely indifferent" to the picturesque landscape, instead taking photographs of bridges and oil tanks with an elite Leica. Another acted like a clown on the train, but Ford saw him bark orders at several other Japanese.

Ford's seven-page report to Captain Zacharias stated that it was plausible the Japanese had scouted every inlet and bay in California. Ford was convinced he had observed a spy ring in action. The United States was already spying on Japan as well. A group of traveling Major League Baseball players had been to Tokyo. Included among them was Moe Berg, a journeyman catcher who was also a brilliant Ivy League attorney. The War Department outfitted him with a long-distance camera and instructions to capture photos of industrial plants, ships, and other potential bombing sites. Jimmy Doolittle's raiders on Tokyo used his photos shortly after Pearl Harbor. Berg was recruited into the Office of Strategic Services (OSS) and, despite being Jewish, was tasked to seek out Nazi scientists before they were captured by the Soviets in the last days of World War II. He was successful, and many of these rocket scientists formed the early U.S. space program.

The Japanese had invaded China in 1931 and were in a heated battle with the United States over an oil embargo imposed by Roosevelt. They were actively aligned with Hitler's Germany, already at war with England and France. Ford decided then and there to make an antifascist film with screenwriter Dudley Nichols. Ford dedicated himself to creating a unit of Hollywood filmmakers tasked with using their particular skills in what he was sure would be a war effort. Wayne had no desire to be involved. Perhaps selfishly, he was interested in building his career on the success of *Stagecoach*. He was roped into a bad contract with Republic Pictures, which, however, was not conducive to his goals.

Wayne received good reviews for his role in *Dark Command*. He was now in a position to command respect, not beg for meetings.

He could call his own shots. He generally did not exact retribution from those who had belittled him in the past, but he had few kind words for Cecil B. DeMille. A few years earlier, DeMille totally disrespected him. Now he was calling with compliments. Wayne did not tell him to jump in a lake, but he did not jump to the mogul's beck and call, either.

Oddly, the political nature of Hollywood beginning in the late 1930s and continuing into the 1940s did not capture Wayne's attention. He was one of the most educated, intelligent people in the business (although his jock-cowboy image belied this, especially with fans) but left social issues to others.

Donald Ogden Stewart, a leading Communist Party organizer, started the Hollywood Anti-Nazi League. One of its members was Herbert Bilberman, a well-known leftist. *The Red Network* was a booklet identifying communists in the industry. Most were screenwriters.

"Screenwriters, who were often the best educated people in Hollywood, generally thought themselves intellectually superior to mere actors, producers, directors, and studio executives," Wayne said. "Many of them belonged to an alliance of liberals and Communists."

"We're up to our necks in politics and morality now," Mary McCall complained in the 1937 issue of *Screen Guild.* "Nobody goes to anybody's house any more to sit and talk and have fun," adding that such gatherings were presided over by a master of ceremonies, and after speeches, a collection plate for whatever cause—the anti-fascists as well as Francisco Franco's side of the Spanish Civil War, the Anti-Nazi League, and Polish Relief—was passed around. What many did not know and what a fair number actually did was that some of these "committees" were communist fronts.

They ranged from fellow travelers who believed, if not in outright communism, at least in a more "equitable" arrangement than capitalism, often referred to as socialism, to outright Moscow-controlled espionage and subversion organizations. Many couched themselves under the umbrella of "relief," motivated to feed the starving of Russia. The news that the millions starving in Russia were starving not because of any natural disaster but as a direct political genocide directed against them by Joseph Stalin, particularly in his native Ukraine, was generally not known, in part because men like Walter Duranty did not tell America about it. Many who were attending these meetings were naive. The communists, as described in Upton Sinclair's *Oil!*, often used women to recruit and seduce pliable men into their cause. Many naively joined or attended because of "a girl" or the honest desire to help starving Eastern Europeans. Many joined and became Communist Party members of their own free will. A fair number were dedicated, paid Soviet agents. John Wayne paid little attention to most of it. Even when World War II started, he was concerned mostly with his next movie project. John Ford, on the other hand, was already dedicated to patriotically helping the American cause.

But what was undeniable was that Hollywood, once almost Republican by nature, was becoming, at least below the mogul level, liberal. Jews incensed by Adolf Hitler supported the Soviet Union, his sworn enemy, but when the Nazis and Soviets signed a nonaggression treaty in 1939, the politics of Hollywood was thrown for a loop. In 1939, Texas congressman Martin Dies chaired a committee to investigate communist infiltration and subversion of Hollywood.

The influential Ernest Hemingway strongly opposed Francisco Franco in Spain, having been on the front lines himself. Ford's *The Grapes of Wrath*, based on John Steinbeck's novel, is considered one of the great liberal works of all time.

"John Ford and I would often talk politics, but Duke didn't express his convictions," recalled the film's star, Henry Fonda. While Fonda found him incurious about it all, he and friend Jimmy Stewart, a conservative, became so heated over political differences that they agreed to never discuss politics again. Oddly, the party animal Ward Bond was at that time far more conservative and political. Wayne even supported the successful state senate candidacy of Democrat Culbert Olson but became disenchanted with the left. Since his good friend John Ford was a liberal fan of the New Deal, Wayne probably maintained silence in order to mollify the man he called "Coach."

"I was young and willing to listen to both sides of the argument," he recalled, adding "as a grown man I found I was more comfortable with Republicanism." Slowly, he was coming to see disturbing trends.

"I noticed something was going wrong in the business around 1937, 1938," he told writer Maurice Zolotow in the 1950s. "The Communists were moving in, and under the guise of being anti-Fascist I saw they were hoaxing a lot of decent men and women on humanitarian grounds," adding that while they were "bleeding heart liberals," they never actually helped the "little guy," which was actually one of Duke's most endearing traits. He heard screenwriters at parties remark that "Russia is the hope of the world" and that America is "shot to hell and patriotism" and a "big joke."

"Hitler and Stalin were the two sides of the same coin," he said. "They both exterminated masses of their own people. So did Mao [Tse-tung] after his Communist reign started in China."

Wayne developed a visceral hatred of communism on all levels. Not only was it an unworkable economic system, but it was a totalitarian dictatorship that put the state ahead of individual liberty, the opposite of Duke's cowboy credo. It was also atheistic, anathema to John Wayne.

"Duke didn't go to church," recalled Pilar Wayne. "He'd been uncomfortable with organized religion since childhood, a feeling which had been reinforced by marriage to the devoted Josephine. But Duke was a believer. He had faith in God and faith in his country. When it came to the United States, Duke was a flag waver who got a tear in his eye when he heard the national anthem or saw the Stars and Stripes outlined against a clear sky."

He believed the "American way" was to "speak out for what they hold dear, to stand up and be counted." She called him a "born-again American" who "saw Communism as an insidious threat that could weaken us from within while attacking our friends and allies on a broad international front."

Russia stood "alone against the insanity of the Nazis," wrote Pilar. "Having voted for Roosevelt, Duke thought of himself as a liberal, a staunch supporter of the principles of Jeffersonian Democracy." But to Duke and the conservatives, their "greatest fear was the industry would be taken over by individuals who secretly belonged to the Communist Party." Duke was called a "right-winger," which Pilar said he called a "bum rap."

Fellow actor Paul Fix recalled Wayne describe "lousy pinkos" and that "something should be done to get rid of them." Director George Sherman recalled Wayne insisting on a script change in *Wyoming Outlaw,* in which his character Ray Corrigan says, "You know, there used to be a time when America meant something. It still does. It stands for freedom and fair play." When British actor George Sanders joked that "the colonial Yankees had been a bunch of fairies," Wayne had to be restrained from knocking him out. Wayne was quoted saying that he wanted his films to warn the American public that they needed to be "prepared to defend their freedom."

In 1941, one of the most legendary small incidents in Hollywood history occurred. Wayne was getting a lot of fan mail and write-ups in the trades. Tay Garnett, a friend of Wayne's at the Emerald Bay Yacht Club, was assigned to direct the legendary German screen siren Marlene Dietrich in *Seven Sinners.* He needed a "big, rugged he-guy type with competent fists, plus sex appeal," recalled producer Joe Pasternak, adding, "T'ain't going to be easy," especially since the hard-to-please Dietrich had casting approval. Garnett wanted Wayne but doubted Marlene wanted him, too. He hatched a plan, which was to have Wayne standing in the Universal commissary when he arrived with the star actress.

With Wayne standing there in all his six-foot-four-inch curly-haired glory, Marlene, "with that wonderful floating walk, passed Wayne as if he were invisible, then paused, made a half-turn, and cased him from cowlick to cowboots," said Garnett. "As she moved on, she said in her characteristic brasso whisper, 'Daddy, buy me THAT.'" The story may be exaggerated, as the line "Daddy, buy me THAT" is from Somerset Maugham's *The Circle,* a film she performed in. But the general idea is achieved; Marlene "approved," and the film represented "Weimar decadence and American innocence," wrote Randy Roberts and James Olson.

Being paired with a decadent sex goddess did little for Wayne's marriage, already stretched thin by culture shock, long location shoots, Ward Bond's influence, drunken fishing trips with John Ford, a million adoring female fans, and the availability of every sexy young thing walking the Hollywood movie lots. Wayne would come back from all that temptation only to find one of the Saenz family priests invited for dinner. It was all too much for him. That said, he was not a philanderer. He claimed he "tried it—but it made me feel cheap and dirty." He was still an old-fashioned Christian gentleman. If he did sleep around at that time, which was hinted at but not verified, he was discreet. His marriage was breaking up out of cultural differences, not infidelity.

But Wayne and Dietrich eventually did become lovers during the *Seven Sinners* shoot. It was a scene straight out of the Old Testament; Marlene, a modern Jezebel who decided she wanted her costar, donned her best garters and exposed herself to him in her dressing room. St. Francis of Assisi would have struggled to resist. Duke was not then and never was St. Francis of Assisi.

He did not succumb to all temptation, however. Joan Crawford, a regular at Clara Bow's parties of the 1920s rumored to have been all-out orgies, tried to seduce Wayne, but he rebuffed her, making her mad that he would sleep with Marlene but not her.

"Gee, ma'am, I'm not that kinda guy," Wayne told her in his most sincere cowboy fashion.

In 1941, the Senate Select Committee on Interstate Commerce's Subcommittee on War Propaganda, headed by D. Worth Clark of Idaho, charged that forty-eight films contained specific elements of interventionist propaganda. Former Republican presidential candidate Wendell Willkie represented Hollywood. At the time, President Franklin Roosevelt was steering money to Great Britain in support of its perilous war effort with Nazi Germany. Spurred by Prime Minister Winston Churchill's inspirational speeches, the British gallantly won the Battle of Britain, an air war fought over the Atlantic and its coastline in 1940. Privately, Roosevelt wanted the United States to enter the war. He was urged to do so by Churchill. He may even have secretly allowed the fleet at Pearl Harbor to be exposed, inviting a Japanese air raid and the necessary national motivation to fight. But in 1940, he specifically campaigned against entering World War II.

Isolationist voices had an anti-Semitic tone to them, led by John F. Kennedy's father, the ambassador to the Court of St. James's, Joseph P. Kennedy. Father Charles Coughlin argued in national radio broadcasts against intervention, asking his audience, "Are you ready to send your boys to bleed and die in Europe to make the world safe for this industry and its financial backers?" That was a direct inference to the Jewish bankers and movie moguls dominating Hollywood.

This was an interesting conundrum. While many Hollywood big shots were indeed Jewish, in the 1930s and 1940s they were predominantly conservative Republicans. While Ambassador Kennedy was a Democrat, prior to World War II most of the opposition to entering the war came from the GOP. They did not trust Roosevelt, expecting that like President Woodrow Wilson, who in 1916 was reelected promising to stay out of World War I, Roosevelt would go back on his word in the same manner. While nobody can truly say for sure, most indications are that even without Pearl Harbor, at some point prior to 1944 Roosevelt would have entered the war. Perhaps the early reports of the Holocaust would have spurred such a decision.

The conundrum is that liberal Democrats were the biggest cheerleaders for America going to war. There have been few if any circumstances throughout American history in which this group wanted to fight—certainly not in Korea, Vietnam, the Persian Gulf, or Iraq. Maybe there was some real consensus on Afghanistan after 9/11 when New York City was targeted, and Muslim terrorists posed a threat to Israel as well as the United States. But in 1941, Adolf Hitler posed an existential threat. Many WASPs and Catholics, knowing it would be their sons who would bear the burden, were unimpressed with a small yet powerful lobby calling for them to march off to war. Stunned by the Hitler–Stalin nonaggression pact, they were after May 1941 again vociferous in their defense of Russia, now under full-scale German invasion.

The Japanese sneak attack occurred on Sunday morning, December 7, 1941, the day after USC tied UCLA, 7–7, at the Coliseum. December is a slow month in the movie industry from a production end. While many premieres do take place, the agents, producers, and executives can often be found lounging in the Palm Springs sun or playing golf. But wild rumors of Japanese naval maneuvers off the coast of California led to blackouts and high alerts. The Rose Bowl had to be moved to North Carolina on January 1.

John Wayne did not want to fight. He knew he probably would not need to go since he was married with four kids, but Henry Fonda, one of his fishing pals from the John Ford cruises, was three years older (thirty-seven) with three kids. He enlisted. Ford was forty-six and called to active duty. Jimmy Stewart had to put on weight just to be eligible and went on to fly missions, eventually attaining the rank of general in the reserves. Gene Autry joined the Army Air Corps. Robert Montgomery joined the navy, Tyrone Power the marines, and William Holden the army. Clark Gable, as big a star as there was, joined the army. David Niven, Laurence Olivier, and Patrick Knowle returned to Great Britain to fight. Of Niven, who flew missions, Winston Churchill remarked that what he did was the highest form of valor, adding that had he not done it, he would have been despicable.

Ronald Reagan was like Ford already a reserve officer. Sterling Hayden, Burgess Meredith, and Gilbert Roland all signed up. Also signing up were directors Frank Capra, William Wyler, Anatole Litvak, John Huston, and William Keighley; producers Hal Roach, Jack Warner, Gene Markey, and Darryl F. Zanuck; writers Garson Kanin and Budd Schulberg; cameraman Gregg Toland; and countless others with less name recognition. Even Joseph P. Kennedy's oldest sons, Joseph Jr. and John, not only served but were bona fide war heroes, with Joe dying in a secret, near-suicide mission (Robert and Edward served in later years).

Baseball stars Joe DiMaggio, Bob Feller, and Jerry Coleman were among numerous athletes who joined up. Ted Williams resisted the calling at first but eventually became a Marine Corps fighter pilot in World War II and again in Korea when his jet was shot down, but he survived. Joe Louis, the highest-paid athlete in history until that time, joined the army. Former Michigan Heisman Trophy winner Tom Harmon's plane was shot down. He survived in the jungles until rescued. USC Olympic track star Lou Zamperini was also shot down, survived on a raft, and then was imprisoned and tortured by the Japanese until the war ended.

Technically, Wayne was not eligible for the draft. He did *not* dodge the draft, but had he chosen to go, he would have been accepted. He was the picture of manly strength, the ex-Trojan football player, still in excellent physical shape. The injury he sustained at Balboa Beach in 1926 had healed long before.

While Fonda, Ford, and others in some cases jumped through hoops to serve when they had safe deferments, many like Wayne were married with kids and, like him, were exempt. The California draft board was quite liberal in its extension of deferments to actors and leading Hollywood players. President Roosevelt explicitly directed the motion picture industry to continue humming along, even calling it a "national security" prerogative. Many argued that "Gary Cooper was more valuable to the war effort as Sergeant York than Sergeant Cooper," according to authors Randy Roberts and James Olson. There were a number of reasons for this. First, it was a tremendous morale booster. Home audiences were reassured of this most American of pastimes continuing to thrive and entertain, giving them respite from their worries, a reason to believe some normalcy still existed in their lives and in their country. Even soldiers fighting overseas, while somewhat resentful of a Hollywood hotshot living the good life while they dodged bullets, still saw films as an example of the American way they were fighting to protect, its continued existence evidence that they were winning. Actresses like Rita Hayworth, whose sexy posters were all the rage with servicemen, indeed symbolized what they were fighting to protect.

The bratty singer Frank Sinatra was despised because of his me-first attitude, the obvious way young girls threw themselves at him—and especially the way he took so many to bed. Many girls wrote their boyfriends with wild descriptions of infatuation for the man who would come to be known as "Ol' Blue Eyes." He was looked upon as a guy stealing their women, a no-no.

But Hollywood was not the only industry that stayed in business during World War II. Schools and colleges all continued unabated, albeit with wartime anomalies. College football continued, although some schools did suspend the sport. Schools like USC were major ROTC training centers, and many a football player from Oregon or other programs suddenly without football found themselves unlikely and, in some cases, very memorable Trojans.

USC–Notre Dame games were suspended. The UCLA game was considered a major terrorism risk. Opponents routinely con-

sisted of St. Mary's Pre-Flight, San Diego Navy, and March Field. Jeff
Cravath coached teams sometimes referred as the "Marine Trojans."

Sam Barry coached baseball, basketball, and football at USC.
"The war started in December 1941," recalled USC and Rose Bowl
Hall of Famer Jim Hardy in *What It Means to Be a Trojan: Southern
Cal's Greatest Players Talk about Trojans Football* (2009). "He gave me
a scholarship around the first part of January. Then, about two
months later, he got called in the Navy, and in March before spring
practice, we hired Jeff Cravath."

Barry returned to USC to coach basketball. He is credited with
inventing the "triangle offense," brought into the National Basketball Association by one his stars, Tex Winter, and made into a championship formula in both Chicago and Los Angeles by coach Phil
Jackson. His successor, Rod Dedeaux was a friend of John Wayne's
who lived in his hometown of Glendale. Dedeaux won eleven national championships, was named Collegiate Baseball Coach of the
Twentieth Century, and turned Troy into the unrivaled greatest program of all time.

"We had a lot of transfers during the war," continued Hardy.
"Oregon dropped football. Washington State and Stanford dropped
football. Their guys would come to USC, Cal, UCLA, or Washington, and we had good material. It was not difficult to win at that
time, but in 1942, Jeff's first year, we had a mediocre season . . .

"We had officer candidates come in. Bill Gray came in from
the Marines. We had transfers from Oregon State to USC. Eddie
Saenz, who later played for the Redskins, came from Loyola. All the
transfers from Santa Clara, Fresno State, and both Oregon schools
came in under the Naval and Marine programs. It was not really a
problem. Some resented not playing more, but they all became Trojans. Some didn't cotton to Cravath, but they became Trojans and
certainly played like it. Nobody asked for anything."

Bill Gray was on the Oregon State team that beat Duke in the
Rose Bowl played at Durham, North Carolina, because of security
concerns on January 1, 1942.

"I was one of those guys who came to the University of Southern California through a military program," recalled the former
all-Coast center. "I was with the Marines, and USC had a contingent

of Marines. We were sent down there to Southern California, to Los Angeles, from Oregon, and I was allowed to go out for football.

"The Pacific Coast Conference at that time was short because some of the schools didn't have enough guys to field football teams. Only schools that had a military contingent, Navy or Army Air Corps, or whatever, could play. I was in the Marine Reserves, and played for Jeff Cravath, who was a fantastic coach and a great guy.

"We beat Washington 29–0 in the 1944 Rose Bowl. We drew 68,000 at the Rose Bowl, and they were very careful; there was a lot of security.

"They were worried about a terrorist operation like later with 9/11. They wanted to do it, but they wanted to be very careful, so we had Army, Navy, and Air Corps personnel protecting the Rose Bowl."

Gray said if a young man entered a collegiate military training program, it delayed entrance into a combat theatre, which was fairly immediate for regular draftees, but "If you waited too long, you got drafted . . .

"I was assigned before the war to the 1st Division, 5th Marines, and they were moving to China, in Peking. We were aligned with Chiang Kai-shek, who was fighting the occupying Japanese while Mao Tse-tung was in the hills waiting for the right time to try and take over. We beat the Japanese, but I never got into action. I was younger, so by the time I got into it, most of the heavy fighting was over." Gray found himself assigned to a force known as "China Marines," made famous by Jimmy Doolittle and Pappy Boyington, but going into the officer-training program at USC saved him from heavy action.

"I went to St. Mary's on a scholarship, but I knew I'd be called in," recalled Gordon Gray, a San Francisco native. "In July, the Navy called me to USC, where they had an officer's training program, and I played football."

Gray played in Rose Bowls during the war. "In 1944 versus Washington, the war was on, so we split the Pacific Coast Conference into Northern and Southern Divisions. Washington was favored by four touchdowns. We beat them 29–0," adding "I did not play in the Rose Bowl versus Alabama after the 1945 season. I was on a destroyer."

The Fighting Irish: Notre Dame Football through the Years by William Gildea and Christopher Jennison has one chapter called "Ecstasies" and another called "Agonies." Included among the "Ecstasies" are Notre Dame's 35–13 win over Army in 1913 (Gus Dorais and Knute Rockne introducing the forward pass); a 20–17 win over Army in 1920; the famed 13–7 victory over Army at the Polo Grounds in 1924 (Grantland Rice coining the term "Four Horsemen of Notre Dame"); a 12–6 upset of the Cadets in 1928 (Rockne's "Win one for the Gipper" speech); and the 0–0 tie with Army at Yankee Stadium in 1946 (securing the national title). While "Agonies" include their fair share of losses to USC (1931, 1964, and 1974), it is noteworthy that other heartbreakers were 59–0 and 48–0 pastings by Army in 1944–1945 and a 19–14 loss to the Great Lakes Naval Training Station played before 22,000 recruits in Illinois on November 27, 1943. The Fighting Irish under coach Frank Leahy were unbeaten and at the height of their storied history, but a service team filled with navy men culled from the national football scene was able to defeat them, ending their bid for a second unbeaten season in three years.

The U.S. Military Academy at West Point, New York, fielded under coach Earl "Red" Blaik, statistically at least, one of the finest college football dynasties of all time during the war years. Featuring back-to-back Heisman Trophy winners Doc Blanchard and Glenn Davis ("Mr. Inside" and "Mr. Outside"), they were unbeaten national champions, averaging almost sixty points per game, in 1944–1945. Only Notre Dame all-American Johnny Lattner's open-field tackle of Blanchard in the 1946 0–0 epic at Yankee Stadium prevented an unprecedented third straight Associated Press number one final ranking. After beating Navy in 1944, General Douglas MacArthur telegraphed Coach Blaik with word that they had "put the war on hold" in order to celebrate the win. It is impossible for modern Americans to truly grasp how important Army football was to pride and morale in World War II. Blaik and his players were giants, admired by the likes of MacArthur, Dwight Eisenhower, George S. Patton, and an adoring public.

The U.S. Army fielded one of the best baseball teams in the world, led by Joe DiMaggio playing in Hawaii, but President Roosevelt was equally clear that he wanted the major leagues to continue, stressing the morale boost to the country. They were down years (although Stan Musial had some memorable seasons in St. Louis), lacking the glamour of Notre Dame–Army, but to soldiers on the front it was very comforting knowing their hometown teams were still in operation. Typical security questions in the field included "Who was the National League batting champ last year?" Asking, "Who won the World Series last season?" led to more than one conversation in a South Pacific jungle or North African combat theater sounding like this: "Aw, Joe, don't remind me of Owen's lettin' Casey's third strike get past him. Cost me ten bucks when Brooklyn lost, doze bums dem."

Army football engendered enormous pride in the nation, big-league ball was comforting, and Hollywood films kept an anxious people entertained. The fact is that the United States could fight a world war on six major, shifting fronts (North Africa, Sicily/Italy, France, Belgium/Germany, the South Pacific, and China, oft on the enemies' "home turf"); in the world's two largest oceans (Atlantic and Pacific); on the land, in the air, and at sea; in brutal heat and brutal snow; in deserts, mountains, forests, and cities; and against the greatest military power ever assembled (Nazi Germany), allied on one side of the world with one of the greatest military powers ever assembled (Japan), on the other side by a nation determined to regain the glory of the Roman Empire (Benito Mussolini's Italy). These were fanatical, implacable foes convinced destiny favored them, willing to go to the most evil lengths in order to prevail. The United States accomplished this while, in addition to sports and movies, running a stock exchange; never abandoning the capitalist system; upholding law and order through a court system; maintaining varied industries, including the farming and infrastructure of a nation; educating its children; maintaining college degree programs; aside from some shortages and occasional blackouts, never depriving the citizenry of basic needs; and a million other hallmarks of American life, all while not insisting its military school students leave college early to fight.

In the history of humanity, this may be the single greatest accomplishment ever.

Some on the left have suggested the Soviet Union really "won" World War II. This is a farce. It is true that 23,400,000 Russian soldiers and citizens died, while "only" 418,000 Americans perished, but if total deaths are somehow considered the mark of "victory," it is news to every military historian and commander in every war college ever. The Soviets threw the bulk of their citizenry into the maw of the Nazi war machine without the slightest regard for cost or importance of human life. Dwight Eisenhower and the United States agonized over every life, constantly planning with the goal of maintaining casualties at as low a number as possible. The Soviets survived and enslaved their neighbors, nothing more. The Americans and British liberated the world. This is real victory, the kind that can lead to the real winners of an ensuing peace.

But it is worth examining the way American life continued relatively unabated, compared to the Soviet Union, Nazi Germany, and Japan, where every able man was thrown into the effort, dragged out of schools, colleges, and jobs. The entire lifeblood of these nations was scrapped in favor of a single purpose: fighting the war. Shortages and starvation—these marked life in these places. Under siege and constant Allied bombardments, it was a 100 percent all-in effort: nationwide "bunker mentalities." The Germans maintained the facade of a peaceful home front for a while, but when their cities were turned to fire and enemies encircled them, that was the end of that. Japan was reduced to committing virtual national suicide.

While the propagandists of these countries did all they could to prevent the citizenry from knowing that the armies destroying them were also rooting for the Chicago Cubs and Notre Dame Fighting Irish, happily playing games on a home front still featuring Saturday afternoon matinees, stockbrokers doing deals, and college boys chasing girls at frat parties, their leaders surely did know these things. Perhaps at first they tried to convince themselves America was unserious and would pay for their unseriousness, but if this was ever contemplated, it was soon replaced by the dizzying reality of carpet bomb strikes, daring assault by Patton's tanks, and "soft" boys who showed the Japanese that, no, the jungle belonged to the old breed, the *Marine Corps.*

"They had service teams throughout the world," recalled Bill Gray. "It was big for morale and for the entertainment of service members. We beat Germany and Japan on two war fronts while playing sports—football, Major League baseball—and they had to look at that and wonder how we did that. Here's these two countries putting every available resource into beating us in a war, and they were getting beat, both of them, by a country that still finds time for sporting activity. Only in America! . . .

"You get back to how strong the U.S. was, how we were defeating Nazi Germany and imperial Japan while our service academies held back their football players and win national championships. What a morale boost for America, and you have to think the German and Japanese high commands looked at that and just thought, *We can't beat these people,* which they couldn't."

While these facts, in totality, help to soften the view of John Wayne's lack of war service, none of this was known when the war began. What is known, though, is that a war is won at home as it is in the jungles, in the skies, on the seas, and on the battlefields. What is also known is that very early on, President Roosevelt urged Hollywood to keep making films for the morale of the citizenry. What is further known is that Hollywood mobilized film units right away tasked with making propaganda documentaries and war films designed to help the cause. Many were assembled at the Hal Roach Studios in Culver City, California (Metro-Goldwyn-Mayer was located in Culver City). Ronald Reagan, already an officer when he moved to the Army Air Force, became a captain in the First Motion Picture Unit, known as "Fort Roach." Among the documentaries made, shown to service members and on screens before features at movie houses, was Frank Capra's *Why We Fight* series, a true masterpiece of patriotism invoking the founding fathers and values making America great.

Finally, it is true that traditional studios, not just the First Motion Picture Unit, did some of the best work done on behalf of the war effort. Major movie companies, operating under a capitalist system and making a profit, its stars earning fame and fortune, were able to do their part. It is problematic to say that a movie mogul, patriotic as he may have been, did as much to help the United States win as a nineteen-year-old grunt killed at Iwo Jima or that John Wayne portraying these men from the safety of Hollywood, California, also did as much. Wayne has his detractors. Many are liberal and found fault with him on this cause less so at the time and more so in later years, when he became outspoken about communism, about the Blacklist, and about the Vietnam War. It was then and often only then that these people resurrected Wayne's lack of a war record.

As for Wayne, he never discussed it on the record. It was off limits. Apparently, if approached on the subject by a reporter, he declined to go into detail. There is no record of his getting worked up on it; he just remained mum. But Pilar Wayne, whom he met and married a decade after the war, did reveal that he suffered great guilt over his lack of service. This was his motivation for becoming a "super patriot." His secretary, Mary St. John, stated Duke suffered "terrible guilt and embarrassment" over the issue.

"Every time he visited a military hospital or base over the years, some young kid would ask him which branch he had served in," she said. "It embarrassed Duke terribly to tell him he had not served. That's why he made up a story about the football injury keeping him out."

"To a man who believed that life largely meant testing one's self, this was the ultimate test untaken," said his daughter, Aissa Wayne.

Even younger brother Bobby Morrison served in the navy, a point their mother Molly made of sticking to Duke.

Again, all of this is true, and again, what is also true is America loved John Wayne. On the balance of deeds done, of service performed, when it comes to public opinion, America long ago and to this day, with the exception of a very small minority, has rendered the judgment that John "Duke" Wayne is a bona fide American hero. The baseball star Ted Williams, after serving two wars as a marine fighter pilot, agreed he was the "real John Wayne," that he did in real life what Duke only did on the screen; but Williams, who was a friend of the Duke's, quickly pointed out that he admired Wayne not just as an actor but as an American patriot as well. If anybody had the right to find fault with Wayne on this issue, it was Williams, but he and millions of others who served, some who were badly hurt, lost friends, and saw horror, feel only love for John Wayne.

Josephine was dead set against his enlistment. Despite their marriage being on the rocks, he was the traditional father of her four children, and she had no desire to see him die. But Wayne also looked at the issue from a practical point of view. It may have been vainglorious, but it was also real. He questioned whether he could serve alongside seventeen- and eighteen-year-old boys reared on his films since, for them, "I was America."

"It became obvious to me I could do more for the troops and boosting their morale than I might have done if I'd been allowed to enlist," he rationalized.

"Such a weak justification, provided a quarter of a century after the end of the war, can be taken on the surface as flimsy, arrogant rationalization," wrote Randy Roberts and James Olson in *John Wayne: American.* "But Duke was not an egotistical or arrogant person. He was an honest man without delusions of grandeur, or self-importance," adding, "The fact he had become a war hero without serving gave every explanation a false, self-serving ring."

Despite his personal anguish, Wayne did really believe Cecil B. DeMille's admonition that "civilians who worked in the motion picture industry had a job and duty every bit as important to the war effort" as the soldiers. *Casablanca,* a 1942 classic that tells a World War II story early in the conflict, albeit one thoroughly absent of the true horrors only time would later reveal, nevertheless demonstrated that cinema could have a tremendous effect on political attitudes. This was the essence of the character change in Humphrey Bogart's Rick.

Compare Wayne with Joseph P. Kennedy, who not only used his connections to avoid military service in World War I but also was a war profiteer before becoming an illegal liquor bootlegger and, finally, again used his power and political influence to try to align America not against but with Adolf Hitler because he was convinced the United States could not beat him. Compare Wayne to President Bill Clinton, who went through every possible gyration to dodge the Vietnam War draft but to do so in a way that made him "politically viable." He certainly did not do civilian work to support the war. In fact, he went to Moscow in 1969.

"John Wayne became a de facto propaganda machine during the war," wrote Roberts and Olson.

In *Flying Tigers*, Wayne is a stand-in for Pappy Boyington in a film depicting Colonel Claire Chennault's legendary American Volunteer Group, flying incredibly dangerous missions against the Japanese for Chiang Kai-shek prior to Pearl Harbor. At the time of its release, the Japanese had lambasted American forces at Corregidor, but the U.S. Navy had responded with vital wins at the Coral Sea and Midway, one of the great turning points in all military history. The timing was perfect. Wayne gave hope and courage to every mother, sister, brother, and wife of a soldier, who saw in him what they wanted to see in their loved ones. For the soldiers, Wayne filled their chests with pride, knowing people looked at them as courageous winners after such a terrible start to the war.

"By God," people began to say, "we might actually win!"

Regardless of how embarrassed or ashamed Duke Wayne might have felt over lack of service, this gift of hope and pride has no price.

He still thought about enlisting, but he was under contract with Republic Pictures and flatly told he would be sued "for every penny you've got" and "every penny you hope to make in the future" if he walked out. Aissa Wayne insisted that he went to Richard Yates, the head of Republic Pictures, and begged out of his contract in order to join the military, but "my father was flatly rebuked."

"You should have thought about all that before you signed a new contract," Yates told him.

"Although he did his best," said his friend and acting coach Paul Fix, "he always felt like a fraud for not getting in uniform, but that was never his fault, despite what some have said."

While watching rushes of *Flying Tiger*, Wayne turned to director David Miller. "Jesus, David, what are people gonna think when they see me winning the war against the Japs when they know I'm a fake?"

"You're not a fake, Duke. You're the real thing. You act with your heart, you give your character honesty and sincerity, and you're going to make Americans feel safer if they can believe that there are men like you fighting the enemy. So stop beating yourself up." But afterward Miller signed up along with Edmund Grainger and said, "I think that only made Duke feel worse."

Duke was chastened by Ford for not serving in the military and, at Josephine's urging, used Ford's influence to try to "save" him from divorce and its religious/Catholic consequences. Wayne *again* considered joining the military. He made one last try before D-Day (June 6, 1944) but was made 2-A by the government ("deferred in support of national, health, safety, or interest").

"It frustrated Duke like hell that he couldn't join up," said George Sherman, adding that he actually was by 1941 "in pretty bad shape" from years of injuries doing his own stunts.

"Frankly, I think the excuse that he didn't enlist because of a shoulder injury was a story the studio put out to justify their own reason for keeping Wayne to his contract and preventing him from enlisting," stated Henry Hathaway, the self-imposed debunker of many John Wayne myths. "I think, knowing Duke as I have for a long time, he would have enlisted if he were able."

He again was dissuaded also by Hollywood opportunity: *The Fighting Seabees.* As soon as Wayne read the screenplay, he knew it would be a tremendous star turn beyond even his previous films. More important, it would have a tremendously positive effect on morale and the war effort. It was a movie he knew would help America when she needed help. If ever he could justify staying home instead of enlisting, this was the movie to do just that. Wayne plays Wedge Donovan, who runs a group of Seabees, professional builders of different ethnic origins, all united by a common American purpose. Not trained as combat soldiers, they are forced to do so by circumstance, triumphing against Japanese forces portrayed as absolutely evil. It was not a sophisticated film, but it was a huge, immediate hit with civilians and military alike.

Had Wayne passed from the scene then and there, *The Fighting Seabees* would have cemented his role as Hollywood's version of the fighting man, a patriot and hero. It is shown regularly on television to this day, enthusiastically received and, to conservatives at least, something that harks back to a time when America was great. While Pilar Wayne would later say her husband was ashamed by his lack of military service, this film justified in the minds of the vast majority of people, in and out of the military, the importance of Duke Wayne to the American cause, something that thoroughly transcends actual official service in the military.

Off the set, Wayne caroused often with Ward Bond, who had also broken up with his wife. This was the essential Duke Wayne, a man far more comfortable in the company of men than women. During the Howard Jones era, Bond and Wayne were regulars on the "special trains" bringing the team and alumni on road trips to South Bend, Indiana; San Francisco; or other locales for big games. They hung out at the Hollywood Athletic Club, where Duke often stayed when he wanted to get away from his wife.

Bond's picture roles emanated from their unusual early rivalry during the train ride to Annapolis, which John Ford saw then and there as future movie scenes, Bond a rival of Wayne's character, a guy who would get in barroom fisticuffs with him over a woman or slight, then after the punches were thrown, they would settle their differences like men, enjoying a shot of whiskey. It was an endearing aspect of the Wayne persona, a scene he repeated not only with Bond but also with other costars over the years, the "manly" consumer of alcohol who could throw as well as take a punch but settle his differences "like men." While Wayne and Bond did not (generally) punch each other out in bar fights, their on-screen characters were not all that different from their off-screen friendship. Now approaching forty, at least when he was with Ward Bond, John Wayne still acted like a juvenile delinquent.

In addition to *The Fighting Seabees*, Wayne went on USO tours, entertaining troops in the company of leggy starlets. Comedian Bob Hope was famed for his patriotic USO shows, a huge hit with the troops. Wayne took some heat from marines who saw obvious flaws in *The Fighting Seabees*, which was far from realistic in the sense of modern war pictures, such as *Saving Private Ryan* or the HBO series *The Pacific*. But any problem he may have had with "the boys," over his movies' lack of reality or his own deferment status, was generally overcome by his popular appeal in front of them overseas. They appreciated his appearance, his being there to cheer them up. He had an irresistible quality. There were, however, rough patches. While filming in San Diego, Wayne got into—and lost—a couple of bar fights with local marines.

OSS commander William "Wild Bill" Donovan actually tasked Wayne with "assessing" the military situation, in particular the performance of General MacArthur, while touring the South Pacific (as Ford had been tasked to observe Japanese "spies" in Baja California while fishing). Wayne never met General MacArthur, and his report was not particularly enlightening. Some who were not officially in the military did some of the most dangerous, important work of the war in the OSS, such as Moe Berg's harrowing rescue of Nazi scientists from the clutches of advancing Soviet troops. Officially, Wayne was given a plaque according him "membership" in the OSS, which certainly would have made up for a lack of military service (think of CIA operatives in Iraq), but he assured all who inquired that it "didn't mean anything."

While Wayne's "performance" onstage was well received, what truly endeared him to the soldiers were his long hours spent in their company, drinking and swapping war stories well into the jungle night. He shared their accommodations, which had no luxuries, then reported upon his return the tremendous sacrifice they made on behalf of the country. It was as telling and realistic as any report from Ernie Pyle or other war correspondents. Americans simply did not realize just how shockingly difficult combat service, particularly in the South Pacific, actually was. This was the domain of the marines. Army pilots were often derided as glamorous "flyboys" who lived in comfortable bases, coming home after missions to party and get the girls. Soldiers in Europe were met by lonely Englishwomen looking for companionship, cheering Dutch and French girls throwing themselves at them, or sexualized Italian women. The "jungle marines" saw little of that kind of thing. In large measure because of the publicity surrounding Wayne's USO tours and his descriptions of life over there, when the war ended the marines who fought in the Pacific were often accorded greater status and respect than anybody else. This would in large measure go a long way toward establishing the Marine Corps as the "elite" American fighting unit—tougher, braver, first in, first to die.

When the United States emerged victorious over Nazi Germany and Imperial Japan in 1945, she stood as the single greatest political and military empire in world history, greater than Alexander's Greece, Julius Caesar's Rome, Napoleon Bonaparte's France, or even the British, on whose colonies the sun never set. The American fighting man was a heroic figure as never before, glorified not only by the pomp and pageantry of parades but also by the new media of screen, radio, and print. Journalists, storytellers, and filmmakers fell over themselves in an effort to glorify the "greatest generation," and none was more glorified than John Wayne, noncombatant.

Duke's divorce was finalized late in 1944. Josie never remarried, acknowledging the civil laws of California made her a divorcee in their eyes, but in the "eyes of God" she remained Mrs. Marion Morrison. His children did not see an American hero, only a father they felt abandoned their mother. It was very difficult for Duke. He understood this and never felt he deserved their forgiveness. Friends all agreed that Wayne never got over his guilt from divorcing Josephine or from not serving in the armed forces. A good psychoanalyst, in observing his actions, his public opinions, and the way he so nakedly exposed himself to what William Shakespeare called "the slings and arrows of outrageous fortune" over the remaining years of an eventful life, may very well trace his motivations to these and his subsequent acts of contrition. Pilar Wayne agreed with this assessment.

It is also not surprising that this period of great guilt, which came in confluence with his attaining great wealth and, still at the height of his physical charms, access to the most beautiful women in the world, resulted in his loss of innocence. He truly had been a Boy Scout type, a freshly scrubbed Christian with midwestern roots, eager to please Howard Jones and John Ford. He was no rube; indeed, he was one of the most educated actors, called an "intellectual" by some, but his pairing with Marlene Dietrich was indeed a metaphor for man's temptation in the Garden of Eden, the cabaret vixen of avant-garde Berlin meeting Clyde Morrison's cowboy son.

Two events mark this change from the Republican Presbyterianism of his youth, the eager-to-please Trojan footballer, the hardworking actor on the make, and the outsider marrying into society money. One was his relationship with a beautiful Mexican girl named Esperanza "Chata" Baur. She may have been a high-priced call girl in the Mexican film industry. Pilar Wayne said she became a prostitute to escape the slums. When she took up with the Duke, the trades pretended she was a Mexican film star.

The second was Wayne's move into the infamous Chateau Marmont Hotel on the Sunset Strip. Wayne was drinking and partying heavily. The Chateau Marmont is the ultimate scene of decadent Hollywood Babylon, where John Belushi overdosed in 1982. It is a place where actors, producers, and big shots meet and party with high-end escorts, often pornographic movie actresses. Anything goes at the Chateau. In the television show *Californication*, the writer played by David Duchovny stays there, encountering every sordid adventure imaginable involving sex, drugs, and rock and roll. It was not as wild when Wayne moved in, but it was no cabbage patch. For John Wayne to choose this den of iniquity meant he was turning a corner of some kind, not necessarily a good one. It all came while he was requesting a divorce, once and for all, from Josephine, expressing to his friends how her Catholicism drove him to distraction. Now he was taking up with a woman with a past.

5

PROPAGANDA, THE BLACKLIST, AND THE HOLLYWOOD RIGHT

"OF ALL THE ARTS, CINEMA IS THE MOST IMPORTANT," SOVIET DICTATOR V. I. Lenin said in 1920. It was very early in the development of this great twentieth-century art form—before sound or color—yet Lenin understood that film could persuade people even more than the stage, more than painting or sculpture, even more than the heart-felt novels of Fyodor Dostoyevsky, Leo Tolstoy, Charles Dickens, Mark Twain, or Upton Sinclair.

It has been referred to as the "American art form," yet it was not invented or initially, even by the 1940s, brought to the full force of its power in America. Created and patented by the Lumière brothers Auguste and Louis in Paris prior to the turn of century, it was the driving force of Nazi propaganda in the 1930s. Leni Riefen-stahl's documentaries of Adolf Hitler at the Nuremberg rallies and the 1936 Berlin Olympics were disturbing triumphs. But it was the Soviets, so backward in so many ways, who got out in front of politi-cal filmmaking.

According to legend, the Russian minister Gregory Potemkin erected fake villages, called "Potemkin villages," on the desolate banks of the Dnieper River. On her visit to Crimea in 1787, "happy villagers" were recruited to wave and pretend all was well in order to fool Empress Catherine II that a military campaign succeeded in enhancing new lands now in Russia's possession. In truth, Crimea was poverty stricken. The lesson of the story, apocryphal or not, was that propaganda had enormous value.

V. I. Lenin and Joseph Stalin, no doubt having seen the benefit of useful idiots like John Reed and Walter Duranty writing glowing pieces in the American press, understood the power of the cinema. It stood above all other arts as a mesmerizing tool of influence. Used correctly, it could move the masses.

Russian cinema reflected pre-Soviet culture, language, and history, mixed with communist dogma. The nation's film industry was fully nationalized and therefore monopolized by the Soviet Communist Party. In a country that experienced famines, strikes, and failed economic theory resulting in genocide, film remains the one thing they actually did well. The artistic strength of the Russian soul flowered even under these oppressive times; then again, the great writers of Russian history had always flowered under oppression of one kind or another.

Russian film introduced a new view of socialist realism. Some subjects did not appear on-screen or appeared only in a coded form. Criticism of the Soviet Union was officially prohibited, but complaint is as Russian as apple pie is American. Unofficial Soviet art, promotion of fascism, and horror films were censored. The communists, who used "free love" as a tool of recruitment meant to liberate the mind from old bourgeois morality, were still unsure of pornography, which on-screen had an effect that they could not control.

In the United States, early film was a ruggedly private industry, as removed from government control as the California gold rush. Its early pioneers were Jewish entrepreneurs freed for the first time in over 2,000 years from the shackles of oppression, Hollywood a promised land of low-hanging fruit in the Hanging Gardens of Babylon. While the Hayes Code would impose government censorship of film and later the studios would cooperate with the House Un-American Activities Committee in the institution of a self-imposed Blacklist, the nature and purpose of movies was entertainment ranging from light comedy to epic drama. This was the polar opposite of both the Soviet and the Nazi film industries, both state controlled, serving the political needs of big government.

The Hollywood that Duke Morrison/John Wayne discovered in the Roaring Twenties and thrived on in the 1930s was mostly devoid of unionization, a free market enterprise that suited Wayne's capitalist credo to a tee.

Oddly, while the filmmakers were under no obligation whatsoever to promote America, they freely chose to "propagandize" in favor of their nation, at odds with international ideologies opposed to theirs. For the early Jewish pioneers, this was a labor of love, to tell the world how much they adored this "land of the free and the home of the brave."

The cowboy films of Wayne's salad days reflected an American mystique that modernists cannot grasp. In a world divided by wars and conflict, before television, the Internet, and the mass flow of information, the image of the American West, especially to foreigners dreaming of deliverance from any number of cruel governments holding them under their heels, embodied by Wayne, was something simply extraordinary, actually *beyond words*. Indeed, here was a landscape of horse and rider, outlined against the sunset, quiet, resolute, and free, answerable only to himself and God Almighty, displayed on big screens in movie theaters built to resemble palaces, the only grand stages capable of capturing its essence.

"Every country in the world loved the folklore of the West," said Wayne.

The Soviets saw the racism brought about by *The Birth of a Nation*, which may very well have been the film motivating Lenin to state, "Of all the arts, cinema is the most important." This told them that the prevailing global notion of America as a wholly wonderful land in which "God sheds His grace on thee" and crowns "thy good with brotherhood" had some serious flaws in its premise.

How to get Americans to accept communism as an international workers' paradise? J. Edgar Hoover came down hard on the anarchism of "Red Emma" Goldman and was cheered for it. There were still living Americans who had come west for the gold rush, fought in the Civil War, and, as with many Duke Wayne characters, lived on the prairie not unlike Wyatt Earp and Doc Holliday. The rugged individualism of America was alive and well, certainly not receptive to communism.

But the communists were masters at subversion, persuasion, and espionage. They used sex, often in the form of "free love," mixed with narcotic stimulants, to lure the unsuspecting. Whittaker Chambers's *Witness* (1952) said they targeted three areas: government, civil rights, and media, with Hollywood included in the media.

There was a substantial revulsion against *The Birth of a Nation* from liberal America. The communists deduced that sympathetic whites and the hated black underclass were prime targets for blackmail, indoctrination, guilt-tripping, and recruitment. Homosexuals were targeted for two reasons. They were easily blackmailed in "repressive" America, and they held a certain distaste for certain jingoistic, "manly" traits associated with patriotism, ranging from war heroics to sports stardom and the great object of it all: getting the girl at the end. Jews were also natural targets, as described in Sinclair's novels. Early feminists were usually open lesbians, often finding the same disdain for traditional American pursuits as male gays.

The entrepreneurs who built Hollywood were rock-solid conservatives like the super-Republican Louis B. Mayer, but most people had not attained his kind of wealth or power. There was still tremendous anti-Semitism emanating from the closed worlds of WASP America: Wall Street boardrooms, country clubs, and college fraternities. The growing rise of Hitler in Germany acted as a catalyst and a prime opportunity for communism to inculcate itself into the arts, particularly the motion picture industry.

John Wayne had been rather apolitical in the 1930s. He concentrated on pleasing his "superiors" in the form of directors and studios, particularly Republic Pictures. He was bothered by a poor marriage that he got out of, wracked with guilt over it and his lack of war service, and then mired in a brief but sordid—by his standard—turn in his lifestyle marked by heavy partying. This included a fair amount of womanizing and then taking up with Chata, described by some as a fallen woman.

But he had not been immune to the political nature of his industry, having "noticed something was going wrong in the business around 1937, 1938." It was the making of *Back to Bataan* under director Edward Dmytryk, later identified as a communist, that opened his eyes wide. Dmytryk laughed at his military advisers, making fun of their Christian faith and singing "The Inernationale," the communist "fight song." Duke despised him. It was not a great film. Some conservatives faulted its attempt to elevate the Filipinos with MacArthur's liberating troops. In truth, President Roosevelt did not want to liberate the Philippines. MacArthur, who was the military commander there prior to the Japanese onslaught, told the Filipinos, "I shall return" when forced to flee. He was determined to fulfill his promise, telling Roosevelt if they did not liberate the islands, the Japanese would use it as a propaganda tool, claiming the Americans were not willing to die for "native peoples." Roosevelt bought the argument. MacArthur did fulfill his pledge, a major source of his historical mystique. It was a strategically important as well as psychologically valuable victory.

It also freed the many captive Americans, most of whom had been killed, the rest left to languish and starve, tortured and humiliated by the Japanese. The hatred Americans felt for the Japanese— and indeed much of the anticommunist attitude toward the "yellow peril" animating Korea, Vietnam, and Red China—stems from portrayals of Japanese atrocities committed on the "Bataan death march." Dmytryk took pains to portray the natives as just as courageous as the Americans fighting there. They were courageous, but not glorifying Americans who suffered so terribly, especially coming from an openly anti-Christian man living the good life courtesy of the red, white, and blue, was not a strong career move for the director. This was a man who told John Wayne if the "masses of the American people want Communism, I think it would be good for the country." The term "masses" was about as communist a phrase as there existed in the 1940s, derided for years by Ronald Reagan. Dmytryk had said this to the wrong guy and would pay for it. His screenwriter, Ben Barzman, shared Dmytryk's politics.

"That was the cause of some problems while we were shooting the picture," costar Anthony Quinn said in 1977. "Duke knew that that Barzman and Dmytryk were far to the left, and when [producer Robert Fellows] introduced Duke to Barzman, Duke said without a smile, 'I'm Duke to my friends.' He paused, then added, 'Also to the people I work with.'

"We had a technical advisor on the set, Colonel George S. Clarke, assigned by the Army to the picture. He was one of the last Americans to leave the Philippines [in 1942] and was a very conservative soldier—someone Duke respected. There were some unfortunate moments when Dmytryk said some things to Clarke which were certainly not of a conservative nature; I never heard those things myself. But I heard that Duke was furious when he found out and he confronted Dmytryk and said, 'Are you a Communist?' Dmytryk said he wasn't."

"Well, to me the word 'masses' is not a term generally used in Western countries, and I just knew he was a Commie," recalled Wayne. "But we had a film to make, and I got on with my job."

"When we started filming I think Wayne knew, through channels, that I was a Communist, but I didn't know," recalled Dmytryk.

"Ben Barzman was another like Dmytryk," added Wayne. "I had to work with these people, but I felt the time was coming when we'd have to do something about it."

The Red Army was completing the encirclement of the Nazis at the time. "You shouldn't keep damning the Russian people," Barzman told Wayne. "Without them we'd be losing the war."

"It's not the Russian people I have a problem with," Wayne replied. "It's Communism. And let's not forget that the Russians are our allies now because the Nazis invaded Russia even though Stalin was happy enough to sign a peace pact with Hitler at the beginning of the war. But I tell you this, when the war's over, it's Stalin's Communist state that will be the biggest threat to us."

"Talk like that is the very thing that causes wars," Barzman replied. "The Russians will be our friends."

"They'll be *your* friends," replied Wayne.

"Wayne was standing up for what was right," recalled stuntman Yakima Canutt, adding, "someone in the Communist Party didn't like it at all." An anonymous letter was sent to Wayne telling him he had "better watch out."

"No God——n Commie's gonna frighten me," Wayne said.

(In 1962, Wayne saw Dmytryk after he spent one year in jail for contempt of Congress. "Jesus Christ, Eddy, why did you do it?" Wayne asked him. "Weren't you making a good living? Weren't you happy with your life? What's the bitch about America?")

"By the end of the war, Americans totally identified John Wayne with that idealized American figure," wrote Randy Roberts and James Olson in *John Wayne: American*. "Americans came to know him through his wartime films, and they absorbed his charter with the films' message. His draft status and his divorce were unimportant to his audience. What mattered on the screen was all that mattered."

An alliance of Hollywood conservatives had been formed in 1944 to rid the industry of communist influence, but Wayne did not join until 1947, by such time as he realized the threat was real, not imagined. To him, it was no longer a free speech issue but a national security concern.

In 1947, President Harry Truman declared America's determination to take "immediate and resolute action" in support of any nation resisting communist aggression. Known as the Truman Doctrine, it was put to the test quickly in Greece and in support of the Berlin Airlift.

"I didn't sign up to the alliance at first because I'm a man who generally likes to beat his own drum," Wayne said. "I was speaking out against Communism in my own way. At Ward Bond's urging, I did some unofficial work for the alliance, working sort of undercover, you might say."

Screenwriter-producer James McGuinness wrote an entire speech for Wayne to deliver to the alliance. "Well, I don't do other people's speeches," Wayne stated. The speech intended for him was actually read by Bond. He did regularly say communism was "a crime, not a means of government" (decades later in the Ronald Reagan documentary *In the Face of Evil*, Stalin's "crimes" were called "incomprehensible," so horrible as to be beyond any pejorative).

"The Communists in Hollywood that were being given full support by the Stalinists were really gunning for Wayne," recalled Canutt. "Why they singled him out, I don't know for sure, but my guess is that they thought him an easier target than anyone who was a part of a great body like the Motion Picture Alliance. Duke kind of stood alone."

Wayne received a phone call and was told by an unidentified caller to keep his "big fat mouth shut, or it'll be shut for good." When he told Canutt this, the stuntman told him he had the best "undercover men in Hollywood" on the case to "ferret out" their identities. Wayne reluctantly agreed but firmly insisted it not be made public. Canutt's men posed as leftists, but little was discovered right away.

Wayne teamed back up with Ford to film *We Were Expendable*, a film personally requested by Secretary of the Navy James Forrestal. It offered a big break to Ward Bond and was the first A-list war film to come out after the war was over. Bond, who had more than a little experience with "party girls," warned Duke not to marry Chata, but he did anyway. It was doomed to fail. Donna Reed also recalled Ford putting Duke down badly because he had not signed up, while the film's star, Robert Montgomery, had earned the Bronze Star. Wayne never got angry, instead putting his arm around Ford and saying, "That's okay, Coach. You just want to make this film the best it can be."

Wayne teamed up with Bruce Cabot in *Angel and the Badman*, which received good reviews. He and Cabot would become friends. It was on the shoot that Duke met the beautiful actress Gail Russell, who he personally insisted be cast at a high price. Naturally, Chata was jealous. After he returned home late one night, she pointed a gun at Wayne.

Then came *Red River* (1948). Directed by Howard Hawkes, it teamed Wayne up with the magnificent Montgomery Clift. Duke had made box office blockbusters and was the most bankable, popular movie star in the world, but this would define Wayne as an actor to be reckoned with. The film's title may have referred to the Red Sea of Exodus in that Wayne leads a cattle drive across a river called the "Red." This symbolized Moses's leading the Israelites to freedom from Egyptian bondage, only to be bound by their own sinful natures.

Wayne plays cattle rancher Thomas Dunson. The film portrays him taking land that Mexicans claim is theirs and his love interest killed by Indian attackers. Dunson adopts an orphaned boy named Matt. He reminds him of the rage he will always feel over what happened. Dunson is a man of single-minded purpose. Fourteen years later, Matt is grown up, played by Clift, just as stubborn. Clift and Wayne did not get along. Clift was homosexual, a brooder, and Wayne thought him "an arrogant little bastard" in an interview with *Life* magazine.

The film centers on a cattle drive from Texas to Kansas City along the famed Chisholm Trail. Dunson and Matt have a dispute. Clift decided this was his big chance to upstage the great John Wayne. Instead, Wayne went off script and tells him coldly yet flatly, "I'm going to kill you, Matt."

(In 1969's *True Grit*, he would say the same thing to Robert Duvall playing "Lucky Ned" Pepper.)

"My good scene certainly went to the devil, didn't it?" Clift told Hawkes outside his trailer.

"Anytime you think you're going to make Wayne look bad, you've got another thing coming," Hawkes replied.

The line was a bold risk for the Duke. He always played the "good guy," and, as he said in interviews, he never wanted to "disappoint my fans." A father threatening to kill his son takes a dark turn away from this, but Duke calculated that his character, like Moses's inflexible commitment to God and harsh attitude toward the Jews when they worship the Golden Calf, represented "wrath" against sin, with Matt representing "rebellious humanity." Whether Wayne really got this deep into biblical thinking is problematic, although film historian Gerald Mast certainly did. Mast went on to compare Dunson and Matt with Moses and Joshua. Who would lead the Israelites into the promised land? In the end, it was not the patriarch Moses but the younger Joshua.

In *Red River*, the final confrontation, with one bound to kill the other, is ended when after a furious fight they are forced at gunpoint to make peace, made to realize they love each other. They indeed do make up, and it ends happily, the way a good western is supposed to.

It was his best film to date, but neither he nor the film received Oscar nominations. Laurence Olivier won for *Hamlet*, and John

Huston won the Best Director honor for *The Treasure of the Sierra Madre*. But when asked what Wayne's "secret" was, John Ford said, "Duke is the best actor in Hollywood, that's all." Quite a statement with the likes of Olivier and Orson Welles in their prime.

In 1949, Duke starred in *The Sands of Iwo Jima*. Filmed largely at the marine base at Camp Pendleton between Orange County and San Diego, California, it was practically a Marine Corps production since they provided so much cooperation it saved nearly $1.5 million in production costs. It remains one of Wayne's most memorable films, often replayed on television (especially around Memorial and Veterans' Days). It holds up well and symbolizes the Wayne image as a "blood-and-guts" military man on screen. It may glorify the Marine Corps more than any single movie ever made and, it could be argued, spurred many to fight in Korea, perhaps even in Vietnam.

Wayne plays Sergeant John Stryker. Kirk Douglas was slated for it, but Wayne wanted it so bad "he could taste it," said producer Edward Grainger. Stryker takes raw marines and molds them into heroes who forge victory in one of the bloodiest conflicts of the war.

"Duke *became* Stryker," recalled Mary St. John. "He really believed in the part."

"Sergeant Stryker was right down Duke's alley," said costar John Agar. "It showed the tough part about him, the soft part about him, it really was very much like him."

For his adoring fans, it cemented in their minds the notion that he *would not disappoint* them. He was reliable. A John Wayne movie could always be counted on to be entertaining, patriotic, and worth the price of admission. He was "money in the bank." Never before and perhaps never after him has an actor been such a sure thing, as they say, "bulletproof." It just got better when he followed that up with the western classic *Rio Grande*. He was equally identified with American victory over evil forces in World War II and the winning of the "wild, wild West" that his own ancestors had been a part of.

He was by now an utter myth, a legend of the very highest order. Only Dwight Eisenhower, Douglas MacArthur, and perhaps a couple of ballplayers, Joe DiMaggio and Ted Williams, were so idolized. The Indians opposing American forces in *Rio Grande* are portrayed as enemies fixed in the American mind as much as the communists who crossed the Thirty-Eighth Parallel, prompting General MacArthur back into action in 1950. That was the mood and politics of the era. Nobody fit that mood or those politics more so than Duke Wayne.

Many in Hollywood were far more outspoken on the left and on the right than Wayne. Ronald Reagan, president of the Screen Actors Guild, was a Democrat, making a conservative turn in reaction to the communist activities he was dismayed to see in Hollywood. Wayne had asked Edward Dmytryk, "Are you a Commie?" However, his politics were mostly on the screen. He let Sergeant Stryker, Lieutenant Ryan, Colonel Madden, and Lieutenant Commander Donovan speak for him. They were unanimous in their support of a jingoistic Americanism, muscular and in keeping with the triumphant times.

But in 1948, his agent, Charlie Feldman, sent him a screenplay submitted by producer-director Robert Rossen. Based on Robert Penn Warren's Pulitzer-winning novel *All the King's Men*, Columbia had paid the princely sum of $200,000 for it with a $1,750,000 budget. Wayne no longer was under Republic's sway, forced to do a string of B movies. It had taken a long time, but he was the biggest star in the constellation. He wrote a letter back to Feldman, not merely turning down the starring role of Willie Stark but also warning that before he sent it to more clients, he should ask whether he wanted to be involved in anything that "smears the machinery of government for no purpose of humor or enlightenment," that "degrades all relationships," featuring "drunken mothers; conniving fathers; double-crossing sweethearts; bad, bad rich people; and bad, bad poor people if they want to get ahead."

"Everything about the film struck an exposed nerve," wrote Randy Roberts and James Olson.

It desecrated the "American way of life," wrote Wayne: family and human dignity. He concluded that Feldman, if he really had gumption, should place the screenplay up Rossen's backside crevice.

The film, based on former Louisiana political figure Huey Long, made a star out of Broderick Crawford and is considered a classic. Oddly, Huey Long was a Democrat and near socialist.

If Wayne wanted to score some points against the Democrats, he would have made the movie while making a big point that it was about a liberal. It is also interesting to note in his letter to Feldman how protective he was of the government. In modern America, the government is not viewed by conservatives as patriotic. Rather, it is seen as corrupt and bloated. It is further of interest that Sean Penn, one of the most left-wing actors in Hollywood history, starred in a pedestrian remake of the movie in 2006. Apparently, the desecration of the "American way of life" so excoriated by Duke Wayne in 1948 was quite favored by Sean Penn fifty-eight years later, which is a microcosm of the larger theme: John Wayne's America no longer exists as a majority view.

It was also a microcosm of Hollywood in 1949–1950 because the film swept the Academy Awards—ahead of *The Sands of Iwo Jima.* "I wouldn't have minded losing so much, if anyone else had won," Wayne said of losing to Crawford.

A mustachioed Wayne also put on a bravura performance as Lieutenant Colonel Kirby Yorke opposite the lovely Maureen O'Hara in *Rio Grande* (1950). He was getting appreciation from the people who really mattered to him, and that was not the Academy. First, there was his legion of fans, an adoring American public. But his role as a soldier taming the Old West impressed a very important fan.

"Young man, you represent the cavalry officer more than any man in uniform," said General Douglas MacArthur.

It was the height of political Hollywood. Labor radicals had threatened Reagan with violence. The House Un-American Activities Committee (HUAC) was in full operation. The Hiss–Chambers case was at its peak. There was no longer any illusion about the Soviet Union being an ally of the United States. The true story of Stalin's genocides, hidden by Walter Duranty of the *New York Times,* was now exposed, and with it the *Times* suddenly found itself criticized by Republicans. The Soviets had enslaved Eastern Europe and blockaded Berlin. Nationalist China was hanging on for dear life against Mao's communists and would fall in 1949. Shortly thereafter, America would be in a shooting war with communist North Koreans and Chinese. The Soviet Union, given atomic secrets by radical left-wingers, would explode the hydrogen bomb.

Rossen, Wayne knew, was rumored to have communist ties. The year 1948 was a pivotal election year. The House of Representatives had gone Republican with a new cast of war veterans in 1946 (Richard Nixon of California and Democrat John Kennedy of Massachusetts). Harry Truman called them the "do nothing Congress." He inherited a presidency that J. Edgar Hoover knew was filled with paid communist traitors. Hoover told Richard Nixon, trying to get traction as Whittaker Chambers's sponsor, that he could not reveal all the spies and traitors of the Democratic Party because investigations were ongoing. If exposed, the Kremlin would pull back, and operations would be lost. But Hoover did tell Congressman Nixon he was on the right track and should pursue the Hiss case no matter how outraged the shrieks of the left.

Hoover knew of the Venona Project. This remains the "trump card," the ultimate Damocles sword the right holds over the historical left. If it were the other way around, Hollywood would have made movies, documentaries, and television shows shouting it from the rooftops. The *New York Times* would try to use the term in all introductions of conservatives. But because it describes treachery undeniably documented in large scale by the left against America, it, like all the movies never made about Democrat spies or the films that will never be made about John Kennedy stealing the 1960 presidential election from Richard Nixon, is treated as if it lacks existence.

In short, during World War II, U.S. military intelligence services began to suspect there were Soviet spies in President Roosevelt's administration. They began to suspect that they were privy to a second Hitler–Stalin pact that would end the war between Germany and the Soviet Union and, worse, suddenly align the communists with the Nazis against the United States in Europe and possibly the Pacific–China theater. Military personnel may take orders from the president, who is the commander in chief, but unlike Nazis sworn to Adolf Hitler, their allegiance is to the eternal U.S. Constitution (MacArthur's argument in disobeying Truman during the Korean War).

Thus, they began to realize that their president or his influential advisers could be traitors. Since if this were true it could directly affect them (i.e., result in their deaths, not to mention the fate of the nation and world), they began to "spy" on Roosevelt's administration. The intelligence centered on monitoring Soviet and State Department cable traffic. It was called Venona. What they discovered was that a large number of Democrats, many working in Roosevelt's Oval Office or other powerful positions (including but not limited to Alger Hiss, Harry Dexter White, and Lauchlin Currie), were paid Soviet espionage agents, complete with handlers and orders from Moscow—pure traitors, enemies of America (although in White's case, he strengthened U.S. monetary policy via the Bretton Woods agreements).

The FBI presented this information to Roosevelt, who told the messenger, "F——k you." He either refused to know about it, did know about it but refused to do anything about it, or worse, did know about it and in fact endorsed it. Hoover knew all of this. He looked upon his job as a keeper of the American flame, "eternal" in a sense like the Constitution, beholden not to a single presidential administration but to the nation, year in and year out, regardless of which political party was in power. He did, however, see that one party—the Democrats—were more likely to (and indeed did) have traitors in their midst, while another party, the Republicans, did not, knew or suspected these traitors existed, and wanted to rid the country of them. In this respect, Hoover was a partisan leaning to the Republicans and thus to Richard Nixon in his quest to expose Alger Hiss.

But few ever did learn of the classified Venona Project. For decades, schools routinely portrayed McCarthyism as "witch hunts," numerous movies were made vilifying Republicans for going after "innocent" filmmakers, and the *New York Times* printed as if it were fact the innocence of Alger Hiss. Finally, after the United States, led by President Ronald Reagan, was able to win the Cold War, knock down the Berlin Wall, dissolve the Soviet Union, and thus open the communist archives, all of this was exposed exactly as described. Everything Chambers had said (and a fair number of Senator Joseph McCarthy's accusations) turned out to be true. The *New York Times*, Hollywood, and the liberal media in the main continue to pretend no such thing as Venona exists.

President Truman was locked in a death struggle with Republican Thomas Dewey, famed for going after the rackets as a later New York political figure, Rudolph Giuliani, would do. Douglas Fairbanks Jr., Humphrey Bogart, Melvyn Douglas, Henry Fonda, Groucho Marx, Lucille Ball, Joan Bennett, and John Garfield openly campaigned for Roosevelt in 1940 and 1944. Robert Montgomery, Ginger Rogers, George Murphy, Adolphe Menjou, Irene Dunn, Hedda Hopper, Gary Cooper, John Wayne, Ward Bond, and Mary Pickford backed Wendell Willkie in 1940 and Dewey in 1944.

By 1948, Roosevelt's New Deal was being framed by the right as tacit communism. Republicans in Washington and the California legislature gained great traction going after suspected communists in the film industry. Hollywood was located in the middle of a conservative state and a conservative city dominated by the ultraright Chandler *Times*. While Nixon was a rising star, California Governor Earl Warren was Dewey's vice-presidential running mate (he later was named to the Supreme Court by President Eisenhower). It was a "coming-out party" for the Golden State, suddenly identified by electoral votes and postwar suburban trends as the most important political and social region of the nation.

Former Vice President Henry Wallace was vilified as a socialist. Conservatives identified groups and expressions as communistic. "One-world" government, the Free World Association, and the Hollywood Popular Front were viewed that way, its expressions and monikers borrowed from leftists of the Spanish Civil War. Billy Graham's Christian Crusades were gaining popularity. Christians increasingly saw themselves as conservatives opposing atheistic communism. The idea of one-world government was anathema to their biblical teachings, in which both the Old and New Testaments plainly speak to individual nations as entities unto themselves, that only Christ Himself "governs" all—and not in this world at that but in the next one.

The FBI identified between 200 and 225 communists at Metro-Goldwyn-Mayer, surely a tragedy for their conservative Republican boss, Louis B. Mayer. Guilds and trade unions of the industry were rife with communist infiltration and influence. Mayer was nearing the end of his career and influence, however. Walt Disney was convinced of "communist agitation, leadership, and activities" leading to a strike at his plant. Films like *Mission to Moscow* and *The North Star* were identified as "eulogies to communism and the Red Army." Screenwriter John Howard Lawson was identified as a member of the Executive Committee of the northwest section of the Communist Party in Los Angeles. Also included were Robert Rossen and labor organizers Herbert Sorrell and William Pomerance. Gary Cooper publicly scolded "the luke-warm Americans who dally with sedition at the guise of being liberals." Clark Gable seconded Cooper's admonition.

Still, during the late 1940s, Wayne did not play an active role in these events. He did not really like politics anyway and felt his lack of war service in some ways disqualified him from speaking out. But he was seeing more and more each day and did not like it. He was getting fed up.

HUAC questioned eleven "unfriendly" witnesses: screenwriters John Howard Lawson, Dalton Trumbo, Albert Maltz, Alvah Bessie, Samuel Ortiz, Ring Lardner Jr., Lester Cole, playwright Bertolt Brecht, directors Herbert Bilberman and Edward Dmytryk, and producer Adrian Scott. They all refused to answer the question "Are you now or have you ever been a member of the Communist Party?" They did not plead the Fifth Amendment right not to incriminate themselves, likely because membership in the Communist Party alone was not illegal. This is different from treason, as in espionage for the Soviet Union (such as in the Hiss case).

Even Lawson, perhaps the most virulent and notorious of the group, could have had his activities argued by a skillful attorney. While he did take orders from Moscow, in terms of his union activities and the subversive messages in his scripts, this may or may not be a crime and may or may not be giving "aid and comfort to the enemy during a time of war." To use two more recent examples, Jane Fonda smiling on a North Vietnamese antiaircraft weapon or even former navy officer John Kerry testifying on the atrocities of his fellow soldiers, which ranged from gross exaggerations to untruths, all during the Vietnam War, could have been argued to be treasonous acts of "aid and comfort." Between 1945 and 1950, the United States was not "at war," and while North Korea and North Vietnam may have been Soviet proxies, we have never been "at war" with the Soviets.

They wanted to avoid the Blacklist, which the major studio heads were in the process of creating and which came with taking the Fifth Amendment. "We used to say if you want to be a martyr you've got to expect to get your side pierced," screenwriter Herman Mankiewicz's anticommunist son Frank observed. "They wanted it both ways; they wanted the glamour of being a martyr and they wanted $5,000 a week for writing trash for the screen."

Brecht left for his native Europe. The rest became the infamous Hollywood Ten, all sentenced to federal penitentiaries for contempt of Congress, Blacklisted by the film industry. This was the moment John Wayne jumped in with both feet.

The communists were "rotten and corrupt," he told Maurice Zolotow, denying anti-Semitism motivated him. "Actually we were the real liberals. We believed in freedom. We believed in the individual and his rights. We hated Soviet Communism because it was against all religion, because it trampled on the individual, because it was a slave society."

It was also during this period that Ronald Reagan met the actress Nancy Davis, his future wife. The meeting was meant to be political in its intent. Miss Davis discovered she was on the Blacklist. She called Reagan, president of the Screen Actors Guild, to clear it up. They met for dinner, where she informed him that she was not a communist; she was the Republican daughter of a very conservative doctor who was warning even then of the dangers of socialized national health care. Reagan looked into the matter and saw that the communist Nancy Davis was another woman of the same name, but romance developed.

Wayne claimed to have flirted with socialism at USC, "but not when I left" because as a man "gets older and gives more thought to his and his fellow man's responsibilities, he finds that can't work out that way—that some people just won't carry their load." He recognized the essential "selfishness of human behavior" and that nothing was going to "stop the greed" with "a bunch of laws."

Bond was really the conservative one, complaining about high taxation while Duke yawned. But by 1949, taxes ranged from 68 to 88.6 and even 94 percent including surcharges, which was theft pure and simple. There were loopholes and ways a rich fellow with a good certified public accountant could reduce exposure, but these rates really mark the beginning of what, over time, became Reagan's conservative revolution. Duke and several of his high-paid Hollywood friends openly asked, "What are we working for?"

By this time, there were a number of Hollywood conservatives who had taken it upon themselves to attend communist cells, acting the "lamb," only to report back to the authorities what they saw and heard. As Wayne heard more and more frightening tales of communist infiltration of his beloved movie business, he finally accepted the presidency of the conservative Motion Picture Alliance of America. This made him a spokesman asked to comment on each successive hallmark of the Cold (and hot) War: China going Red, the Soviets detonating "the Bomb," the convictions of the Rosenbergs and Hiss, Korea, and McCarthyism.

While Wayne's anticommunism was popular, the Blacklist fully endorsed by a majority of moguls, when Louis B. Mayer left MGM and was replaced by the liberal Dore Schary in 1948, a kickback, a debate about the merits of anticommunist investigation, began. It was estimated that some 300 communists operated in the industry, seen as a far higher percentage than in America in general. There were plenty of liberals around to defend them.

It is hard to say just what Wayne's political activism meant to his career. It is difficult to conceive that it could have been better than it was. His lack of Academy Awards was from the beginning attributed not to anticommunism but to anticowboyism. His politics were American politics of the 1950s. His voice for the Silent Majority, the conservative right in later years, may have made him more popular. But he made enemies in Hollywood for sure.

"I was a victim of a mud-slinging campaign like you wouldn't believe," he told Zolotow. "I was called a drunk, a pervert, a woman-chaser, a lousy B picture Western bit player, an unfaithful husband, an uneducated jerk, a tool of the studio heads." He considered communism a "clear and present danger and called for registration of members so they could not operate in the quiet." Wayne called them "country club communists" who made $5,000 a week but joined commie cells.

"The overwhelming majority of HUAC's immediate targets *were* Communists and former Communists," journalist and authority on the subject Victor Navasky commented. "Although it served the party's interest to present the 'witch hunters' as indiscriminate smearers, in fact HUAC came to specialize in Red-baiting Reds and former Reds. The real vice of HUAC was not that it bagged the wrong quarry but that it had no moral, political, or constitutionally legitimate hunting license in the first place."

Navasky has a point. Again, *being* a communist or fellow traveler was not then nor is it now against the law any more than it is against the law to be a Nazi or a member of the Ku Klux Klan. The real laws broken—espionage and, with it, treason (the Rosenbergs and Hiss)—were hard to prosecute and in most cases not publicly identified until Venona in the 1990s. J. Edgar Hoover was less interested in prosecuting individual members of President Roosevelt's staff than he was in following the trails they led his investigators on, "big fish" in the Soviet hierarchy who were part of the "long game" marking the Cold War. Richard Nixon certainly burnished anticommunist credentials all his career, but his nailing Hiss and elevating Chambers to heroic status was not so much an act of legal justice as it was political ambition, leading to his 1952 vice-presidential nomination and beyond. Republican anticommunist Congressman J. Parnell Thomas ended up in jail on corruption charges. Later, Joe McCarthy's personal foibles deeply undercut his "moral legitimacy."

Next came the most controversial episode of the Blacklist period: naming names. Fifty-eight of 110 Hollywood workers named names. This, as much as any single episode, explains the cancerous division of America found today, the divide separating conservatives from the liberal wing of President Barack Obama's Democratic Party. Much water has gone under the bridge and many other issues have inflamed passions, but this is the benchmark that led to a liberal media and, with a liberal media, a sea change in attitudes. It certainly spurred Hollywood from its original quasi Republicanism, then unifying World War II patriotism, into what it has became: utterly and absolutely left wing.

In examining the naming of names, it is important to maintain an understanding of what communism was and still is. While its roots stretch back to the French Revolution, it officially began in Russia in 1917. It became international, spreading to China, North Korea, Vietnam, and Cuba, with proxies, revolutions, wars, and offshoots taking root and losing steam at various times throughout the Third World. It has resulted in the *murder* of some 110 million to 120 million human beings (a recent Mao biography "upgrades" his death toll from 55 million to 70 million in China, 35 million in the Soviet Union, 2 million in Vietnam, 2 million in Cuba, 1.5 million in Cambodia, and the rest in North Korea; further estimates vary widely for Eastern Europe, East Germany, and elsewhere). Nobody will ever have a true accounting of the horrors. Murder is defined as firing squad, hanging, forced starvation, forced famine, being worked to death, and other methods.

Twelve million died in Adolf Hitler's Final Solution. Six million were Jews. Of the 35 million murdered by V. I. Lenin, Joseph Stalin, and subsequent Soviet dictators, it is more than likely the number of Russian Jews murdered surpasses those killed by Hitler. Hitler started World War II, in which some 60 million perished in all forms. The Soviets conquered and subjugated all of Eastern Europe. Multiple millions died. Stalin did not murder only Jews, Christians, and dissidents; he also killed the best and the brightest of the Soviet military hierarchy because he was worried a charismatic officer might emerge more popular than he and challenge him. Out of megalomania, he killed thousands of political figures and "allies" he suspected of treason and betrayal. The CIA reports that what they did to the civilian Muslim population of Afghanistan in the 1980s is among the worst atrocities in all of history.

Some of this was not known by those asked to name names by HUAC in the early 1950s, but much was. They were educated people, not ignorant of world events. What was known was that over 10 million peasants died of forced starvation and slave labor in the 1930s, mostly in Ukraine. Multiple thousands of Soviet officers were purged by Stalin to promote his "cult of personality" in the 1930s. The Red Army raped and pillaged on a scale above all previous armies, ranging from Genghis Khan to the Romans and beyond. They conquered all of Eastern Europe, creating an "Iron Curtain." They tried to starve western Berlin. An odd purge of Jewish doctors was already under way, an oddity of Stalin's madness without the kind of "motivation" Hitler had, which was to exact revenge from his youth as a failed painter and belief World War I Germany was sold out by Jews and communists. How much of this purge against

Jewish doctors was really known is problematic, but he was a mass murderer of multiple millions, well recorded as fact by this time. By this statistical analysis, at this point communism was without doubt every bit as evil as Nazism and on its way to becoming far deadlier.

If in the late 1930s those who joined the American Nazi Party, attended Nazi meetings, sympathized with the Nazis, and were paid Nazi spies and traitors were questioned by the U.S. government, that government would have been well within its right to ask, "Are you now or have you ever been a member of the Nazi Party?" Failure to answer or evasion would have resulted in jail or deportation, cheered on by the forces of righteousness. Had these men been found and questioned after the war started and particularly after facts of the Holocaust started coming out, the justification would have increased tenfold. A suspension of habeas corpus and the imposition of martial law, once initiated by Abraham Lincoln upon citizens of the United States, would have been justified.

Yet somehow, despite being identified with a political ideology that is statistically and in reality the most evil in all of human existence, a tool of Satan if such a thing can be conceived, a large segment of not only American but also world society somehow believes questioning these people and asking them to provide information they can use in an intelligence-gathering operation vital to the security of Mother Earth herself is somehow a "witch hunt" in the historical mind, taught as such in public schools. It is somehow viewed as a violation of "civil rights," to be despised and lied about. A single industry (modern Hollywood) and a political ideology (for lack of a better term, liberalism) have used their considerable power of persuasion, propaganda, media, historical revisionism, academe, and dramatic depiction to perpetuate a monstrous lie upon humanity.

Why? The only explanation is to state the obvious, which is that on some level, if not in wholesale manner, liberalism identifies with and favors communism. Psychological justification or means of explaining such a thing does not exist within the framework of common sense and decency. To the religious, this seems evidence that this philosophy is actually evil, the tool of ancient dark forces haunting the Earth, manifest in the age we live in as today's weapon of choice against the righteous. All Democrats were not traitors. All the traitors were Democrats. There was no animating Nazi spy or "fellow traveler" or subversive wing existing within the American right despite the lingering lie of the left that such a correlation exists. The first hallmark of conservatism dispels this notion in a matter of seconds. Small government and individual liberty motivate conservatism. Perhaps it is self-serving for conservatives to say that, left to their own devices with nobody to stop them from grabbing total power, they would rewrite the U.S. Constitution, except that history verifies this as an actual event (today a growing liberal outcry in the courts and politics actively tries to weaken the Constitution). Leftists and socialists worshipping big government as a nationalist god, ranging from Lenin to Stalin to Mao Tse-tung to Kim Il-Sung to Fidel Castro to Pol Pot to Hugo Chavez, have, once given total power, become mass murderers or, at best, dictators. If one examines all of this honestly and without all the preconceived prejudices that drive people away from the truth, then it becomes apparent these statements are not opinion but factual statements that can be arrived using Socratic logic.

Never through the travail of ages has any political notion been more about big government and less about individual liberty than Nazism. The real reason no "Republican Nazis" were found and prosecuted by the Democrat Franklin Roosevelt is because none existed. The most prominent American Nazi sympathizer was the Democrat and father of President John Kennedy, Joseph P. Kennedy.

Perhaps the future was somehow envisioned, dreamt in a nightmare, or prophesied in private by John "Duke" Wayne. While many on the right went after the accused communists for personal political gain, this future may well have been the primary motivation of a fair number of them, particularly those who had read Rousseau's *The Social Contract* and seen how it led to the genocide of the French Revolution, or Karl Marx's *The Communist Manifesto* and seen how it led to the Russian Revolution, or Hitler's *Mein Kampf* and seen how it led to the Holocaust. The thinking leader in politics had a duty to read, understand, and try to use these lessons, these road maps of history, in an effort to prevent future catastrophe.

By mid-century, the American cinema was the most powerful, popular art form in world history. If a leader looked at this art form and, to paraphrase the philosopher George Santayana, failed to "remember the past," then he very well could be dooming his country "to repeat it." Nevertheless, there do not appear to be any Prophet Isaiahs saving us from the "Big Lie."

The great director Elia Kazan was a good liberal but from immigrant stock. He made a film about persecuted people kissing the ground upon arrival in America. His talent was stupendous, but to this day he is treated like those persecuted rabble from the Old Country his ancestors escaped from because he named names. Budd Schulberg and Lee J. Cobb, fellow talents in *On the Waterfront*, named names. The Blacklist has been compared to the Spanish Inquisition by the left, an American genocide. Nobody was killed. Most of those jailed were released in relatively short order. Ann Coulter, who engenders as much hatred as any right-wing pundit, infuriated the left when she detailed numerous Hollywood figures Blacklisted, only to live in luxury on the Riviera, participating in the French New Wave with such atheists as Jean Luc-Godard. Many were quoted saying this period of "persecution" was indeed some of the best years of their lives.

"During that decade, purging Communism was as American as motherhood, baseball, and apple pie," wrote Randy Roberts and James Olson.

The baseball star Jackie Robinson, a friend of Richard Nixon's who was a constituent in Nixon's old congressional district in the Los Angeles suburbs, told the committee that the communists tried to usurp the civil rights movement. African American actors Harry Belafonte and Sidney Poitier fell completely under the sway of black singer and communist Paul Robeson. Belafonte's radicalism remains to this day. Poitier, tasting stardom and its fruits, stayed away from politics the rest of his life.

"If anything, Hollywood was more forgiving of former Communists and more willing to bring them back within the fold than was the rest of the country," wrote Roberts and Olson, adding that in the manner of Christian redemption, once a man renounced his "sins," he could be "forgiven his trespasses." The unrepentant radical would compare this to Chinese authorities who tell an innocent man "it will go better for you if you admit your crimes."

Larry Parks (*The Al Jolson Story*) refused to name names out of principle because they included friends of his. He was a fairly tangential witness anyway but found himself Blacklisted. Even though he did not give Congress what they wanted, he begged his case to John Wayne, asking forgiveness from the film community. Wayne understood the man's reluctance to "rat on his friends," according to Roberts/Olson, and wished to remove his name from the Blacklist. Conservative columnist Hedda Hopper berated Wayne, stating that while he might "feel sorry" for Parks, she felt sorry for the mothers of 55,000 American boys dead at the hands of communists in Korea. Other conservatives were with Hopper, essentially saying that if a man had been a communist, he could not be trusted. Only a true and real conversion, the kind that happens when a man suddenly knows the divinity of Christ, as happened with Whittaker Chambers before he decided to turn in Alger Hiss, was acceptable in this climate.

Actress Geraldine Page, who starred in *Hondo* with Wayne and Ward Bond, felt Wayne "would talk so sensibly," while Bond was a reactionary right-winger. Wayne basically thought these left-wingers were misguided and could be made to see reason. The notion that he was a force for good in a cosmic struggle against real spiritual evil did not occur to him or at least did not seem to in the 1950s.

"He felt protective of his country and its way of life," wrote Randy Roberts and James Olson.

"I never felt I needed to apologize for my patriotism," Wayne said. "I felt that if there were Communists in the business—and I knew there were—then they ought to go over to Russia and try enjoying freedom there."

Wayne began to study the films his industry was churning out, dissecting them for social content he felt deviated from the essential goodness of the American character. He did not advocate censorship but did exercise his own right of free speech to publicly criticize much of what he saw. He responded with his own pro-American World War II, Western, and Cold War messages: *Jet Pilot, Operation Pacific, Flying Leathernecks,* and *Big Jim McLain.* John Ford urged him to tone down his rhetoric. This time Duke did not obey the old "Coach."

"We were just good Americans, and we demanded the right to speak our minds," he said. "After all, the Communists in Hollywood were speaking theirs. If you're in a fight, you must fight to win, and in those early years of the Cold War I strongly believed that our country's fundamental values were in jeopardy. I think that the Communists proved my point over the years."

Speaking at the Crusade for Freedom rally in 1949, Wayne announced, "The past ten years the disciples of dictatorship have had the most to say and have said it louder and more often. All over the world [the communists] pour their mouthings into the ears of the people, wearing down their resistance by repeated hammerings of half-truths. That's where our Crusade for Freedom comes in."

His term "half-truths" is particularly poignant, underscoring the subversive affect of the communist filmmakers and others who over the years have tried to tear down American history. On the issue of American Indians, for instance, while it is true they were lied to, had land stolen, and were treated miserably, it is also *not true* that they were wiped out in genocidal manner, while the Spanish Inquisition, communists, Nazis, Muslims, and others throughout history *did* wipe out minorities and "enemies" in genocidal manner. On the issue of slavery, as a second instance, while it is true the "peculiar institution" did exist in constitutional America between 1787 and 1863, it is also true that America is where slavery came to die. While it is true terrible racism existed in America during and after slavery, it is also most likely, using just a few historical examples—communism, Nazism, the Ottoman genocide of Armenians, the Cambodian "killing fields," and genocides in Africa—that no other nation in the world could have absorbed into their culture and system the enormous number of Africans absorbed into America with less bloodshed. To imagine Germany, France, Spain, Russia, Mexico, Japan, China, or virtually any number of nations suddenly confronted with 4 million black people in their midst, in 1865 or 1900, is to imagine the carnage of millions. There was Jim Crow, there were nightriders, there was voter suppression, there were segregated drinking fountains, there was a color barrier in baseball, but there was no carnage.

Ronald Reagan appeared before the HUAC at the height of the commission's most controversial work, the Alger Hiss case, on October 23, 1947, along with "friendly" witnesses Robert Taylor, Gary Cooper,

Ginger Rogers, and Adolphe Menjou. He agreed a "small clique" of guild members associated with "tactics" of the Communist Party but did not advocate outlawing communism. He said people had the right to choose their politics, claiming Americans fought and died for that right. He told the committee he did not think the communists really permeated the industry, ostensibly because *there were too many patriots like him to allow such a thing to happen,* which was certainly true.

"I hope we are never prompted by either fear or resentment of Communism in compromising our Democratic principles in order to fight it," he said. Reagan was extremely fair, almost liberal, on the issue. He was lauded for his open-mindedness. It is important to note, however, that in October 1947, the Hiss case had by no means revealed his guilt; the FBI was still holding back what it knew about communist infiltration almost everywhere within the levers of American power; the sound barrier was broken only that month, so the space race and arms races were not yet under way; China was not Red, and the Soviet Union had not demonstrated the Bomb; the Soviets were still thought of as war allies; the Berlin Airlift was a year away; the worst abuses against Eastern Europe were not yet happening; and the wholesale mass murders of communism, resulting in over 100 million dead, were not yet known. In light of this, Reagan can be excused for his fairness if not naïveté, regardless of how he claimed his innocence was already gone when he saw the union tactics used against him.

But, again, Reagan's appeal to HUAC that communist infiltration was not quite as terrible as they might think because *there were too many patriots like himself to allow such a thing to happen* in many ways is a single blanket statement describing conservatism, which has often been, for lack of a better term, a "victim of its own success."

Looking at the twentieth century, had there been a strong conservative element operating in Russia in 1917, it may very well have stopped the Bolsheviks before they could create a nationwide revolt. Or if "guys like Reagan" existed in ample supply, would Hitler have risen in Germany? Had these movements been stopped early, later alarmists warning of the threats of communism or Nazism may have been called "alarmists" or "warmongers," frightening the population with wild conspiracy theories.

6

DUKE GETS HIS DUE

THEN CAME JOHN WAYNE'S PERFORMANCE AS SEAN THORNTON, OPPOSITE the beautiful Maureen O'Hara, in *The Quiet Man* (1952). It was his greatest performance, perhaps the best he ever gave before or after. It seemed to represent the Duke in a personal way; a gentle man of intellect, not wont to fight, who can use his fists when he needs to. The film won a number of Academy Awards, but Duke was not so much as nominated. Bond was convinced communists in the industry prevented his nomination.

"Duke's politics definitely hurt him that year," said Mary St. John.

Recognition was long overdue, but for John Wayne it came from a far more respected source than a movie critic, *Variety* magazine, or even the Academy Awards. It came from the American public and from a titan of American journalism, Henry Luce, the all-powerful head of *Time* and *Life*. Luce championed Chiang Kai-shek and had desperately propped him up in a battle against Mao Tse-tung's communists in the Chinese Civil War. He knew the value of "propaganda," fighting endlessly with his top reporter, Theodore White, who wrote of Chiang's corruption. Just as critics felt Wayne's *The Flying Tigers* failed to show the weaknesses of Chiang's Kuomin-tang army, which military censors insisted during the war not be exposed, Luce argued we were still at war against international communism. But hostilities having ceased, the Soviets still a nominal "ally," it was an age in which reporters felt compelled to reveal the "truth." Years later, after Mao won and 70 million Chinese had been murdered, the wisdom of White's "honest" reporting versus Luce's "moral duty" seems to weigh toward Luce. This single conflict further marks the great divide of America, along with the Alger Hiss affair and McCarthyism, that by 1966 (ironically the year Mao's Cultural Revolution started), with Vietnam raging, marks that point in which America was no longer John Wayne's country, leading to that point when it would become, arguably at least, Barack Obama's country.

By 1952, Wayne was among that class of conservative Hollywood figures who men like Luce, who employed Hiss's accuser, Whittaker Chambers, as a *Time* magazine editor, saw as opposing the evils of communism.

Luce decided three or four times a year that his magazine cover should be graced by a movie figure, preferably a beautiful woman. It was the age of military heroes and politicians wielding power unseen since the days of Caesar Augustus; beribboned images of Dwight Eisenhower or Douglas MacArthur mixed with statesmen such as Harry Truman and George C. Marshall. Often photographed from below, they appeared more like Washington monuments than flesh-and-blood people. Hollywood stars provided a relative human touch.

Luce assigned movie writer Jim Murray, his most talented scribe, to picking out the "next big thing" in showbiz. To be selected for a *Time* cover story was tantamount to instant success and credibility. Murray found himself mingling with and courted by the likes of Cary Grant or Marilyn Monroe. He had aisle seats for the Academy Awards and invitations to the hot premieres.

"It was pretty hard to keep your feet on the ground in that rarefied atmosphere and I'm not sure I did," he wrote.

John Wayne was a big star but was not considered an actor of depth along the lines of a Fonda or a Bogart. But Murray's job was to keep tabs on box office records. He knew that Wayne was the most popular actor in the world. The elites of Hollywood and New

York favored more stylized artists, but in the "sticks," which were pretty much everywhere else, the Duke was number one. Murray began lobbying for big John Wayne coverage, but most of his New York bosses did not know who he was.

"Nobody in Rye or Mamaroneck or Old Greenwich ever went to one," he wrote of Wayne's movies. "It was a hard sell. The editors wanted to put Kate Hepburn or Claire Bloom on the cover, somebody they wouldn't have to apologize for at the Harvard Club."

But Luce knew who he was. Finally, *Time* gave Wayne his due for *The Quiet Man.* Murray loved him, a man's man who lived in a man's world of poker, cronies, and Baja pigeon shooting. Murray felt Wayne in part posed as a rugged macho man in order to cover up for his given name of Marion. His size and football background added to the image, but Murray discovered an intellectual under his muscles. Wayne never said "ain't" until a movie script made him say it. Murray discovered that Wayne was an A student, a high school valedictorian who made excellent marks at USC. Wayne was deeply patriotic and, like another conservative, Ronald Reagan, enmeshed in politics.

"He was as Right-wing as Bank of America," wrote Murray.

John Ford had a real "sadistic" streak, according to Murray. Ford bullied Murray during an interview, but when the writer threatened to walk away, Ford laughed, admiring Murray's willingness to stand up for himself.

Despite Wayne's desire to use movies as a tool of patriotic propaganda favoring America, Murray found him uncomplicated, self-deprecating, and funny. Wayne never made more of his movies than what they were, joking that he "won" the war playing heroic figures, but the pinstripers at Foggy Bottom "gave it all back at the peace table."

He said Hollywood publicists named him all-American after being a second-stringer.

Wayne always played characters the public rooted for with one exception: when he let Montgomery Clift be the heroic figure of *Red River.* He was approachable, a trait Murray said many stars had in those days only when they needed the press.

Wayne constantly fought ex-teammate Ward Bond on screen. Bond was always the friendly Irish priest or saloon keeper who, after a punch-up with the Duke, shared a shot of whiskey with him. It was still an innocent time.

Murray's admiration for Duke was returned. "Lots of fellows don't put in the care and effort that you do yours," Wayne wrote to Murray in a letter dated February 28, 1952.

Murray found Humphrey Bogart the opposite of Wayne. With the Duke, what you saw was what you got. Bogart resented his Park Avenue upbringing. The son of a doctor, he pretended he was a "dead-end kid."

"He was about as tough as a ballroom dancer," said Murray, who loved Wayne's image of rugged individualism. Murray noted that it cannot be overstated how tremendous was the impact of the cowboy on the world's psyche. Such a figure was a wholly unique, new character on the world stage. Europeans of the twentieth century especially were enamored of this romantic image, embodied by the Duke. Living in huddled masses with nameless faces and being automatons and merely numbers in mass crowd scenes bowing in fealty to a totalitarian dictator like Adolf Hitler or Joseph Stalin, they saw in the cowboy a master of his own destiny. The easterner Murray admired this individualist, living off the land in prairie splendor, answerable only to his own willingness to make do; such a concept was unthinkable through 2,000 years of monarchs and militarists forcing farmers to pay homage and tribute to their pagan idols. Such was the most iconic of American characters; it was in the West where he thrived, and his name was John Wayne.

After *The Quiet Man*, Duke started his own production company. He was not happy with the tax policies in America, claiming to a *Look* magazine writer in 1953 that the previous year he made $500,000 but after expenses and taxes kept only $60,000. Claiming, "I spend $65,000," he added, "You see where that leaves me. Sure, I'm broke, but I don't owe a dime in taxes." He certainly did not live lavishly. His home was modest, and he did not throw huge parties. His idea of a good time was still a night of drinking or a Trojans football game with Ward Bond.

Wayne originally supported Ohio Republican Senator Robert Taft for president in 1952. He promised to dismantle the New Deal, but the more moderate General Dwight Eisenhower was a lock as soon as he declared his candidacy. His choice for vice president was Richard Nixon, who had been elected to the Senate in 1950. This was further proof of both California's postwar political importance (Governor Warren having been Thomas Dewey's 1948 running mate) and the anticommunist issue. Nixon was, along with Senator McCarthy, at the height of his popularity and influence, the leading Red-baiter of the right. Hollywood followed the trend. While there might have been enough "communists" to form a conspiracy to deprive Wayne of an Oscar for *The Quiet Man*, according to Ward Bond, the powers that be green-lit a series of anticommunist films during this era.

"They were part of Hollywood's ritual of atonement and appeasement," claimed film critic Norma Sayre, "and were aimed at an uninformed audience in a decade when almost anything that middle America feared could be related to Communism." She added that communists were depicted as "haggard and disgracefully pudgy . . . occasionally effeminate."

While Sayre's descriptions are accurate, she was talking about a political ideology that by then had already murdered at least 30 million people, a little less than a third of the tally existing today. People capable of committing such crimes *are* more likely to look like the "hit men" or "gangsters" she complained they resembled. These sorts of stereotypes have certainly been turned around in the years since. The modern-day conservative, Republican, and Christian is more often made to look stiff, unrelenting, and humorless, a direct form of backlash against McCarthyism and the Blacklist.

Big Jim McLain was a story of FBI investigation of communism. Liberals did all they could to put down the film, which was made by Wayne's production company on budget. It did not receive good reviews, but America lapped it up, raking in solid box office profits.

During this time, Wayne's marriage to Chata broke up, and he met a Peruvian actress named Pilar Palette. Although Wayne had a fling with the decidedly Teutonic Marlene Dietrich, for some reason this rugged WASP man was attracted to swarthy Latinas. He would marry her and have three more children: Aissa, Ethan, and Marissa. It was the end of his "wild child" period, marked by an affair with a

German sex goddess, drunken revelry at the Château Marmont, and ill-advised marriage to a "sick" woman, Chata, who symbolized the scorn and depravity of fallen womanhood.

Duke made *Hondo* in Mexico with Geraldine Page. "He's a terribly honest man, you see," Page said of him. "And that comes across, underlined by the kind of parts he plays. He always plays an honest man, and his honesty feeds into it, and the simplicity of his acting." This, she added, was what endeared him to the public and made them wish to see him "again and again."

After *The High and the Mighty*, Duke went completely out of character in *The Conqueror*, a screenplay originally written for Marlon Brando. It was ridiculed in some quarters and obviously not his best work. But the film had a profound impact on his life. Filmed in St. George, Utah, in 1954, it fell within range of a series of atomic bombs tested and exploded in nearby Nevada. A strong wind carried much of the fallout to St. George, where a fine ash descended upon the set. Incredibly, much of the dirt from the scenes, still highly radioactive, was trucked back to Culver City to make sure interior scenes had the same color and texture. Some ninety of the cast and crew, including John Wayne, would get cancer, a number three times greater than actuarial tables suggest is probable. Several prominent cast members died. Wayne himself would battle cancer, surviving lung cancer in 1964 but dying of stomach cancer in 1979. This is Shakespearean irony; the symbol of America, no doubt a supporter of the dropping of atom bombs on Japan to end World War II, favoring nuclear superiority in the arms race with the Soviet Union throughout his years, dying apparently from the very weapons he advocated, the power he in part embodied as a symbol of the American Empire at its heights.

Wayne starred with Lauren Bacall in *Blood Alley*. She and her husband, Humphrey Bogart, had been investigated by HUAC and were liberal. She thought she would clash with Wayne but was "very surprised when I found Duke to be a very warm person, very friendly and amiable. After Bogie was diagnosed with cancer, Duke, who didn't really know Bogie at all, was among the first people to send his best wishes."

The Searchers (1956) starred Wayne as Ethan Edwards in a John Ford classic. He was paired with the Wood sisters, Natalie and Lana, his nieces who are kidnapped by marauding Comanches. Wayne is a Confederate veteran who returns to West Texas only to find his brother's family slaughtered. He teams with Ward Bond as a Texas Ranger to find the girls. It was a dark, brooding western, absent the sort of "good triumphs over evil" theme most of his movies represented. Wayne's character openly rejects Christian faith in favor of brute force and revenge. It was also typical of the genre John Wayne is remembered for—the Indian fighter, the tough white man versus the savage red man—although Ethan's obsession drives him to near insanity. Films like these played a role in the American Indian movement, propelled in large measure some years later by Marlon Brando. On set, Bond was up to his old shenanigans, lusting openly for Vera Miles, who somehow rejected his advances, which included exposing himself.

"I think it was the greatest performance Duke ever gave," Harry Carey Jr. said of *The Searchers*.

The end of *The Searchers* contrasts with the "politically correct" *Dances with Wolves* (1990). He finally finds Debbie (Natalie Wood), by now married to the Comanche chief. The Indians are now "my people," she tells him. Ethan prepares to kill her, blinded by hatred and racism, but at the last second kindness enters his heart—perhaps the Christianity he has heretofore rejected?—and he takes her in his arms.

"Let's go home, Debbie," he says, and they ride off into the sunset. French director Jean Luc-Goddard, who stood for everything John Wayne does not, who "hated" Wayne, was moved to tears when he saw the film, transformed into a fan.

"He was never better," remarked Mary St. John.

The *Hollywood Reporter* called it "undoubtedly the greatest Western ever made." Wayne was "an anti-hero worthy of the James Dean and Marlon Brando rebels of the 1950s," wrote Randy Roberts and James Olson in *John Wayne: American*. Indeed, one of his greatest (if not the greatest) roles was against his long-held type. John Milius, who wrote such classics featuring antiheroic, lonely, obsessed men as *Dirty Harry* (1971), *Jeremiah Johnson* (1972), *Magnum Force* (1973), and *Apocalypse Now* (1979), called it his greatest influence.

Rio Bravo was another box office hit. Duke then played a Union cavalryman in *The Horse Soldiers*. During filming, Pilar attempted but recovered from a suicide attempt. It was a mystery to Duke. She seemingly had everything but was brought low by depression, a condition Wayne had "no clue" how to understand, said Mary St. John. The film was further darkened by the death of Fred Kennedy, killed when he landed poorly in a horse scene.

Ward Bond "appeared in hundreds of films, but he is probably most famous for his role as Major Seth Adams in television's *Wagon Train*, in which he starred from 1957 until his death of a heart attack at age 57 in 1960," wrote Jim Gigliotti in *Stadium Stories: USC Trojans*, a short history of the school's football tradition. Indeed, Bond forced his way, literally, into the movie business when he argued his way past Duke Morrison onto the train bound for Annapolis, Maryland, and the filming of *Salute*. Discovered by John Ford, eventually befriending Duke, his claim to fame was to be John Wayne's sidekick, both on- and off-screen. Fellow USC football players, they shared a love of the game and their alma mater, some of their most uproarious times spent on the Trojan special trains carrying fans to and from USC road games. If people thought Wayne to be right wing, he had nothing on Bond, who saw communist conspiracies—often industry ones designed to keep Duke down to deny him or his films Oscars—around every corner.

But Bond was not merely Wayne's drinking buddy. He had talent, most ably displayed by his believable Irish brogue in the role as a friendly Irish priest in *The Quiet Man*. Finally, he had *his* role, a claim to stardom separate from Duke Wayne's shadow. But he was a party animal and womanizer of the first order. His ignoring of doctor's orders to slow down alcohol consumption, pill popping, and a Ruthian zest for living caught up to him at a relatively early age.

"We were the closest of friends, from school days right on through," recalled Wayne at his funeral. "This is just the way Ward would have wanted it—to look out on the faces of good friends. He was a wonderful, generous, big-hearted man."

"I had never seen him so preoccupied, so subdued, so quiet, so depressed," said Mary St. John of Duke's reaction to Bond's passing. "He lost fifteen pounds over the next two weeks because he didn't want to eat. It was as if someone had cut out his heart."

Wayne's world was slowly dissolving. The deaths of Fred Kennedy and Ward Bond, Pilar's strange myopia, and encroaching liberalism in Hollywood seemingly aimed directly at him were all taking their toll. But instead of giving in and giving up, he went the opposite direction: he reloaded and, like Rooster Cogburn telling "Lucky Ned" Pepper to "fill your hand'" with lead, charged forward.

In 1962, Duke starred in *Hatari!*, a Howard Hawkes feature costarring Bruce Cabot, who in some ways was "replacing" Ward Bond as one of the Duke's sidekicks. It was a melancholy experience, as he had long planned to bring Bond with him and had an elaborate practical joke all set to play on his friend. Instead, Bond was gone. The film was shot in Tanganyika, an African country in the throes of unshackling itself from colonialism at the time. Wayne was unimpressed with its leader, Julius Nyerere, a nationalist with "half-baked Socialist" ideas.

"The whole damn place won't be worth a s——t in ten years," he said of the nation later known as Tanzania. He was right; Nyerere became a dictator. Wayne observed that while 8 million blacks lived there, if they endorsed capitalist principles, with its abundant natural resources they could grow enough food to support 60 million instead of enduring constant famine. It "could quite possibly have served as a breadbasket to the world," wrote Randy Roberts and James Olson. The biographer also noted that while Wayne's views would have been considered mainstream throughout most of the century, by the 1960s they were becoming a minority opinion.

After returning from Africa, another of Wayne's close pals, publicist Bev Barnett, passed away. It was another jolt to a man who saw the world changing too fast for his liking. Many leading men of Wayne's vintage were dying or retiring, but Wayne had lost money on *The Alamo* and needed to keep working.

The Comancheros was a film set in the Texas of the 1840s, also costarring Bruce Cabot. Son Patrick and daughter Aissa had roles.

After that came *The Man Who Shot Liberty Valance, Donovan's Reef, McLintock!, Circus World,* and *In Harm's Way.* They were standard John Wayne vehicles, although each seemed to veer further from the changing mores of Hollywood filmmaking and culture. During these years, films like *The Manchurian Candidate, Seven Days in May, Dr. Strangelove,* and *Fail-Safe* were released.

In *The Man Who Shot Liberty Valance,* Wayne conflicted with his old friend John Ford, who ridiculed his lack of military service in World War II, contrasting that with Woody Strode, the black ex-UCLA football star, who did serve. Then Wayne and Strode almost came to blows, stemming from a scene in which Wayne lost control of his horse.

"John was working the reins, but he couldn't get the horse to stop," recalled Strode. "I reached up to grab the reins to help him, and John swung and knocked me away. When the horses finally stopped, he fell out of the wagon. I jumped down and was ready to kick his ass." Strode was forty-seven, still in football shape. Wayne was fifty-five but overweight. Ford pleaded with Strode not to hit Wayne. Filming stopped until the men cooled down. Duke's role was ambiguous, but as he later declared, "I don't trust ambiguity."

In 1962, Wayne starred, albeit as part of a larger all-star cast, in two of the greatest films ever made. He played General William T. Sherman in *How the West Was Won* and Lieutenant Colonel Benjamin Vandervoort in *The Longest Day.* Both were, like *Lawrence of Arabia,* Hollywood epics, the kind of enormous extravaganzas that marked the 1950s and early 1960s but, after the failure of *Cleopatra,* disappeared as a genre. While Sherman had nothing to do with the great quest to take the American West, wresting it from the control of Indians and Mother Nature, the film represented pure Manifest Destiny. In that respect, it and John Wayne were absolutely in sync with each other. The movie is not wholly jingoistic, as it makes a cursory attempt to show government duplicity in dealing with Native Americans. A scene with George Peppard and Richard Widmark represents competing points of view. Peppard's Zeb Rawlings, a former Union soldier who actually saves the life of Wayne's Sherman and Harry Morgan's General U. S. Grant in a fictionalized scene, is a scout assigned to the railroad. After a treaty is broken, the Indians attack, leaving many dead, including the mother of a crying baby. Widmark's hard-core railroad man Mike King is asked by Rawlings, "Can you live with that? Because I can't." King replies, "That ain't cryin'. That's life goin' on." This represented the view of an inexorable empire on the march and was still in those days the predominant attitude of most Americans.

Producer Darryl F. Zanuck paid Wayne $250,000 for a two-day shoot in his masterpiece, *The Longest Day*. It was a phenomenal rendering of the Allied invasion of Normandy, which to this day, like *How the West Was Won*, holds up very well and is arguably as good as the "semi-remake" *Saving Private Ryan*. Thus in one year did John Wayne star or costar in two movies that he represented beyond all other American actors: the western and the war picture. Neither was ambiguous, and both were emotional, evoking pure patriotism and pride in the greatest nation of all time. *How the West Was Won*, like *The Magnificent Seven* and later *True Grit*, were marked by panoramic, picturesque color; fabulous location shots; and soaring sound tracks (*The Longest Day* was one of the last great black-and-white movies).

While *Red River* remains a classic and later westerns such as *Unforgiven*, among others, rank with the all-time greats, four made in the 1960s, two starring Wayne (*How the West Was Won* and *True Grit*), plus *The Magnificent Seven* and *Butch Cassidy and the Sundance Kid*, may be the best in film history. Any short list of best-ever war films, which might include the likes of *Patton*, *A Bridge Too Far*, *Apocalypse Now*, *The Thin Red Line*, and *Saving Private Ryan*, would not be complete without including *The Longest Day*. It was most likely the best war picture ever made until that time, surpassing Wayne's own *The Fighting Seabees* and *The Sands of Iwo Jima* along with *From Here to Eternity* and *The Bridge on the River Kwai*.

Bruce Cabot had a small role in *McLintock!* (based on William Shakespeare's *The Taming of the Shrew*), in which Duke teamed up with *The Quiet Man* costar Maureen O'Hara. She was one of his all-time favorite women, his "ideal" according to biographers Randy Roberts and James Olson, although the two were never romantic.

"It was a friendship that never, fortunately, turned into a marriage," recalled Mary St. John. "They are the strongest two people I have ever known. They would have been like oil and water as man and wife."

Wayne plays G. W. McLintock, who expresses the essential American notion that government governs only by consent of the citizenry, when confronted by homesteaders telling him the government *gives* them land.

"The government never *gave* anybody a thing," McLintock bellows. Later, when an Indian chief refuses to accept a government offer of relocation, McLintock approves, saying, "Charity is for widows and children, not for men."

When his son Patrick (playing Dev Warren) thanks him for *giving* him a job, McLintock states that he never gives anything away. "I hire men!" he states. "You will work hard, and I will pay you for it. You won't owe me a thing, and I won't owe you a thing!"

After *McLintock!*, Wayne played a cameo in *The Greatest Story Ever Told*. Raised a churchgoing Presbyterian, he was a Christian all his life, but Hollywood had lapsed him a great deal. There was the alcohol, the ribald times with John Ford and Ward Bond. Wayne was never a womanizer by most Hollywood standards, whether those standards are Bond or Errol Flynn, but he strayed. He certainly fell hard for Marlene Dietrich, at least for a while (while married to Josephine). He grew very tired of his first wife's Catholicism and all the family priests coming over for dinner. His natural Scotch-Irish background, which included ancestors who had fought Catholics in the Old Country, certainly would not have led him to convert. He divorced two women, breaking a sacred vow in all forms of Christianity.

He was not a churchgoer, at least regularly throughout his adult life, but he believed in God. It was part of the American experience for him and millions like him. He despised communist atheism and was unimpressed with the fact so many of the Soviet spies and fellow travelers were Jewish.

Offered $25,000 (a paltry sum compared to his fee for appearing in *The Longest Day*), Wayne was happy to declare the divinity of Jesus Christ publicly, on-screen, uttering some of the most famous biblical words ever stated.

Duke portrays the Roman centurion who witnesses the crucifixion of Christ and, as God's wrath is displayed amid darkening skies and an earthquake, states, "Truly, this man was the son of God." Director George Stevens asked for "a little more awe," so Duke jokingly restated the line in an exaggerated cowboy drawl, mimicking himself. After getting a good laugh, he nailed it on the third take. While far from his best work, there is symbolism in his playing this role, which always goes to famed gentile actors in various film interpretations (Ernest Borgnine, among others). The Roman centurion is the first recognized European gentile to turn from the Greco-Roman gods of monotheism, accepting or, more precisely, having the one true God fill him with Holy Spirit (the Bible is not precise; he probably is the same centurion who earlier asked Christ to heal his servant). While Christianity started as a Jewish cult and spread in a land of what would be called Arab Muslims, it was in Europe, among white Europeans, where it would grow in power and influence. This power and influence would be the heart of Western civilization, which birthed the American ideal that Duke Wayne so embodied.

"Wayne's popularity with his audience was not ebbing," wrote Randy Roberts and James Olson. Each of his recent films had done well at the box office. But the country was changing. While filming *In Harm's Way*, Duke was diagnosed with cancer. A young hospital technician accidentally told him before the doctor did. Wayne comforted the chagrined technician, then feigned surprise when the doctor gave him the "bad news" a short while later. It was one of his greatest acting jobs, wrote Roberts and Olson. At first, Wayne even thought about suicide. Cancer in 1964 was a death sentence, but incredibly he beat it. The tumor was relatively small, being caught before it spread and contained. A checkup at the Scripps Clinic in La Jolla, California, indicated it had not returned. An article in the *Los Angeles Herald-Examiner* revealed the story. More than 100,000 letters poured in, a testament to his huge popularity.

He did *The Sons of Katie Elder*, set in West Texas, with Dean Martin. When CBS television announced a *Tribute to John Wayne*, he did not much care for it, thinking it a send-off to a dying man.

"What are they trying to do, bury me?" he told Hedda Hopper and Mary St. John. "Tell them to forget it. I've just got my second wind."

In Harm's Way, directed by Otto Preminger, costarring Kirk Douglas, was filmed in large part at Pearl Harbor. It was about the U.S. Navy's heroic response to the Japanese sneak attack and ranks among Wayne's great performances. It came amid great turmoil and was a kickback of sorts to the kind of antiwar, antiauthority, perhaps even anti-*American* films that had been produced at least since the influence of John Howard Lawson, the Hollywood Popular Front, and communist infiltration of Hollywood took root in the 1930s and 1940s. But now, after such blockbuster antihero films as *The Manchurian Candidate* and *Dr. Strangelove* and liberal-themed films like *Seven Days in May* and *Fail-Safe*, a movie like *In Harm's Way* threatened to be an anachronism. It was not, saved from such a fate by virtue of Duke Wayne's screen authority.

In fact, the changing times were proving to be not a liability to his career but a benefit as he recovered from lung cancer.

"For those who longed for the old John Wayne, the one they were used to . . . Wayne was back, king of a mountain where doubt and uncertainty had been conquered," wrote Randy Roberts and James Olson.

In the 1966 film *El Dorado*, Wayne found himself working with an actor who would go on to a reputation as one of the most outspoken liberals in the business.

"I was leery of him," recalled Ed Asner. "For our first scene Howard Hawks went over the lines with the Duke and me. The scene has him returning money I have given him to kill Robert Mitchum. He comes up to the ranch house on his horse and he throws the money back at me. That was our first scene. I suggested a couple word changes to Hawks, which he liked.

"Wayne didn't say anything. Hawks says, 'It'll take a long time to set up the shot. You can go back to your trailer or whatever you want to do.' So I was walking around, too God——n nervous to go sit in my trailer. I look over and there's an army of grips and crew moving mumbo jumbo fast. So instead of taking a long walk I changed direction and walked toward the ranch house.

"There at the ranch house is John Wayne cavorting on his appaloosa. He's practically looking right at me and he says, 'Where's that New York actor? Where's that New York actor?' Well, I had been on the West Coast for several years by that point and did not consider myself a New York actor. But I took that to be an anti-Semitic comment. I walked toward him and said, 'You mean me?'

"He mumbled something incoherent. I never discussed politics with him. One time I was with Jimmy Caan sitting around and he started asking John Wayne all kinds of political questions. Wayne gets so roused with questions about Patton, questions about McCarthy, he starts whipping his hat against his thigh to burn off some of his anger. I was sitting there skulking, thinking, 'Jesus Christ, Jimmy, you sure provoke.' They weren't even liberal questions, just points of information. Wayne gave it to him in spades."

Asner found himself on the receiving end of Hawks's displeasure but said "John Wayne's make-up man, Larry Butterworth," gave him great advice.

"I always find that if you write somebody a letter—it tends to be effective," Butterworth told Asner. Asner took Butterworth's advice, to good effect, and went on to a great career on-screen and in television.

Asner's anecdote about Wayne asking, "Where's that New York actor?," which he took to be anti-Semitic, was at some issue in the 1960s. He was working with many Jewish actors. The old Hollywood preferred Englishmen and WASP leading men, but after World War II, New York acting coaches began to adopt what they perceived to be a style known as "the method," purportedly taught in Russia by Constantin Stanislavski. Lee Strasberg was the leading proponent of this new teaching tool. Out of it, a new "leading man" emerged, embodied in part by the antihero roles of Marlon Brando. Suddenly, actors with longer hair, swarthier complexions, and less traditional physical appearances took star turns. Some were physically beautiful to the point of resembling Greek sculpture, as with Tony Curtis and in particular Kirk Douglas's chiseled visage in *Spartacus*. But actors like Ed Asner and Eli Wallach often portrayed villains, characters, and wise guys. Many came out of Strasberg's New York acting studio. This no doubt propelled Wayne's demands of a "New York actor." He certainly was not one. He was a movie star and all that entailed, bred in Los Angeles from his youth, with no New York identification. He was of the American West all the way.

Wayne's was a world where "a man could move free, could make his own code and live by it; a world in which, if a man did what he had to do, he could one day take a girl and go riding through the draw and find himself home free," wrote Joan Didion.

Wayne's WASP reputation and conservative politics may have made some think him anti-Semitic, but he was not. Screenwriter and director Melville Shavelson, a Jew, did not share Wayne's politics, but he did share his passion for a story. Knowing Wayne to be a fair man, he approached him about David "Mickey" Marcus, a high-ranking U.S. Army officer who lent military expertise—and with it U.S. support—to the fledgling Israeli army fighting for the independence of their tiny nation in 1947. Wayne felt that to Shavelson, this story was what *The Alamo* had been for him. He agreed to help finance *Cast a Giant Shadow*, with his son Michael as a producer. The film featured an all-star cast, including Kirk Douglas as Marcus, Yul Brynner, Frank Sinatra, Angie Dickinson, Senta Berger, and Topol.

The story is viewed through the eyes of General Mike Randolph, played in a secondary yet very important role by the Duke. It begins with General Randolph witnessing a liberated death camp at the end of World War II. Shavelson did not think he could capture the horror of the Holocaust and relied on Wayne, without a word, "seeing" the camp. His reaction was a magnificent acting job that profoundly moved Shavelson and was a trademark of Wayne's skill in some of his greatest scenes.

"Ordinarily, he is one of the kindest and most level-headed men," Shavelson recalled. "But when he is crossed, and particularly when he is double-crossed, he can make a nuclear explosion seem like a baby's sigh."

7

REPUBLICAN DUKE

JOHN WAYNE WAS DISPLEASED THAT HIS AGENT, CHARLIE FELDMAN, HELPED Sinatra's friend, presidential candidate John Kennedy, "find girls" during trips to Los Angeles.

"The country's going soft," he exclaimed.

He supported Vice President Nixon in his campaign against Kennedy, whom he despised for his "lace curtain arrogance and unctuous liberalism." He felt Kennedy was just a product of his father's money machine, lacking moral vision, a "snot-nosed kid who couldn't keep his dick in his pants." Disgusted when he heard that Kennedy had won a Pulitzer Prize for a book he did not write (Theodore Sorenson penned *Profiles in Courage*), he paid $152,000 for a full-page advertisement in Henry Luce's July edition of *Life* magazine, urging the nation to uphold its traditional values.

The Republicans, staunch defenders of freedom from the communist threat, were called the witch-hunters of McCarthyism, losing the presidential election in 1960, senatorial midterms in 1962, and then virtually everything in 1964. Nixon, who kept a paid Soviet spy, Alger Hiss, from possibly becoming secretary-general of the United Nations, was held in the crosshairs of the left for more than two decades until he was hunted down and disgraced for doing precisely what Attorney General Robert Kennedy did seven years earlier. The newspaper that made Nixon a crusade (the *Washington Post*), employer of the two reporters (Robert Woodward and Carl Bernstein) who dogged him like Ahab chasing the great white whale, was the same organization that, twelve years earlier, was like the three monkeys who "see no evil" when right under their own noses John F. Kennedy, Joseph P. Kennedy, Lyndon Johnson, Mayor Richard Daley, and the Democratic Party stole the 1960 presidential election from Nixon ("They stole it fair and square," Nixon aide Murray Chotiner famously said in Oliver Stone's *Nixon*).

John Kennedy in the White House and the rise of the civil rights movement added luster to Hollywood liberalism. The cultural critics "continued to rise." The American right bided its time.

Boston Red Sox legend Ted Williams retired from baseball a little over a month before Kennedy was elected. This represented a true changing of the guard, one Boston superstar stepping aside after a lifetime of sports accomplishment, matched by few, if any, while a new Bostonian ascended to the Oval Office.

Williams had feuded with the Boston press for twenty-one years. They hounded him for not visiting his mother in the offseason, for fishing in the Florida Keys when his wife was giving birth, for not joining the military as fast as Bob Feller, for not tipping his cap, for spitting in the wind, and for arguing with writers. Williams had joined the military. Unlike Joe DiMaggio, who played baseball in Hawaii, or Willie Mays, who set stateside camp home-run records for the U.S. Army team during the Korean War, Williams signed on as a marine fighter pilot. The odds of even making it past flight school were long, but they needed pilots and took men who had not gone to college (like George H. W. Bush, a Connecticut prep school graduate who did not play baseball at Yale until after the war). Williams served first during World War II, then was recalled for Korea. By that time, marine pilots were flying jets, so flight school was tougher than before. Again, he made it. He flew numerous missions, was shot down, but refused to eject, fearing at his height that his kneecaps would be lost, not to mention the dread fear of being a celebrity prisoner of war in the hands of Kim Il-Sung.

He survived and returned to wild cheering throngs at Fenway Park. Between 1939 and 1960, he hit 521 home runs, with 2,654 hits and a .344 batting average. This included missing all of the 1943, 1944, and 1945 seasons (ages twenty-four to twenty-six), then the 1952 and 1953 seasons (ages thirty-three to thirty-four). Prior to his first tour, in 1943, he batted .356 with thirty-six home runs and 137 runs batted in (RBIs). Upon his return in 1946, he won the Most Valuable Player award, leading the Red Sox to the World Series with a .342 average, thirty-eight homers, and 123 RBIs. Before leaving for Korea, he hit thirty home runs with 126 RBIs; upon his return, he batted .345. He essentially lost five years to military service. Had he played those years, he most likely would have passed Babe Ruth's all-time home-run record of 714 and finished with 3,600 hits. It is generally considered by baseball experts to this day that he attained his childhood goal of "walking down the street and having people say, 'There goes the greatest hitter who ever lived.'"

Williams was movie star handsome yet a curmudgeonly, rock-ribbed southern California Republican of the Chandler era. He feuded with the Kennedyites and Harvard boys of the Boston press, whom he dubbed the "knights of the keyboard." Williams was perhaps the most outspoken, opinionated athlete of the twentieth century. Joe DiMaggio, who, if he had opinions, kept them to himself, regularly hung out with New York Mafiosi, but nobody knew this until Richard Ben Cramer revealed it in his 1999 biography.

Williams admired John Kennedy's heroism in the South Pacific during the war but was not impressed that the young lieutenant let the *PT-109* get rammed out of incompetence. He did not appreciate the fact that his own fishing trip to Florida, coinciding with his wife giving premature birth, was splattered all over the front pages while Kennedy's tryst with girls on friend George Smathers's boat in Florida, while Jacqueline Kennedy was giving well-planned birth, was treated like a national secret by his media protectors. Williams abhorred cheating and dishonesty, the essence of "Old Man Joe" Kennedy. He was not happy with reports that the 1960 election had been stolen by a cabal including mob boys with ties to "Old Man Joe" and Frank Sinatra; Chicago Mayor Richard Daley (the most corrupt politician in the nation) delivering Cook County, Illinois,

via dead voters on the rolls; or Vice President Lyndon Johnson similarly rolling out the same Texas "tombstone vote" that first delivered
his 1948 Senate seat (as described in Robert Caro's *Master of the Senate*). While Vice President Nixon never authorized a full recount,
by most accounts the money and methods employed by Kennedy's
viciously corrupt father did him in.

John F. Kennedy, said the man known as the "Splendid Splin-
ter," was "overrated" in that he shared the same opinion with the
man he was compared to often, Duke Wayne. The two shared the
same politics and the same feuding ways with a media out to get
them, in large measure for political revenge. They represented
a conservative America that was increasingly curmudgeonly, having lost the public relations battle over McCarthyism. Now, the
press was dubbing the handsome Kennedy and his glamorous wife
"American royalty" as they assembled the "best and the brightest" to
what historian Theodore White would call "Camelot." Inherent in
this flowery language was the notion that Dwight David Eisenhower
and the men he assembled first to defeat Nazi Germany and then to
run America during eight years of peace and prosperity had, in Kennedy's words, failed to "get America moving again."

Kennedy's stealing the election away from Nixon created
profound changes in the global landscape. In his first term, Kennedy had met Nikita Khrushchev at Vienna. Kennedy, who used his
looks and charm to his advantage his entire life, entered the summit
thinking he could do the same. He felt that reasonable argument
would prevail and made a major point of indicating to the Soviet
premier that if the two countries engaged in nuclear war, 70 million people would die. Khrushchev just looked at him as if to say,
"So what?" After all, V. I. Lenin had once said it would not matter
if most of the world's population perished as long as the survivors
were communists. Joseph Stalin used *New York Times* reporter Walter
Duranty to put it in American terms, stating that in order to win this
worldwide revolutionary "omelet," it would be necessary to "break a
few eggs."

Khrushchev, the hero of Stalingrad, had seen more war than
any man should ever see. He had no desire to see more. But he
decided to hard-line Kennedy, to make the young president think

that no sacrifice was too great in the name of the communist cause. This was the big trump card of Marxist-Leninist theory, the idea that people in the present were never more important than the goal, the plan, or the future—some utopian land that everybody would occupy once "purification" had rid it of the bourgeoisie.

Kennedy had tried to convey a tough message in his inauguration speech, espousing the idea that the United States would tackle any task, help any friend, and oppose any foe. But Khrushchev knew that Kennedy was bluffing. At Vienna, he sized up Kennedy and determined that he was still a "playboy" and "a rookie," controlled by his father, part of a political philosophy that had aided and comforted communism during the McCarthy era, and not willing to put his prestige on the line to oppose him.

This decision manifested itself in two areas: the Cuban missile crisis and Vietnam. After the Bay of Pigs, Kennedy was on his heels. He was not prepared to launch any military offensives against communism after the Cuban fiasco. Khrushchev knew it.

The question is, *What would have happened if Nixon had been in the White House?* Nixon was the most ardent, hard-line anticommunist politician in America. While McCarthy was posturing, Nixon was doing detective work, rooting out communists. His big prize was Alger Hiss.

Nixon demonstrated a hard line time after time after Hiss. He called Helen Gahagan Douglas the "pink lady." He proposed "battlefield nukes" at Dien Bien Phu. Nixon stood up to communists in face-to-face confrontations in Latin America and earned heroic status for his bravery. He met Khrushchev and debated him in Russia and the United States, including the famous "kitchen debate," in which the two matched the relative merits of their respective systems while standing in a kitchen that they were touring. He was intimately involved in plots by the Central Intelligence Agency (CIA) to disrupt communism in the Third World. He was the driving force behind the plans to invade Cuba after Fidel Castro's revolution, which were the early stages of Operation Mongoose, orchestrated by the CIA to eliminate the Cuban despot.

During the 1960 election, Nixon pointed out that 800 million people lived under communism and that only 500 million lived under freedom. He lost many votes because he was unable to discuss the top secret plans to topple Castro, and when goaded by Kennedy about it, he held his tongue.

Nixon was not a man to be trifled with when it came to the communist threat. Nobody understood that better than the communists themselves. Nixon learned a valuable lesson, too. His enemies (foreign and domestic) thought of him as slightly unhinged and more than a little bloodthirsty. Nixon did not try to play that image down. He let it work for him. In prosecuting war and peace with an enemy who respected only force, it was *his* best trump card.

Had he taken office in 1961, history may very well have been written much differently. This "what if?" scenario involves the assassinations of both John and Robert Kennedy, the Bay of Pigs, the Berlin Wall, the Cuban missile crisis and Fidel Castro, the CIA-authorized coup and assassination of Ngo Dinh Diem, and of course the Vietnam War, Chappaquiddick and Watergate, the political futures of both Edward "Teddy" Kennedy and Ronald Reagan, and the Cold War.

"I have been told that my father had great dislike for all the Kennedy men, but the only ill will I witnessed myself was toward Teddy," recalled Aissa Wayne. "Even before Chappaquiddick in 1969, my father watched Ted Kennedy on television and branded him a liar and a phony."

"This guy says he only cares about issues," Wayne would shout at the television. "Bull———t. He cares about getting power, and he'll say and do whatever he has to do to get it—just like every other politician. If he'd just admit he's like everyone else. Ted Kennedy's so fake he makes me sick."

Of Chappaquiddick, when Senator Kennedy allowed a girl riding in his car to drown in order to avoid embarrassment and a drunk-driving charge, Wayne was livid.

"Jesus Christ, it's a cover-up! Anyone else would at least get indicted! They're letting him off because he's a Kennedy. That family's got too much God———n pull!"

"He snatched a metal paperweight, hurling it straight at Ted Kennedy's visage, shattering our expensive TV," recalled Aissa. "My father, I surmised, was not a rational man when it came to the senator from Massachusetts," adding, "I'd never seen him so worked up," and he "went ballistic."

"Everything goes the Kennedys' way," was the saying at least until November 22, 1963, in Dallas, Texas. Some have speculated on the wrath of God, karma, some sort of cosmic retribution for Joe Kennedy's terrible misdeeds over the decades. Indeed, after his eldest son, Joe, died flying a heroic air mission in World War II, Joe was later rendered mute by a stroke shortly after his son's inauguration. He was forced to sit in silent agony watching two of his sons felled by assassins' bullets and Edward's political future destroyed by Chappaquiddick, unable to speak while he contemplated whether he had brought it all upon his family in the worst tradition of Shakespeare and Greek tragedy.

But Richard Nixon was no saint. His misdeeds would be paid for in the form of public embarrassment, which the Christian philosopher would say is a lot better to endure in this life, when one can pray and ask God for forgiveness, than to suffer your punishments in the next, when it is too late.

But it did not go Nixon's way in 1960. Instead of Nixon possibly blowing the communists "back to the Stone Age," as many on the right, including Chairman of the Joint Chiefs of Staff Curtis LeMay, advocated at the time, ending the conflict before it started—a very real possibility but also a potential disaster with Third World War implications—after Kennedy's 1963 assassination Lyndon Johnson escalated American involvement in Vietnam, as Speaker Sam Rayburn said, "by inches."

Ultimately, Shakespeare said it best, as he most often did:

> The fault, dear Brutus, is not in our stars,
> But in ourselves, that we are underlings.

Wayne, who really was something of a "quiet man" until he assumed a political role during the early years of the Blacklist, was not quiet anymore. He appeared on a television talk show hosted by *Sun-Times* columnist Irv Kupcinet, hosting a discussion of America along with University of Chicago sociologist Herman Finer.

"American heroes are really American legends," Finer said. He meant it not in a laudatory way but rather as a pejorative; "legend" was a stand-in for "lie." The "heroes" of great battles, of the cowboy range, of the struggle against communism, were not really heroes. The heroes, Finer might have identified, were civil rights victims or targeted by Senator McCarthy and HUAC.

The professor went on to say that "my wife and daughter can't even walk the streets at night." This statement seemed to favor the conservative viewpoint; liberal civil rights enforcement created a lack of law and order, with the result being blacks no longer working or marrying the mothers of their children. This led to more crime, which was why a man like Professor Finer found the streets of the Windy City unsafe for his family.

Despite being a tenured college professor living a comfortable life, Finer attributed the government as the only source of his income (the University of Chicago is a private school, ironically home of conservative economist Milton Friedman and the well-regarded "Chicago school" of economic thought, a direct refutation of Keynesianism). Duke took the professor's criticism of crime-laden streets as tacit criticism of America herself and of course got his back up over the notion that government was the source of largesse as opposed to good old Tocquevillean capitalism. Leaning forward, visibly irritated, he waited until Professor Finer was done, then got in his face.

"The people who developed Chicago didn't know whether they were going to be alive the next day, or whether their kids would be chopped up by Indians, or whether they could raise enough and develop this place for you," he shouted. This may have been a thinly veiled reference to the professor's background since it was highly unlikely his immigrant ancestors had anything to do with the development of Chicago, a place pacified, organized, built, and made prosperous by nineteenth-century pioneers, ready-made as it were by the time immigrants arrived. "And now you're whining, sitting in your easy chair over at the university teaching kids philosophy."

Wayne was not finished. "You professors kiss ass for years to get a Ph.D. and tenure. Then you spend the rest of your life trying to change the values of 18-year-olds. How pathetic!"

"Duke feels pretty strongly about these things," Professor Finer stated.

John Wayne (as Sergeant John Stryker), with John Agar (as Private First Class Peter Conway) in *Sands of Iwo Jima* (1949). Republic Pictures©/Photofest.

Wayne as Lieutenant Colonel Benjamin Vandervoort in *The Longest Day* (1962). 20th Century Fox©/Photofest.

Wayne in *The War Wagon* (1967). Universal Pictures©/Photofest.

Wayne as Colonel Mike Kirby in *The Green Berets* (1968). Warner Bros©/Photofest.

USC coach Howard "Head Man" Jones, directing practice (Duke Morrison is seen standing, middle), was larger than life; he won four national championships at USC. Courtesy of USC and XOS Digital.

After a surfing injury, Duke may have lost his starting job to Brice Taylor, an African American and USC's first all-American. Courtesy of USC and XOS Digital.

1966 VARSITY FOOTBALL ROSTER

No.	Name	Cl.	Pos.	Age	Hgt.	Wgt.	Exp.	Hometown (High School)	High School Coach	No.
52	Adams, Bill	Jr.	C	20	6-2	220	JC	Santa Monica	Don Kramer	52
66	Allmon, Dick	So.	DE	20	6-0	220	Fr.	La Jolla	Gene Edwards	66
51	Baccitich, John	Jr.	C	21	6-1	205	1V	San Francisco (St. Ignatius)	Vince Tringali	51
64	*Barry, Steve	Sr.	RG	22	6-2	210	2V	Los Angeles (Loyola)	Lew Stueck	64
17	Battle, Mike	So.	DH-S	19	5-11	170	JC	Lawndale	Dick Braunbeck	17
63	Blanche, John	So.	LG	19	6-2	215	Fr.	Claremont	Len Cohn	63
78	Born, Dennis	Jr.	LT	20	6-1	235	JC	Whittier (La Serna)	Tom Keough	78
31	Bowie, Wilson	So.	LH	20	6-1	193	Fr.	New Orleans, La. (Carver)	Enos Hicks	31
72	Brucker, Bill	So.	LT	19	6-3	240	Fr.	Van Nuys (Birmingham)	George Goff	72
26	Cahill, Ray	Sr.	LE	21	6-1	203	2V	Los Angeles (Manual Arts)	Jim Blewett	26
30	Cashman, Pat	Jr.	Rov	19	5-11	190	JC	Long Beach (Wilson)	Skip Rowland	30
47	Cooper, Sam	So.	RH	19	6-2	210	JC	West Covina	Mal Eaton	47
94	Crane, Dennis	Jr.	RT	21	6-5	240	JC	Colton	John Odenbaugh	94
81	Curtis, Mike	Jr.	RE	20	6-1	205	1V	Los Angeles (Loyola)	Mario DeMuro	81
33	Dale, Steve	So.	RH	19	5-11	185	Fr.	Yakima, Wash. (Eisenhower)	Clayton Frazier	33
83	Drake, Ron	Jr.	LE	20	6-0	175	JC	Pico Rivera (El Rancho)	Ernie Johnson	83
74	Everling, Rod	So.	RT	19	6-5	276	JC	Long Beach (Wilson)	Skip Rowland	74
59	Ferguson, Jim	Jr.	LB	24	6-4	230	JC	Long Beach (Excelsior)	Les Billinger	59
65	Garland, Cal	So.	RG	20	6-1	210	Fr.	Pasadena	Tom Hamilton	65
21	Grady, Steve	Jr.	LH	21	6-0	200	1V	Los Angeles (Loyola)	Lew Stueck	21
73	*Hayhoe, Jerry	Jr.	LT	22	6-4	230	2V	Van Nuys (Birmingham)	George Goff	73
85	Hayhoe, Bill	So.	RE	20	6-8	235	1V	Van Nuys (Birmingham)	George Goff	85
90	Hoffman, John	Jr.	DT	23	6-6	240	1V	Studio City ((Western, Anaheim)		90
69	*Homan, Jim	Sr.	RG	21	6-2	230	1V	Long Beach (St. Anthony)	Tom Carroll	69
16	Hough, Dick	So.	QB	20	6-0	175	JC	Anaheim	Clare Van Hoorebeke	16
23	*Hull, Mike	Jr.	FB	20	6-4	210	1V	La Crescenta (Crescenta Valley)	Gary Hess	23
25	*Hunter, Mike	Sr.	S	22	5-9	160	1V	Newport Beach (Anaheim)	Clare Van Hoorebeke	25
41	Jaroncyk, Bill	Jr.	DH	19	6-1	188	JC	Encinitas (San Dieguito)		41
29	Keithly, John	So.	LH	19	6-0	195	Fr.	Long Beach (Wilson)	Skip Rowland	29
46	**King, Eddie	Sr.	Rov	22	6-3	220	2V	Fresno (Bullard)	Robin Rush	46
84	Klein, Bob	So.	RE	19	6-5	230	Fr.	Pacific Palisades (St. Monica's)	Woody Bray	84
37	Kochinas, Tony	So.	DH	19	5-9	175	JV	Los Angeles (Lincoln)	Skip Giancanelli	37
28	Lawrence, Jim	So.	RH	20	5-11	190	JV	Buena Park	H. L. Looney	28
27	**Lee, Phil	Sr.	DH	21	5-10	185	2V	Stockton (Edison)	Lowell Herbert	27
82	Leon, Rich	Jr.	LE	19	6-1	190	JC	Whittier (Sierra)	Don Stillwell	82
36	*McCall, Don	Sr.	LH	22	5-11	195	1V	Los Angeles (Fremont)	Frank Nobbe	36
22	McCullouch, Earl	Jr.	S	20	5-11	170	JC	Long Beach (Poly)	Bill Mulligan	22
60	Maeding, Dale	So.	LG	19	6-2	200	JC	Santa Ana (Santa Ana Valley)	Dick Hill	60
75	*Magner, Gary	Jr.	DT	21	6-3	220	1V	Costa Mesa (Mater Dei)	Dick Coury	75
67	*May, Ray	Sr.	DE	21	6-2	230	1V	Los Angeles	Jim Pendleton	67
86	Miller, Bob	So.	RE	20	6-4	220	1V	Compton (Dominguez)	Bob Spindola	86
71	*Moore, Denis	Jr.	DT	22	6-5	220	2V	Los Angeles (Westchester)	Bill Young	71
24	Motley, Marv	Jr.	LH	20	5-9	180	JC	Long Beach (Poly)	Bill Mulligan	24
91	Murphy, Jim	Jr.	DT	20	6-1	225	JV	Los Angeles (St. John Vianney)	Fred Aldrich	91
18	Nungesser, Kendall	So.	DH-Rov	19	6-2	195	Fr.	San Gabriel	Howard Hunt	18
79	O'Malley, Jack	Jr.	DT	20	6-4	245	1V	Wilmington (Banning)	Paul Huebner	79
15	Page, Toby	Jr.	QB	20	6-0	190	1V	Santa Ana (Mater Dei)	Dick Coury	15
61	*Petrill, Larry	Sr.	MG	21	6-0	205	1V	Redondo Beach (Morningside, Serra)	Jay Roelen, Hub Maikowski	61
88	*Rossovich, Tim	Jr.	DE	20	6-5	220	1V	Mt. View (St. Francis)	Angelo Aguiar	88
80	*Salness, Ty	Jr.	Rov-DE	21	6-1	200	1V	Anaheim	Clare Van Hoorebeke	80
76	*Scarpace, Mike	Jr.	LT	20	6-1	245	1V	Van Nuys (Birmingham)	George Goff	76
38	Scott, Dan	So.	FB	19	5-10	205	JC	Pico Rivera (El Rancho)	Ernie Johnson	38
96	Scott, Willard	So.	MG	19	6-1	230	JC	Los Angeles (Manual Arts)	Gil Rozadilla	96
89	**Shaw, Nate	Sr.	DH	21	6-2	205	2V	San Diego (Lincoln)	Shan Deniston	89
12	**Sherman, Rod	Sr.	RH	21	6-0	190	2V	Pasadena (Muir)	Don Hunt	12
35	Sims, Leonard	Jr.	RH	20	5-10	190	JV	Garden Grove (Santiago)	Tom Avery	35
55	Snow, Jim	So.	LB	19	5-11	215	JV	San Diego	Joe Duke	55
14	Sogge, Steve	So.	QB	19	5-10	170	Fr.	Gardena	Stan Smith	14
58	Swanson, Steve	Jr.	LB	20	5-10	200	JC	Pico Rivera (El Rancho)	Ernie Johnson	58
49	Treadwell, Lee	So.	LB	19	6-2	200	Fr.	Tipton (Tulare)	Tom Yost	49
87	Truman, Phil	Jr.	LE	20	6-5	195	JV	Rosemead	Jim Ellis	87
95	Taylor, Mike	Jr.	RT	20	6-4	260	JC	San Francisco (Lowell)	Bill Felling	95
70	*Wells, Harry	Sr.	DT	21	6-1	230	1V	Los Angeles (Manual Arts)	Jim Blewett	70
92	Westphal, Mike	Jr.	DT	21	6-6	250	JC	Long Beach (Jordan)	Walt Anderson	92
44	*Williams, Homer	Sr.	FB	22	6-1	220	1V	Long Beach (St. Anthony)	Leo Haggerty, Tom Carroll	44
10	*Winslow, Troy	Sr.	QB	22	6-0	183	2V	Inglewood	Bill Peters	10
57	Wojcik, Greg	Jr.	C	20	6-5	245	JC	Huntington Beach	Ken Moats	57
68	Woudenberg, Dana	So.	LG	20	6-1	220	JV	Scottsdale, Ariz. (Arcadia, Phoenix)	Bob Hendricks	68
77	*Yary, Ron	Jr.	RT	20	6-1	265	1V	Bellflower	Don Ashton	77
50	*Young, Adrian	Jr.	LB	20	6-1	210	1V	La Mirada (Bishop Amat)	Phil Cantwell	50

*Number of varsity letters won.

The 1966 Trojans lost the Rose Bowl to Bob Griese and Purdue, 14–13, when McKay went for two but missed. Courtesy of USC Athletics.

The USC track team that Harley Tinkham ran for was a perennial NCAA champ under Coach Dean Cromwell. Courtesy of Amanda Tinkham Boltax.

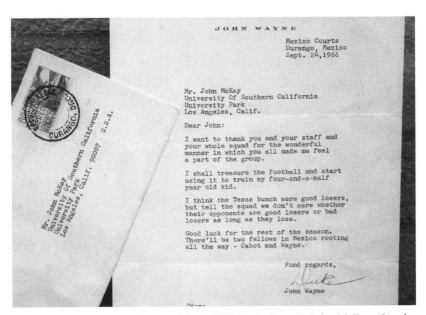

The letter Duke wrote to his new friend, USC football coach John McKay, after the 1966 USC–Texas game. Courtesy of J. K. McKay.

L.A. Times scribe Harley "Ace" Tinkham (right, with his wife and daughter on the USC campus, early 1980s) apparently got into a mythic scuffle with Wayne in Austin in 1966. Courtesy of Amanda Tinkham Boltax.

8

THE DUKE OF ORANGE COUNTY

WHEN THE WATTS SECTION OF LOS ANGELES WENT UP IN FLAMES IN 1965, many felt the riots were a justified expression of black rage. But many more were disgusted, especially since the blacks harmed and killed mainly themselves, burning down their own homes and businesses. But many whites in Los Angeles decided to flee. Wayne biographer Michael Munn, during press interviews for his book *John Wayne: The Man behind the Myth* (2003), speculated that the move to a "big house with walls around it" was motivated partly by these and other events as well. The Waynes' Encino house was a five-and-a-half-acre estate, but the riots coincided with these other events that Wayne found disturbing, motivating him to move.

In 1965, Duke heard little Aissa Wayne scream in their Encino home. He grabbed his gun and ran, confronting a burglar whom he chased out of the house. The police were called and found the man, a deranged, out-of-work carpenter named Dennis Lee Parker. With the man detained, Wayne confronted him. Parker asked Wayne a favor; he had taken a taxi and hoped he would have stolen money to pay for it. Wayne paid the taxi driver the $20 for the cab ride, explaining he did not want him to be stiffed.

After the break-in, he said gun control people would be "glad to have a gun around" if their homes were broken into. Then he announced he was selling his home to Walt Disney's daughter and moving his family out of Los Angeles.

Actually, according to biographers, it was Pilar Wayne who bought a new home in Newport Beach without even asking Duke for "permission" while he was filming on location.

"However, this house had a magnificent view of the bay from the back patio," Pilar recalled. "I could imagine Duke sitting outdoors with our children, enjoying the wonderful sea air while we watched the sun set." According to her, she did ask Duke first, calling him in Durango on *The Sons of Katie Elder* set.

"If you think it's right, buy it," he told her.

"Your mother and I are thinking of moving to Newport Beach, not far from where the boat is," Duke told Aissa. "We want to know what you think. Would you like to move to Newport?"

She was mainly happy to be included in the discussion, her opinion valued enough to be asked even if the move was already a done deal.

"For me it was easy," she recalled. "Partial to the cool climes of the beach, wary of living life on a hill behind ten-foot walls, pleased that my father was so solicitous of my feelings on such an important matter, I told him yes, moving sounded wonderful."

All packed and ready to go, Wayne remembered one last item before departing Encino: a portrait of liberal Minnesota Senator-turned-Vice President Hubert Humphrey. Humphrey wrote, "Dear Duke, Thanks for your continued support." Wayne taped it to the toilet tank in his guest bathroom for comedic purposes. He almost left it behind but remembered to retrieve it before leaving.

When the Waynes moved to Newport Beach, it was a natural. It was "Trojan country." It was John Wayne country. Many film people lived in Encino, as did many other professionals: doctors, attorneys, and certified public accountants. It was a part of the city (technically, due to water grabs and land incorporation, it, like most of the San Fernando Valley, was officially Los Angeles) where an increasingly large group of UCLA graduates, the great rival of Duke's beloved USC Trojans, made their residences. It was increasingly liberal, and as the burglary incident indicated, the crime of urban Los Angeles was creeping closer. The freeways were clogging up, and it no longer had that country feel of a decade earlier. Smog in the valley, where intense heat is trapped by mountain ranges absent cooling Pacific breezes, was brutal.

Newport Beach, in southern Orange County, was a dream come true. Close enough to the Long Beach–Los Angeles corridor to call itself a suburban bedroom community, it was far enough away, with a physical environment and lifestyle unique enough, to have its own identity. Richard Nixon was born in Yorba Linda in northern Orange County and grew up amid orange groves in a rural environment. After World War II, the population grew tremendously, but it still had a small-town feel to it. Nixon's anticommunist politics were the politics of Orange County, home of the John Birch Society. It was reactionary and grew in large measure as a result of "white flight" after the Watts riots, but a sense of "California cool" pervaded the place, tamping down the sort of virulent racism still found in other parts of America.

While "white flight" and freeways grew "the O.C.," it was the opening of Disneyland (1955) that jumped the population from 688,290 in 1960 to 1,110,210 in 1965, with far greater growth ahead. Disneyland did not merely bring jobs, people, and schools to Orange County—it was its identity. That identity was white, Protestant, Republican, Christian, wholesome, clean, and honest, not to mention, in the case of girls especially, blond, tanned, athletic, and full figured. When the Beach Boys sang of "California Girls," no place on earth represented that image more than Orange County.

In 1964, the moderate Republican governor of New York, Nelson Rockefeller, was favored to capture the GOP nomination. He was challenged by right-wing U.S. Senator Barry Goldwater (R–Arizona). The party nomination came down to California. Orange County gave Goldwater (who also owned a home in Newport) the votes he needed to secure the nomination at San Francisco's Cow Palace. Three California Republicans dominated the state party's political scene, none of them elected officials. Former Vice President Richard Nixon, after losing to incumbent Edmund "Pat" Brown in the state's 1962 gubernatorial campaign, was now practicing law in New York City, a kind of "exile" as he pondered his next move.

The other two prominent Republicans were actors: Ronald Reagan and John Wayne. Reagan had not and would not move to Orange County, Nixon's boyhood home and Wayne's new home. But the politics of Nixon, Reagan, and Wayne would come to be identified as "Orange County Republicanism," a sort of attractive extremism, rabid in its anticommunism, absent the racism of the equally anticommunist Jim Crow South, still operating under the official cover of the Ku Klux Klan and the Democratic Party. When people thought of Orange County Republican politics, the images of flag-waving Birchers was mixed with images of Duke Wayne on horseback and the smiling visage of a handsome Ronnie Reagan, not to mention Jimi Hendrix going electric, big-wave surfing, and a coastline etched by God Himself, complete with bikini-clad babes who looked to have stepped right out of the pages of *Playboy* magazine. It was paradise.

Asked to give a speech for the flagging Goldwater, Reagan dazzled a southern California crowd and national television audience with his manifesto, a marvelous explanation of conservatism then and now. Known simply as "the Speech," it launched his career but could not save Goldwater from a brutal defeat at the hands of President Lyndon Johnson.

There was a fourth important Republican in 1964, also an actor. George Murphy would be an elected official before Reagan. The former song-and-dance man, once Shirley Temple's "second fiddle," defeated former President Kennedy's press secretary, Pierre Salinger, for the U.S. Senate, a rare GOP victory in a year of Democrat dominance.

(For that matter, Shirley Temple, thirty-six years old in 1964, was already a Republican with a future as a diplomat, serving under multiple presidents.)

In 1966, Gene "the Singin' Cowboy" Autry, of John Wayne's movie vintage, moved his Los Angeles Angels from Dodger Stadium to Anaheim Stadium. This move profoundly changed the Angel image. In Los Angeles, led by wild-partying pitchers Bo Belinsky and Dean Chance, they had a reputation as swinging bachelors haunting the Sunset Strip. Belinsky was dealt to Philadelphia, and the Angels of Anaheim lost all their color and character in the suburbs. But the move, coming on the heels of Disneyland's success and Goldwater's voter bloc, put the county on the map. Growth continued unabated.

Extending sporadically around Orange County and then north to the massive Long Beach naval facilities and shipyards, there started a thirty-mile trek through San Pedro, Torrance, Carson, and El Segundo, ending at the Santa Monica Municipal Airport. This area could be considered headquarters of the twentieth-century military-industrial complex, dominated by the billionaire filmmaker and aviation pioneer Howard Hughes—to the south the sprawling Camp Pendleton marine base and beyond that San Diego, the ultimate navy town. In the middle of the county was the Marine Corps Air Station El Toro. It was at a swinging bar near the El Toro base where in the early 1960s a young band regularly played a romantic ballad called "You've Lost That Lovin' Feelin'." A black marine jumped up upon the song's conclusion, declaring to his buddies, "That was *righteous*, brothers!" Thus was born the name of a classic American group. This seemed to epitomize Orange County cool: paradise mixed with the American military empire at the height of the Cold War.

Of all places in Orange County, none was more magnificent than Newport Beach. It offered palatial homes, sweeping ocean views, towering seaside cliffs, the endless strand with monster surf, an "Orange coast" of clean ocean air and cool breezes, and a happening nightlife, all an ocean apart from the stifling heat of Encino. Its residents were aerospace engineers, FBI agents, military officers, attorneys, captains of industry, and all other symbols of American success. Most were WASPs, and a disproportionate number had blond hair, especially their daughters, who made up, along with San Marino "old money," the famed "daddy's girls" forming the heart of USC's sorority row.

The trendiest shopping centers dotted the landscape. Office towers were going up in Newport near the 405/San Diego Freeway and in nearby Costa Mesa and Irvine. The Irvine Company became one of the biggest developers in the nation. All the major law firms and many top corporations set up businesses there. It was not a very environmentally conscious atmosphere, yet despite much freeway expansion, population growth, and construction, the land was and remains to this day abundant enough to absorb it all without blight.

It was not known as a movie colony, but Duke Wayne was welcomed there. Like the rest of the county, it was airtight conservative Republican. Whatever the Chandlers had envisioned Los Angeles to be—indeed, had shaped it into becoming but had been lost to the 1960s and encroaching liberalism—Newport Beach was tenfold. Newport's politics were Duke's and vice versa.

He bought a home on Balboa Bay, not far from the infamous "Wedge," where as a young man he dislocated his shoulder, leading to his losing his job on coach Howard Jones's 1926 USC Trojans; this in turn meant the loss of scholarship money, leading to his dropping out of school and going to Fox studios, and the rest was history. It was at the outlet of the Santa Ana River, an area long known as San Joaquin Bay because it was already part of Rancho San Joaquin.

The 9,000-square-foot, seven-bedroom house on Bayshore Drive had a boat launch for the *Wild Goose* and was three doors down from Jimmy Cagney's brother. Cagney would come down, and everybody would pile onto Duke's boat for a day of sailing, drinking, and fun; maybe a few broads would tag along to lend some curvature to the earth. It was perfect for Wayne, who always loved the sea since his youth and had spent decades sailing up and down the coast with John Ford. The only problem was any boater on the bay could pull up to the dock, but Aissa recalled that Newport Beach, despite its massive wealth and opulence, was, compared to the Hollywood community, a homespun sort of place, much more to her father's liking.

She recalled his speaking of "doctrinaire liberals" who were "not in touch with the American people." Wayne was, and he felt most at home in this Orange County enclave. Aissa pointed out one particular incident she said personified the difference between Hollywood and Newport and between Duke and the showbiz crowd.

Once out with her dad, she saw Rita Hayworth act condescending and nasty to busboys and waiters when she dined with Duke during the 1963 filming of *Circus World*. This behavior was "anathema to my father."

"Never lose the common touch," he told her afterward. "Never think anyone is better than you, but never assume you're superior to anyone else. Try and be decent to everyone, until they give you a reason not to."

"Home prices began their spectacular ascent, and Orange County became the centerpiece of the 'California Dream'—fair weather, beaches, mountains, cars, malls, and lots of home equity," wrote Randy Roberts and James Olson, adding that the Orange County John Wayne found in the mid-1960s looked "a lot like Glendale in 1910" (plus the addition of bikinis).

A few years later, President Richard Nixon, who owned a mansion called Casa Pacifica down the coast at San Clemente (known as the "Western White House"), hosted Soviet leader Leonid Brezhnev. After arriving at El Toro, Brezhnev and Nixon flew by helicopter down the coast south to San Clemente. Brezhnev stared out the window at the magnificent estates dotting the beaches for mile after mile. He remarked to Nixon that surely this was a trick, a "Potemkin village" of a sort, or special "dachas," where only the elites of the U.S. government were able to live in such luxury. Nixon smiled and said, no, these were middle-class families who, by dint of the capitalist work ethos, owned these homes and raised families there. Brezhnev was dumbstruck that average people lived like that.

Wayne, a native Angeleno who grew up in the shadow of Hollywood proper, attended the most "Hollywood" of all schools, USC, where countless celebrities sent their kids, and was the most popular actor who ever lived yet never felt at home among the elites, the snobs, indeed the very outsiders who flocked to his town year after year looking to attain stardom. He and Pilar, however, were American royalty in Newport Beach, immediately listed in *The Orange Book*, the county's social register (in Los Angeles, such a thing was reserved for the Chandlers and the Saenz family). No town could have been more perfectly suited for a man. For all his success and achievement prior to the move, it defined his identity in many ways as much as anything he ever did in his career.

9

DUKE VS. STALIN

JOHN WAYNE ACCEPTED THE DOMINO THEORY THAT IF ONE NATION FELL INTO communist hands, the nation next to it would, until all nations in the region fell. He had followed the activities of communist guerrillas in British Malaya, French Indochina, Dutch Indonesia, and the Philippines. He was prepared to accept the premise that Vietnam was the place to take a stand against this pernicious disease.

It was during this time—the apex of the Blacklist, McCarthyism, and the struggle between the forces of freedom and the forces of communism taking shape on the battlefields of Korea, in the rice paddies of Indochina, in the hearts and minds of the Chinese people, in Eastern Europe, and in Hollywood—that John Wayne, anticommunist, faced his greatest threat.

He knew how much the communists hated him and like thinkers. Union thugs and communists infiltrating the film industry had menaced Screen Actors Guild president Ronald Reagan with bodily harm. Whittaker Chambers, Richard Nixon, McCarthy, HUAC, Reagan, John Wayne—these people were throwing a monkey wrench, exposing some of Soviet dictator Joseph Stalin's most insidious conspiracies.

While filming *Hondo*, the FBI and studio security began notic-ing unusual activity surrounding Duke Wayne. Unknown men were making inquiries of his whereabouts, his habits, and his communi-cations and of movie schedules and locations. His estranged wife Chata hired detectives to get dirt on him, as she desired not merely to profit from their divorce but also to destroy his reputation.

But according to film historian Michael Munn's *John Wayne: The Man behind the Myth*, somebody else was trailing him. British actor Peter Cushing heard stories from Chinese immigrants about Soviet dictator Joseph Stalin and Chinese Chairman Mao Tse-tung plotting to have a "big American film star killed." He told this story to Michael Munn in 1973 or 1974.

"He is known to hate Communists, and he's famous for being a screen cowboy," Cushing said of the target of the assassination. "The first name that comes to mind I say is John Wayne. But surely that can't be true. Yet that's what these wonderful Chinese people told me. I wonder if it *was* John Wayne they meant."

Munn spoke to Wayne during a visit to his film trailer a short while later. The subject of communism came up.

"You just can't let the Communists do what they want, which is to rule the world," he said to Munn in the 1970s. "Make no mistake. I *know*. Khrushchev told me what he was going to do. And we can't let 'em do it. It's unthinkable. There are people who'll tell you that the Communists are no threat. Believe me, they are. I tell you, I *know*."

"Is that because they tried to kill you?" Munn asked him.

"Why'd you say that?" replied Duke. He shrugged and sighed.

"I'll tell you something," Duke went on, resigned to the story. "I'll tell you why it's got to be like that after I tell you what hap-pened," adding, "Once the genie's out of the bottle, how ya gonna get it back in again?" Munn quoted Wayne saying to him, when asked, if the plot was true.

"Kid, I've been criticized for years because I've made my feel-ings known about those pinko bastards. I said it during the '50s and I've said it in the '60s, and I've stood up and said we were right to be in Vietnam. But those Lefties, those so-called liberals, have tried to crucify me. Well, ya know something. They can't lay a glove on me with their mean-spirited words because I've faced worse than them.

"I'll be straight with you 'cos I like you, and you already know more than anyone should. This is between you and me. The Communists have been trying to kill me since 1949. But as you can see, they didn't do a very good job of it. I licked the Big C—and I licked those Commie bastards."

With the help of the FBI, plus two good friends, screenwriter Jimmy Grant and stuntman Yakima Canutt, "attempts on his life on American soil," wrote Munn, were also foiled. "I owe my life to Yak," Wayne said. "The agents told me I needed special protection. I said, 'Hell, I'm not gonna hide away for the rest of my life. This is the land of the free, and that's the way I'm gonna stay.' I'd say up to this point, I've succeeded right well," adding, "As far as I'm concerned, I've always been safe. I'm not going through life looking over my shoulder."

Then Wayne asked Munn, "How in hell did you know?"

Munn told Duke the story told him by Cushing.

"What your friend Mr. Cushing said was true," replied Wayne. "I don't know for sure how long that God——n Chairman Mao wanted me out of the way, but it turned out he did. I had an idea there was a Communist conspiracy, but I kept it to myself. Never wanted my family living in fear that anything untoward would ever happen. Thanks to Yak, some of his best cowboys and some men from the government, I was okay on American soil, so I never told my family. And if you ever meet Yak, you can get him to tell you what I mean."

After Wayne's 1979 passing, Munn heard confirmation of the story from none other than acclaimed actor Orson Welles in 1983. He said he heard it from Soviet film director Sergei Bondarchuk while making *Waterloo* (1970).

"That took you by surprise, didn't it?" asked Welles.

"Stalin was mad, of course. Should have been put in a straitjacket. Only a madman like Joseph Stalin would have tried to have John Wayne killed."

According to Welles, Stalin's vendetta against John Wayne stemmed from events going back to 1936.

"There was a noted Russian screenwriter called Alexei Kapler who just happened to be a Jew," Welles recalled. "Now, Joseph Stalin hated Jews, but he tried his best to keep his hatred to himself, although those closest to him knew he was completely anti-Semitic. Stalin knew of the advantage propaganda could play in motion pictures, and he decided that a film must be made about Lenin.

"And so he invited Kapler to his dacha in Kuntsevo, and commissioned him to write the screenplay. Kapler was a Jew, but he was also one of the very best screenwriters in the Soviet Union. Stalin decided that Mikhail Romm, one of the most prominent of Soviet film directors, would direct the film. Stalin frequently discussed the script with Kapler and Romm, offering his own advice, which neither Kapler nor Romm was foolish enough to turn down."

Kapler's screenplay turned out to be not one but two movies: *Lenin in October* (1937) and *Lenin in 1918* (1939). However, when Stalin's young daughter developed a mad crush on the handsome thirty-four-year-old Kapler, Stalin had him sent to the gulag at Vorkuta.

According to the story line, Stalin apparently learned of Wayne's popularity from the Russian filmmaker Sergei Gerasimov, who attended a peace conference in New York in 1949.

"He . . . heard that an actor named John Wayne was publicly denouncing Stalin and the Communist Party," said Welles. "He was also denouncing the newly created People's Republic of China and its leader Mao Tse-tung."

Gerasimov told Stalin of Wayne's fervent anticommunist beliefs.

"In 1949 there was a great deal of brouhaha in Moscow when Gerasimov returned to Moscow and brought to Stalin's ears the news that John Wayne was leading the war to crush Communism in America, and in the American motion picture industry. Wayne had been elected president of the Motion Picture Alliance for the Preservation of American Ideals, and its main objective was to fight all that was anti-American, and that meant Communism. Despite all the efforts of Soviet infiltrators, the Communists had failed to fully penetrate the American film industry, and people who had become sympathetic to the cause and those who had fully joined in the cause had been Blacklisted by Hollywood. Some had even gone to jail."

Frustrated by this, Stalin ordered a hit on the Duke, but word of this unusual act filtered through the Soviet film community. That was how Kapler, languishing in the gulag, heard of it. The way Kapler heard it, Stalin planned to send Wayne a "warning that if he continued to urge the American people to wage war on Soviet Russia, he would die," said Welles. Kapler managed to get a message through some of his dissident "Jewish friends in the Soviet film industry" to warn U.S. intelligence of the plan, said Welles.

By 1949, according to Welles, Stalin "came to hate" the name John Wayne. "He feared it. He felt that the name had become a major threat to him and his ideals," adding that to the Soviet despot Wayne was an American "secret weapon, more subtle than a nuclear bomb, but just as destructive to Stalin's ideals and his dreams of world domination."

Welles told Munn that Stalin urged Chairman Mao, fresh off victory over Chiang Kai-shek's Kuomintang forces, to join in the conspiracy to kill Wayne. Mao agreed but only if Stalin mounted World War III against the West. Stalin agreed, but apparently it was a double cross. Nevertheless, a second order to Chinese hit men was authorized. This would expand to North Korean and North Vietnamese assassins.

Stalin was so angered by Wayne's anticommunism that he plotted several attempts on the actor's life in the 1950s. In one instance, two Russian hit men posing as FBI agents visited Wayne at his office in Hollywood. Real agents who knew about the plot stopped the attack before it could be carried out.

Munn told BBC News Online of his conversations with Orson Welles and Wayne himself over thirty years and added that Stalin's motivation was Hollywood's Blacklisting of Soviet sympathizers.

"Stalin decided Wayne had to die," Munn said.

When two hit men called at Wayne's office at Warner Brothers studios in 1951, they were captured and later requested asylum in the united States. According to *John Wayne: The Man behind the Myth*, "Big John Wayne stood a meter or two behind the kneeling men, a gun in his hand. Next to him stood his partner, a broad, short man with a crew cut, also with a gun in his hand. The weapons were aimed at the back of the heads of the two kneeling men who uttered pathetically in Russian. Wayne assumed they were saying their last prayers to whichever god Soviet Communists revered."

The "other man" was screenwriter James Edward Grant. According to the story told by Yakima Canutt to Michael Munn in a

London hotel in 1976, Wayne counted to three and fired but did not kill them. Wayne then turned to the FBI men and said, "You can have them now."

He held up his gun to the would-be assassins.

"Blanks," he explained, then told the FBI men they could "send them back to Russia."

"No! Please! Don't send us back to Stalin," they begged. "We will both die."

"Don't worry," the FBI man said. "You won't be going back . . . yet. We've a few questions we want answered. And then—maybe—we'll let Stalin have you back."

"But you don't need to interrogate us," they pleaded. "We can help you. We can work for you."

"Seems they're more afraid of their beloved Stalin than they are of you," Wayne said. "Welcome to the land of the free."

To the agents he added, "You won't forget our deal, will ya? I don't care what you have to tell [J. Edgar] Hoover, but you'll keep my name out of this."

"If that's what you really want, Mr. Wayne. But these Commies came here to kill you. They failed this time, but those f——g Russkies may try again."

"Like I told you, I got a wife, and four kids, and I don't want any of them knowing and having to worry for the rest of their lives. These Commies f——d up this time. Maybe they'll think twice before trying again."

"Maybe, Mr. Wayne."

"The name's Duke."

"Suppose they do try again?" Grant asked.

"You'd better hope they don't, otherwise you might never work again."

"Yakima told me that the FBI had discovered there were agents sent to Hollywood to kill John Wayne," said Munn in 2003. "He said the FBI had come to tell John about the plot. John told the FBI to let the men show up and he would deal with them."

"American intelligence was pretty smart to discover Russian agents had arrived in America," Canutt told Munn in *John Wayne: The Man behind the Myth.* "FBI agents had infiltrated a lot of Commu-

nist groups—and I mean groups of real hard-liners who were sponsored by Stalin and who played host to the agents Russia sent over.
They had nothing to do with the film industry. The Communists in
the business were just trying to follow a policy that they believed in,
although they were naïve to do so.

"The FBI were able to discover the time and place, which was
at Wayne's office at Warner Brothers, where he and Jimmy Grant
would be working on the script [for *Big Jim McLain*]. The KGB
agents would be masquerading as FBI agents. John had decided to
set up a 'sting' for his would-be assassins.

"The FBI agents were prepared to be with John and Jimmy
when the KGB turned up. Wayne prepared for the KGB's arrival
by telling the guard at the studio gate that he was expecting two
agents, so they were able to drive straight in and up to John's office. They spent the rest of the day and into the evening waiting for
the KGB to turn up. No one knew how the Russians would get into
John's office.

"The FBI agents said they'd have to make a report back to J.
Edgar Hoover. John said, 'Just so long as it's all hushed up.' Years
later, we all found out Hoover had his famous 'secret files.'

"John told them that he and Jimmy would scare 'the living
s——t' out of the Russians and he worked out with Grant how they
would take them to a remote beach John had in mind. I mean, this
was literally scripted, written by James Grant. They'd have guns
armed with blanks, and John and Jimmy would act out an execution
on them. After the FBI could do what they liked. Well, the agents
thought this was just a great idea.

"John had them hide out in another room. It was dark when
the two Russian agents turned up. I suppose they were KGB. They
spoke with perfect American accents and had FBI badges and
were able to convince the guard at the gate that they needed to
see Wayne because his life was in danger. When the guard phoned
through to John's office, he told the guard to let them in, and then
he told the FBI agents to be ready.

"When the Russians came into John's office, the FBI agents
came into the room and held them at gunpoint. Then they got into
cars and drove up the coast until they came to the place where John

planned to carry out the mock execution. He told me, 'I just wanted them Commies to know they didn't scare me.'"

Afterward, though, John shunned FBI protection and did not want his family to know. When Stalin died on March 2, 1953, many imprisoned by him were released, including Alexei Kapler, who told Sergei Bondarchuk about it, "and Gerasimov told Bondarchuk how Stalin tried to kill John Wayne, Bondarchuk told it to me, and now I tell you," Welles said to Michael Munn in 1983.

Unbeknownst to Wayne at the time, Stalin's order was rescinded after his 1953 passing. Despite that, American communists headquartered in Burbank, California, a major film industry town and home to the NBC studios, still wanted Wayne killed. They decided to act on their own. In 1955, they intended to carry out their plot, but a group of stuntmen (led by Yakima Canutt) loyal to Duke raided the premises and "ran them out of town." They had infiltrated their cells.

Canutt told Munn, "Wayne later learned that those Russian agents were so afraid of going back to Russia that they happily began working for our side, and they were able to provide a lot of useful information. John thought he was safe after that. But a bit later, I learned from my own network of undercover guys—my stuntmen—that the danger wasn't over."

Canutt learned about those plots in part because he was looking into Chata's detectives following Duke while he filmed in Mexico. "I learned from my own undercover boys that some of the investigators were Communists out to get Wayne. This time they were not Russians, but American citizens.

"I got in touch with John and told him that there were Communists heading his way, and *those* were the men the police were ready and able to dispose of. When Duke told the police to make sure they left the country, he didn't just mean they should get them out of Mexico. He meant they should be sent to Russia. And that's what the police did, rounding up these guys and getting them on a plane for Russia at gunpoint.

"Duke said to me, 'I guess this Khrushchev fellow still wants me out of the way.'

"I said, 'I'm not so sure. My guy who got me this tip says that the American Commies are making their own decisions. All the same, you better expect more trouble sometime.'"

Canutt's trusted friend Cliff Lyons had infiltrated the "most hard-core group of Communists in Los Angeles," added Canutt, emphasizing it was not a government operation; therefore, they did not have FBI protection. "We didn't know who we could trust, and we didn't want anything to jeopardize our plan and put Duke's life at risk."

While many "limousine communists" may have believed in some esoteric form of communism, the men Canutt's group unearthed were "Stalinists" and "dangerous people, not the Hollywood Ten. These guys were the Stalinists who were brainwashed to believe they were the true government of America in waiting then." Canutt and Wayne assumed that Stalin's standing order to have him offed still stood and that these people, whether directed by Moscow or just out of rabid belief in the cause, were intent on carrying it out.

Whittaker Chambers described this form of fanaticism in *Witness* (1952). It was also displayed in Frank Sinatra's *The Manchurian Candidate* (1962). While Nazi evils were easily identified, first in a direct U.S.–German war, then in the unearthing of the death camps, the U.S.–communist confrontation failed to capture this sort of intensity for most. There were proxy wars, a missile crisis, varying forms of threat and confrontation, and the Cold War, but the kind of evil represented in the mass extinction of over 100 million people has, for some reason, never been fully illustrated to the American people, a certain segment of which, for some odd reason, then and now seem to varying degrees to identify with it. But for John Wayne, he saw it up close and personal—first Stalin's agents, then the American group tracking him to Mexico, and now again on his home soil.

They operated out of a printing company in Burbank, not far from the Warner lot where the FBI had apprehended Stalin's assassins. They were apparently motivated to kill Wayne because *Blood Alley* was an anticommunist movie.

"They'd tried before when Duke was in Mexico making *Hondo*, so this time they were going to get him in his own home," said Canutt.

John Wayne was apparently the real deal, just as Ted Williams was the real deal. He did not show fear. He did not back down or hide. He was in real life as he portrayed on screen, military service or no military service.

"They show so much as their little pinkies, I'll blow them all to Kingdom Come," Wayne said.

"Look, John, I think we can stop them, but what if we can't?" asked the stuntman.

"I've got enough guns to arm the 7th Cavalry," responded the Duke.

"John, the 7th Cavalry were wiped out at Little Big Horn."

"You'd better make sure they don't get here."

Cliff Lyon and Canutt rounded up "our most trusted stunt guys who were all cowboys," and off they went to what Yakima called "the bloody battle of Burbank." According to him, armed to the teeth, they entered the meeting place, at which point the communists realized Lyons had set them up and they were surrounded. Without firing a shot, the cowboys "went straight into action and we just lay into them," using chairs and tables in an "almighty fight." The stuntmen beat them to a bloody pulp, then "drew our guns . . . there was a lot of blood spilled, and I reckon it was lucky nobody got killed."

The communists began to plead for their lives when Canutt told them that if they "like your precious Stalin so much, you can join him," presumably in death.

"No one's gonna die if you do as we say," Canutt then told them.

Canutt produced plane tickets to Russia, drove them to the airport, and saw them board planes. There is no explanation regarding passports, visas, or other necessities of international flight, shedding some question on Canutt's claims made to Michael Munn over the course of several meetings and described in his 2003 Wayne biography. However, travel rules were different in the mid-1950s, particularly for Americans, who were essentially free to fly anywhere they liked without restriction. Also, Canutt may have worked the deal out with the government, but his statement to Munn indicates he did not.

"As far as I know, the cops never knew what we'd done, nor the intelligence guys," he said. "We kept it a secret."

Wayne certainly did not want any of this publicized and kept it from his family.

"Fortunately, as time passed, it all went very quiet. I think we must have driven out the most dangerous Communists in Hollywood. What we didn't know was that Mao Tse-tung was gonna later try the same thing, so for a long time Duke thought it was all over. He's lucky he's still alive," Canutt told Munn in the 1970s.

"I am quite convinced that it was not propagated by John or his inner circle," Munn added.

In 1958, Wayne and Khrushchev met. Two years earlier, the Soviet leader had taken his shoe off and pounded it on the podium at the United Nations, declaring his country would "bury you."

"President Eisenhower invited Nikita Khrushchev to the United States," Duke told Michael Munn in 1974. "The President sent me word that Khrushchev wanted to meet me. Seems that he had seen many of my films which he pirated across the Iron Curtain and had dubbed into Russian just for his own pleasure. When I got word from the President that the Soviet leader wanted to meet me, I accepted because I certainly didn't want to embarrass the President.

"I guess I was curious to know what a Communist leader was like. I knew he was not another Stalin who was a God——n monster, but these people were still enemies of freedom. Although it hadn't happened yet, Khrushchev was the guy who sent all those nuclear missiles to Cuba and aimed them at us. And yet the guy I met didn't seem the type to want to blow up any country, but that's what he was always threatening to do. So anyway, we met up at a function thrown by Spyros Skouras who was the president of Twentieth Century Fox, and we talked a while through interpreters, but it was about as private a conversation as two people can have with another person standing there interpreting everything and surrounded by film and political bigwigs, not to mention the security agents all over the place.

"We decided to make the conversation more private by going to a private bar—with the interpreter—and Khrushchev said to me, 'I am told you like to drink and that you can hold your liquor.' I said, 'That is right.' He said that he also liked a drink and could hold his liquor, and I said, 'I had heard as much.' We went on to compare the virtues of Russian vodka and Mexican tequila, and then we matched each other drink for drink. If he hadn't been a Communist, the man might have impressed me. But even though he was no Stalin, he was still a Communist, and I'll tell you what's bad about that. Khrushchev said something with a big smile on his face and laughed, and I was smiling as I said to the interpreter, 'What did he say?' The interpreter said, 'He is the leader of the biggest state in the world and will one day rule the world.' I laughed politely and said, still smiling, 'And I'm gonna knock him on his sorry f——g ass.' The interpreter said something and Khrushchev laughed, so I said, 'What did you tell him I said?' He said, 'I told him you would buy him a drink the day he rules America.' And then the guy said, 'We have to maintain diplomatic relations here.' So I just laughed and raised my glass."

While there is no evidence that John Wayne and Francis Ford Coppola were ever friends in the 1960s, it is possible this story made its way around film circles and may have reached Coppola. It sounds very much like the scene at the end of *Patton* (1970) in which George C. Scott as the general is introduced to a Soviet general during a celebration over the fall of Germany. In that scene, Patton is asked if he would like to share a drink with the communist. Smilingly, he tells the interpreter, "My compliments to the general. Please inform him that I do not care to drink with him or any other Russian son of a bitch."

"Sir, I, I cannot tell the general that," the nervous translator replies.

"You tell him that. Tell him word for word."

After the translator does so, the general frowns and says in Russian (translated by the interpreter) that Patton "is a son of a bitch, too."

Laughing, Patton then says, "Okay. I'll drink to that; one son of a bitch to another."

This John Wayne "scene" and another one in 1966 would mysteriously "appear" in *Patton*.

Canutt added further insight into the Khrushchev–Wayne meeting.

"Duke called me and said, 'What do you think? Khrushchev wants to meet me. Says he liked my pictures.' I said, 'Maybe he does, I think it's worth seeing him—if only to ask him face-to-face why he is trying to kill you.' Duke said, 'That's just what I was thinking.'

"So when Duke met Khrushchev, once he got over the formalities and was able to speak to him in private, he asked him outright why he was trying the hell to kill him. And Khrushchev apparently looked very grim and said, 'That was the last decision of Stalin during five mad years. When Stalin died, I rescinded the order.' Duke said, 'Then how come after Stalin died some of your guys over here tried to bump me off?' Khrushchev said he knew nothing about it but that there had been a number of Communist cells around the world who refused to denounce Stalinism. He said that he had taken steps to remove those people.

"Duke was fascinated to hear about the machinations of Stalin's government and its secrets, and Duke was impressed with Khrushchev because he was trying to make the Soviet Union a country based on pure Communism and not Stalinism. Of course, Duke didn't think Communism was good in any form, and he told Khrushchev just that. So Khrushchev changed the conversation and brought up the subject of drinking.

"He warned Duke, though, that he should not let his guard down. He said that Mao Tse-tung was like Stalin and he kept trying to push the Soviet Union into a war with the West. Khrushchev told Duke that Mao was in on the conspiracy. Duke said that Khrushchev seemed concerned but gave no guarantees.

"Duke finally said to him, 'Do you really watch my pictures?' and Khrushchev said, 'Yes, I especially like the ones about the U.S. Cavalry. They remind me of how the white Americans oppressed the true natives of America.' Duke said he wanted to punch Khrushchev in the mouth but thought the better of it. Then Khrushchev said, 'Our Russian actors do not do a very good impression of you. Now I have heard you speak, I will try to imagine how you would say your lines.'

"Duke said he had to pretend he liked the leader of the Soviet Union because it suited the President's PR men to say that even John Wayne liked the president of the U.S.S.R. Duke didn't mind so long as it helped ease tension between East and West. But, of course, it didn't help a damn."

Michael Munn asked Canutt what the interpreter's reaction was to the subject of assassination. "John said that the interpreter told him *he* wouldn't be the one to tell the president that the Russians had been trying to kill John Wayne, and John told him, 'That's fine by me. Because if you did ever say it was discussed, I'll deny it, and I'm sure you won't get old Iron Curtain Pants here to back you up.' John had a way of putting things that made people do what he told them—*asked* them." Wayne made it clear that all of this needed to remain secret, and it did so throughout his life and the Cold War, which ended with the fall of the Berlin Wall in 1989, but it still could have leaked, maybe even becoming an urban legend of sorts among USC film students like John Milius and his Bruin pal Francis Ford Coppola.

After the 1958 Wayne–Khrushchev meeting, the two exchanged gifts. One day, a large crate arrived at Wayne's office.

"'Hell, Mary, open it up,' Duke said to Mary St. John. 'It's too damn big to be a bomb.' So we opened it with a crowbar and inside were several cases of top-quality bottles of Russian vodka and a note which read, 'Duke, Merry Christmas, Nikita.' I reciprocated by sending him a couple of cases of Sauza Conmemorativo Tequila, and wrote a note saying, 'To Nikita. Thanks. Duke.'

"Bearing in mind that the Communists were still our greatest enemy, I felt that it would be great if all conflicts could be settled that way. Of course, that's idealistic bull——t, but it's kind of nice of a thought. Anyway, it was a good piece of propaganda for the press."

Wayne did an interview with Hedda Hopper, who asked about Khrushchev.

"He is always trying to belittle this country, to downgrade it, to sneer and boast and toss out insults and to brawl and threaten," Wayne said. "Why don't Kennedy and Nixon take this yelling and bragging boor apart? When Nixon was in Moscow he took him on in his own backyard and made him like it . . . I'm proud the President of the United States is a gentleman; but I wouldn't care if he walked up and punched Khrushchev in the nose. I'd applaud and holler, 'Attaboy Ike!'"

10

DUKE VS. CHAIRMAN MAO

JOHN WAYNE HAD SURVIVED AN ASSASSINATION ATTEMPT BY JOSEPH STALIN and several by Los Angeles communists and exchanged gifts with his "big fan" Nikita Khrushchev, but the threat to his life was not over. The Soviet leader had warned that Chairman Mao still wanted him dead, and by the 1960s the Soviets and Chinese had split. The Soviets had no control over Red China and Mao if, indeed, they ever did.

Wayne was diagnosed with cancer in 1964 but managed to beat it back. Afterward, he said he would go to Vietnam "just to shake hands with those kids we'd sent over. I did it for their fathers in the last world war, and I'd do it for them because whatever war it is, we all owe a debt to the men who fight for our freedom."

In June 1966, Wayne visited American troops in Vietnam on a three-week USO tour. *Photoplay* writer Paul Keyes told Maurice Zolotow soldiers "felt this giant hand on their shoulder and voice saying: 'Hello, soldier. I'm John Wayne and I just want you to know a hell of a lot of folks back home appreciate what you're doing.' Soldiers would tear up in his presence. He spent fourteen hours a day doing this, from six A.M. to ten at night."

"I can't dance and I can't sing—but I can sure as hell shake a lot of hands," Duke said.

"I'd come out of the Rex Hotel and the Vietnamese people would just stop their cars, and they'd be shouting, 'John Wayne! Number One Cowboy!' I didn't think they'd know who I was . . . ," he recalled. He literally stopped traffic in Saigon.

At Pleiku in the central highlands, he watched *Fort Apache* with some Green Berets. Also watching were some Montagnards who did not speak English but were fierce anticommunist fighters. Everyone was startled when during a scene in which Indians attack the U.S. Cavalry, they cheered.

"They knew nothing about United States history," Wayne recalled, "but they knew what they liked: brown people killing white people . . .

"I wanted to see for myself what was going on out in the boondocks. So they sent me to a little village, and I could hear a lot gunfire going on not far off."

At the marine base camp at Chu Lai, snipers came within a few feet of his location. It was generally assumed to be either "normal" sniper fire or possibly aimed at Wayne when word filtered out that he was in the vicinity. But after the failed attempts on his life, by Soviet hit men and homegrown communists in the 1950s, there remained the possibility that this was a more planned, coordinated effort to kill the anticommunist Duke Wayne than just random sniper fire. In conversation with Michael Munn some years later, Wayne lumped all these incidents together.

"The Communists have been trying to kill me since 1949," he was quoted saying.

"The 3rd Battalion was based there, and I was signing autographs and the usual stuff when bullets began hitting the ground near us. I didn't notice and just kept signing autographs, but the Marines automatically scrambled for cover. So I took cover, 'cos I'm not stupid enough to stand out there and be a sitting duck.

"I thought, 'Jesus, the God——n Commies nearly got me again.' Ya see . . . back in the '50s . . . look, if you ever see Yakima Canutt, just ask him. He saved my life a couple times, but he wasn't out there in Vietnam to save me. Fortunately, I had the Marines, which is the next best thing to Yak . . .

"But in Vietnam I almost walked into a sniper's bullet that had my name on it," adding he could hear the bullets "whistling past our ears," that he could "feel the wind as they fly by," and after that "you *know* you've just made a narrow escape. I don't mind admitting, this time I shook. Scared the hell out of me."

"One of the snipers was captured," said Munn in an interview, "and said there was a price on John's head, put there by Mao Tse-tung."

At first, Wayne thought it was "just another sniper aiming at Americans," he said, but the marines "caught the son of a bitch. Turned out he was some kind of elite sniper from China working with the Viet Cong. I don't know what kind of interrogation they gave him, but they said to me, 'You better come and listen to this.'"

Wayne entered the hut and looked him in the eye.

"I was trying to kill *you*," he told Wayne via a translator.

Wayne looked behind him to see who was there; surely *he* was not the target. He was. "He said I was the big American movie star who his beloved Chairman Mao had said was the chief devil of the great Satan America, or some such Maoist crap. Well, I've been called all kinds of sons of a bitch, but never that. The word had gone out that I was in Vietnam. Seems there was someone who saw me coming out of the hotel in Saigon, who was a spy or something, and the news of me [being there] got back to Mao Tse-tung. He had promised a great reward for the man who killed me. What was so pathetic was this sniper said that Mao promised that the reward would be great glory, but he also said he had heard there was a financial reward too, and this sniper needed the fortune more than the glory because his family back in China was so poor. So when he saw me, he figured he'd collect on the reward.

"Don't know what happened to the poor bastard. I suspect he didn't live to tell the tale. And if that sounds shocking, you need to know that the Viet Cong were doing the most unimaginable things to our men. Things I wasn't allowed to show in *The Green Berets*. But I knew what was happening out there."

"Duke was furious when the press called him a hero, exaggerating the danger he'd been in," said Pilar, apparently in the dark during his lifetime regarding communist assassination attempts, although the one in Vietnam could not be hidden: there were marine witnesses. He hated how the left labeled our heroic soldiers as "cold-blooded murderers."

James Grant died a painful death in 1966. This was another blow, coming six years after Ward Bonds's passing. Duke was with him often in the last days. Perhaps the loss of his good friend, who helped save his life when communists tried to kill him at Warner Brothers, spurred him to visit the troops and eventually do even more than that.

"When Duke returned from that trip I could see he was a man with a mission . . . I wasn't surprised when Duke told me he intended to make a movie about Vietnam, one that would pay tribute to the Green Berets," recalled Pilar Wayne.

While John Wayne saw the Vietnam War in black-and-white terms, the forces of freedom trying to stop the forces of evil, having already killed 40 million to 50 million humans, from killing 40 million to 60 million more, several theorists and political apologists were emerging with the opposite viewpoint. One was Noam Chomsky, the college professor-author who twisted history, using moral relativism to "justify" communist expansion as some kind of "normal" act of "progress," or reaction to Western "imperialism."

While indeed Duke would make a movie about the troops fighting in Vietnam, and his reaction to both the Vietnam trip and the assassination attempts was part of his motivation, there were other events in the 1960s further motivating him.

11

DUKE'S TROJAN WAR

ON MARCH 24, 1965, THERE WAS A "SIT-IN" AT THE UNIVERSITY OF MICHIGAN. More than 3,500 attended the event. Michigan was the alma mater of Tom Hayden, who organized the Student Nonviolent Coordinating Committee and the Students for a Democratic Society. His Port Huron Statement had been a clarion call of the civil rights and now the antiwar movement.

For such an event to occur at Michigan was rather meaningful. It was and largely still is a traditional campus, full of football ardor, in a state full of hunters, autoworkers who believed in the superiority of American products, and general patriots. Early antiwar demonstrations had begun at Columbia University in New York and on the University of California campus in Berkeley. This was not a surprise. New York's Greenwich Village was already the East Coast "headquarters" of the counterculture. On the West Coast, the beats originated in San Francisco's North Beach, once a traditional Italian American enclave and home of baseball great Joe DiMaggio, among many other diamond stars. By the 1950s, however, it was a flourishing haven for drug users, homosexuals, communists, and the new, bearded face of the left embodied by poet Allen Ginsberg. This would give rise to the "hippies," who flooded Golden Gate Park during the

"Summer of Love" and naturally made their way to Berkeley, located just across the San Francisco–Oakland Bay Bridge.

Many who made their way to Berkeley were outside agitators. Communist front groups, some homegrown and some controlled by Moscow, funded much of the agitation. J. Edgar Hoover and later California Governor Ronald Reagan investigated Cal President Clark Kerr for being so accommodating to the protesters, letting them use his campus to "aid and comfort" the enemies of America. But regardless of whether the protestors were funded by Moscow or Kerr was sympathetic to communism, there was genuine hatred of the Vietnam War, whether agitated, funded, or not.

Hollywood was still resistant to the antiwar movement. It was still a business, even though many will laughingly say that "showbiz is not a business," but it was still in the last vestiges of the studio system, which would be broken down a few years later by new blood in the form of Robert Evans, Francis Ford Coppola, and USC film school stars like George Lucas.

There were "message" movies, such as *Sweet Smell of Success, Spartacus, Seven Days in May, Dr. Strangelove,* and the television series *The Twilight Zone,* but the old potentates who felt it was their duty to promote a country that saved them from the shtetels their ancestors suffered in for centuries were still making John Wayne westerns, war pictures, and biblical epics.

Similarly, the Los Angeles of the Chandler *Times,* a city built largely via southern evangelism and midwestern Republicanism, resisted the movement. UCLA was quiet, a laconic campus more interested in beautiful girls, beach parties, and Bruins basketball. USC was downright right wing.

But when John Wayne appeared with Bob Hope on a program benefiting USC's scholarship endowment, he was stunned to find out that despite its Republican image, the school had been the scene of a number of sit-ins, teach-ins, bomb scares, boycotts, and protests.

College students of the 1960s were the most privileged, well-to-do kids ever. The age of the GI Bill generation, of World War II and Korean veterans returning to campus, was over. These were the children of the "greatest generation." They reminded Wayne of Hollywood liberals of the 1930s and 1940s who benefited from capitalism yet seemed to want to "shoot the golden goose."

"What's their bitch about America?" he asked Mary St. John on different occasions.

With more than 10,000 people on hand at USC, amid much arguing, chanting, and obscene catcalling, Wayne decided to get tough. He showed Hope some changes in his prepared remarks. Hope suddenly resembled a real-life "paleface," the role he played for laughs with Jane Russell in 1948.

"You can't give a speech like that here, Duke, unless you intend to turn those kids out there into a lynch mob howling for your blood," he said.

"I don't give a s——t. . . . It's about time someone talked turkey to those kids. Let 'em lynch me."

Duke said if the producer did not want him to use the changes he would not. He okayed it without really reading it.

"Duke Wayne was a former student of USC so it was appropriate that he be among the guests to deliver a short speech before I got up and said my piece," Bob Hope told Michael Munn when Munn was a messenger on the set of *How to Commit Marriage* at the New Victoria Theatre in London in 1969. "But he was not impressed by some of the students who had staged a number of anti-war protests and boycotts.

"If Mount Rushmore could sprout legs and walk, that's what Duke would be like. You'd want to get out of the way pretty quick. Well, when we were rehearsing, some of the students would look in and shout obscenities and chant their protests, and this was really getting to Duke. He decided he'd make some changes to his speech, and when he showed me, I said, 'My God, Duke, if you say those things you'll turn those kids into a lynch mob.' And Duke said, 'I don't give a s——t!' and I thought, Well, I'm not standing in his way."

"A university should be a quiet place where you go to learn, not to destroy property belonging to someone else," Wayne told the assembled students and faculty. "Getting an education is a privilege, not a right. Your professors and administrators should be treated with courtesy and respect. While you're here you ought to be learning a sense of responsibility. We aren't going to sit by and let you destroy our schools and system. This is a great university. You owe it your best. Thank you very much." He left to a standing ovation.

"So on the night, there were kids in the audience who gave catcalls as Duke walked on stage," added Hope. "He just stood there and he just kind of subdued them into silence by his very presence. And he told them what he thought, and they gave him a rousing ovation."

"There were a lot of people in that audience that obviously didn't feel the same way those who were catcalling did, because I got a standing ovation," Wayne said, reinforcing the image of USC as conservative, many of its students part of the Silent Majority.

"As I came off I said to Bob, who was waiting in the wings, 'I hope I haven't stolen all your thunder, Bob.' He said, 'The next time I tell you something's a bad idea, just ignore me.' I said, 'I always do, Bob.' Anyway, Bob went out there and entertained the audience, and we raised a lot of money.

"But you know? I hate to think of our endeavors going to help students who, like me when I was a kid, couldn't afford to attend without a scholarship—but they turn out to be the ones who go out and burn the American flag."

"I recall the night of the show with special clarity," recalled Pilar Wayne. "Debate over the Vietnam War had led to a series of violent confrontations on campuses across the country, and USC wasn't immune to the turmoil. Riots and sit-ins which demonstrated contempt for the nation's leaders and the university administration were as much a part of campus life as panty raids had been in the '50s. When Duke took the stage he would be facing a new breed of college student, young men and women who felt alienated from any authority figure."

These were kids whose motto was "You can't trust anyone over thirty."

"Instead, he chose to lecture his young audience about their duties and responsibilities as college students," continued Pilar. "Hope turned white as he read what Duke had written. . . . He made them aware that the property they'd been destroying belonged to tax payers of the state and not to the students. . . . There had been a few scattered boos and hisses as Duke began his speech. As he finished 10,000 people rose to their feet cheering."

"Don't look so concerned," Duke told his wife. "All those kids wanted was some leadership with a different point of view. The only people they ever hear are the liberal-thinking malcontents."

"Duke, you're probably the only person in the world who could have gotten away with what you said tonight," she responded.

"Duke didn't see it that way," she wrote in *My Life with the Duke: John Wayne* (1989). "He was convinced that U.S. youths were being led astray by a very liberal minority group of radical liberals who may have even been infiltrated by Communists. Duke believed in the inherent goodness of the nation's youth and thought they would willingly listen to someone who could give them the other side of the story. Unfortunately for my peace of mind, he saw himself as the ideal candidate for the job, and he never turned away from an opportunity to face down a crowd of angry demonstrators."

"It's kind of a sad thing when normal love of country makes you a super patriot," Wayne said in 1974.

In August 1965, Duke returned from shooting *Cast a Giant Shadow* in Rome and Israel. He had to attend a meeting at the Shrine Temple to discuss plans for a charity event. The Shrine Temple, erected in 1926 when Wayne was a student at USC, was not officially part of the USC campus but was, like the Los Angeles Memorial Coliseum on the other side of the college, right across the street. For all practical purposes, both the Shrine and the Coliseum were part of the university. Both embodied the school: the Coliseum as scene of Trojan glory, the Shrine Temple (site of numerous Oscar ceremonies) a symbol of private enterprise, entrepreneurial spirit, and noble charity dispersed. The school always represented both of these. It was integral to the growth and history of Los Angeles, a unique city that by the 1960s was surpassing Chicago as the second most populous while eclipsing New York—its Sinatra swank fading and awash in racial strife, crime, corruption, union intransigence, and, for the first time, a bad Yankees team—as the great American metropolis.

Wayne and Mary St. John strolled across Jefferson Boulevard to the campus. During the Howard Jones era, he and Ward Bond were regulars at Trojan football games, taking the special train with the team to Notre Dame or to San Francisco for the California or Stanford weekend. Over the years, Wayne still attended USC football games. He had children who attended the university over the years. He was a friend of Trojans baseball coach Rod Dedeaux, who played for a rival high school team of Marion Morrison's Glendale Dynamitors, the Hollywood High Sheiks, before starring at USC before a brief stint with the Brooklyn Dodgers. Now Dedeaux, a resident of Wayne's hometown of Glendale and member of Lakeside Golf Club, was coach of the greatest college baseball program in the nation, the four-time College World Series champion Trojans. Wayne occasionally attended USC baseball games, which by the mid-1960s were also frequented by Dedeaux's manager at Brooklyn, now a Glendale banker named Casey Stengel.

"Casey, Rod Dedeaux and John Wayne frequently socialized," said Stengel's personal manager the last decade of his life, Bob Case, a childhood friend of Dedeaux's son Justin, who, after becoming the clubhouse attendant for the Los Angeles Angels, befriended many players, including Bo Belinsky, and has one of the great collections of sports memorabilia in the nation. "Wayne was a class act, a truly great, sincere man who loved USC."

But with Bond's passing, an era seemed to have come to an end. Wayne was recognized wherever he went, and while Los Angeles is more laid back than other cities when it comes to celebrity sightings, with many frequently spotted at the Coliseum, Dodger Stadium, the Forum, and Staples Center, this was no ordinary celeb: this was *John Wayne*. The Duke enjoyed meeting his fans, but he was a private man, protective of his wife and family. Crowd scenes were a bit much. He scaled back his attendance and involvement with his alma mater.

But on a hot, smoggy summer day in 1965, in between the summer session and the bustle of the fall semester, with football season looming but the campus not quite at full steam, he strolled its tree-lined lanes with Mary St. John. Hot Santa Ana winds blew in. His shirt stuck to his skin, but the beautiful campus made him feel good with its green lawns, eucalyptus trees, and traditional brick buildings.

Duke and Mary were staring at the ornate Doheny Library, such a symbol of USC tradition. Edward Doheny, who also had a major Hollywood thoroughfare named after him, was the oilman who helped orchestrate the Teapot Dome scandal, the villain of Upton Sinclair's left-wing diatribe against capitalism, with the despised Southern Pacific University a stand-in for USC.

Suddenly, there was a commotion. A student group had set up tables and posters to protest the Vietnam War. America had been involved in Indochina, Laos, and now Vietnam for years, but after a period of "police actions" involving the Special Forces, first ordered in by President Eisenhower and escalated by President Kennedy, one year prior President Johnson had made it a full-scale war after the Gulf of Tonkin incident.

Wayne looked on, dismayed. Other schools protested: Berkeley, Columbia, Ann Arbor—but USC? His school? It seemed incongruous, but John Wayne had long ago learned the United States was changing. Many thought like him and loved him for his views, but he was not in lockstep with an entire nation, if ever he had been. Besides, it was free speech. Nobody believed in free speech more than the Duke.

Then he saw a young marine corporal dressed in crisply ironed khakis, black shoes shined to a high degree, not so much walking but marching across the beautiful campus. He was bemedaled and beribboned: the Navy and Marine Corps Overseas Service Ribbon, a National Defense Service Medal, a Vietnam Service Medal, a Combat Action Ribbon, an ARVN (Army of the Republic of Vietnam) Campaign Medal, a Sea Service Deployment Ribbon, and—a *Purple Heart.*

Wayne could not believe what he was seeing.

The protestors were heckling him.

"I thank God every day I wake up as a citizen of the United States," he said, "but it seems there are some Americans who don't feel as I do. Things began changing in the mid-'60s and during the Vietnam conflict. I saw it happening for the first time after I'd made *Cast a Giant Shadow,* which I made because I wanted to remind Americans what their country had done for another little country. Well, we were in Vietnam giving lives for another little country.

"I'd gone into Los Angeles to discuss plans for a charity benefit in aid of burn patients at a children's hospital, and there were a lot of meetings . . . so I took a break and went over to the old USC campus for a stroll with my secretary. I saw a group of students protesting against the Vietnam War. It's only natural that young people should protest against the idea of war. Hell there were plenty of Americans who opposed our country's entry into the Second World War. But you gotta do what's right. You gotta know what you're protesting about.

"What got my goat was these students were heckling a young Marine, a corporal, who was going by and heading for his car. He walked with his back straight as a rod, and he wore his uniform with pride. Then I noticed that where his right arm should have been there was only an empty sleeve which was neatly folded and pinned down.

"Turned out he was one of the 9th Marine Brigade which were the first ground troops America sent to Vietnam. He had a chest full of medals and ribbons."

This was the worst thing his eyes had ever witnessed. He had seen communism in Hollywood up close and personal. He had felt its wrath and hatred. He had been the target of an assassination ordered by no less than Joseph Stalin himself. He knew there were traitors in President Roosevelt's White House, that McCarthy in some part had the right idea, that treason was a sin loosed upon this clean land, but he had never really seen anything like this. This was open hostility toward a young patriot who served this great nation, obviously a combat veteran.

Then he saw the right sleeve pinned against his uniform to keep it from flapping. A Vietcong booby trap had taken it. He left it halfway across the world. The 9th Marine Expeditionary Brigade was a force of 3,000 deployed by President Johnson to the hot spot of DaNang, South Vietnam, in March 1965, early on in the conflict.

After an operation, a hospital stay, and convalescence, he was attending USC on the GI Bill.

Instead of admonishing the protestors, Wayne approached the marine.

"Why do you take that from those sons of bitches?" he asked him.

The marine stopped, recognizing that he was in the presence of Sergeant Stryker from *The Sands of Iwo Jima*, the Duke in the flesh.

"My drill instructor taught me to ignore impolite slimy civilians," he replied. "Maintain tack and bearing. Don't give the scum the satisfaction of noticing them."

"Well," drawled Wayne, "thank you for your service to the country, corporal."

"Thank you, sir."

Wayne walked him to the car, giving him an autographed card.

"I waved to him as he drove away," Duke recalled. "And my blood was boiling."

"I knew all hell was going to break loose," Mary St. John recalled.

As the car pulled away, Wayne jogged back across the street.

He arrived at the protestors' table, slamming both fists on it, and screamed into their startled faces.

"You stupid bastards!" he yelled through clenched teeth. "Blame Johnson if you must; blame that sonofabitch Kennedy; blame Eisenhower or Truman or God——n f——ing Roosevelt, but don't blame that kid. Not any of those kids. They served! Jesus, the kid's arm is gone."

The protestors obviously disagreed with him but were cowed by the mere presence of John Wayne. He turned, lifted his arms, letting them fall by his sides, and exclaimed to nobody in particular, "What the hell is happening to this country?"

Duke Wayne's Trojan war was on.

12

"THE EYES OF TEXAS"

W‌HEN THE U‌NIVERSITY OF T‌EXAS STUDENT COUNCIL HEARD THAT John "Duke" Wayne, star and director of *The Alamo*, would be back in the state of Texas while filming *The War Wagon* in Mexico and that the USC Trojans would be in Austin at the same time to take on the Longhorns (September 17, 1966), they issued an invitation to the Duke to come be their guest. Duke accepted. He was asked to make an appearance on the field, introduced to the UT faithful and whatever Trojans were in attendance. USC has a diverse nationwide, even worldwide, alumni, draws and "travels well" for most road games, especially openers, games against powerhouse opponents, and crucial games. This tradition was established by the Trojan special railroad convoys that Wayne and Ward Bond so enjoyed going on, often engaging in great hijinks.

As for Wayne, he had not been as active with his alma mater in recent years. The death of Bond put a crimp in his regular attendance at the Coliseum or road games. His celebrity was such that merely attending a crowded football game was a hassle for him and whatever security was on hand. He had battled cancer, been active in politics, and of course increased his workload, directing, producing, and starring in films, many on location. This was a chance for him to reconnect.

"John Wayne," a USC friend said once, "never forgets. He always mentions the fact he's a Trojan."

He would also be not in the stands, surrounded by autograph seekers, but rather on the sidelines, seen by many but not in a position to be approached by every glad-hander at Memorial Stadium.

John Wayne, whose on-screen character once called these people "Texicans," was as popular in the state as any figure. By 1966, with Texas turning against the Great Society and the first negative reports from Vietnam beginning to filter home, the state was beginning to elect the first wave of Republicans who would transfer the South into a GOP stronghold. Wayne was arguably more popular than President Johnson by then, a conundrum of sorts in that Wayne at the time was developing *The Green Berets* with the cooperation of Johnson's Department of Defense while at the same time campaigning for Ronald Reagan for governor of California and other Republicans staunchly opposing if not the war then most certainly the president's domestic agenda.

The USC–Texas game was the opener for both teams. Ninth-ranked USC was 2–0 against the Longhorns historically, both wins coming in the home-and-home arrangement of 1955 and 1956. African American Trojan running back C. R. Roberts's enormous game at Austin in 1956 still stuck in the craw, a grudge forming and revenge hoped for. No greater slayer of dragons could have emerged to take on this challenge than the great Darrell Royal himself, restorer of Longhorns pride and glory. It was a battle of coaches, two of the hottest young stars of the profession at that time, Royal versus John McKay.

As *Los Angeles Times* sports columnist Jim Murray had the temerity to point out, this was relatively rare: a game between an integrated team from outside Dixie against an all-white southern school. But it was not that rare for McKay or USC, as the 1955–1956 games with Texas indicated. McKay's teams lost to Texas Christian and Baylor on the road and beat Georgia at home (1960), lost to Georgia Tech and beat Southern Methodist University (SMU) at home (1961), beat Duke at home and SMU on the road (1962), lost to Oklahoma at home (1963), and beat Oklahoma on the road and Texas A&M at home (1964). They had a home-and-home arrangement scheduled against Texas (1966–1967) and Miami (1966 and 1968), plus a 1969 home game with Georgia Tech on the horizon.

(The 1970 USC–Alabama game would not be scheduled until early that year when the NCAA allowed a first-ever eleventh game.)

Wayne did things big, with a style and flourish worthy of a state as big as Texas itself. In Texas filming *The War Wagon*, he purchased a 1966 International Harvester Travelall, inspired by vehicles built for *Hatari* (1962). Ray Gaskin of Pasadena built it to spec for use on Wayne's Red Eye Ranch. It was antichopped six inches, Gaskin raising the roof six inches so that Wayne could pop out through a hatch and shoot at a comfortable height while hunting antelope—and also so he could wear his cowboy hat. It had a five-speed International 460 engine and a hydraulic clutch. The back included a medicine cabinet; underneath were heavy-duty shocks, extra spring leaves, and additional room for hunting guns. It had extended steel bumpers on both ends, including a 10,000-pound winch in front, and inside was air conditioning (unusual at the time) and an electric rear window. Wayne's son Ethan gave it *The War Wagon* name, written in red on the sides along with the moniker "Red River Land Co." It had spot lamps, a tubular roof rack, roll bars, and Arizona license plates. Described as "a monster and a piece of history," in recent years a Texas state legislator had it up for sale at a bid of $1 million.

Wayne's arrival in Austin on Friday, September 8, 1966, is verified, as was his appearance at the game the next day and also the fact that when he left, he filmed *The War Wagon* in Mexico, which was released in 1967. Michael Munn's biography was titled *John Wayne: The Man behind the Myth*. This was not apocryphal; Wayne was in many ways every bit as much a myth, a legend, and a story as he was a flesh-and-blood American citizen who got up every day, made movies, protected his family, and loved his country.

Wayne's life has been dissected up one side and down the other. He cooperated with Maurice Zolotow on a biography in the mid-1970s. He even wrote a rough, typewritten autobiography that is in the possession of Claude Zachary, the archivist of USC history at the Doheny Library on campus, that remains unpublished for reasons not made clear.

Many others have written at great length of the Duke. Interviews with actors and movie people, such as Ed Asner, often end up being about John Wayne when the interviewer discovers the subject once made a film with Wayne, as Asner did on *El Dorado*. There are movie histories, collections of his films, compendiums, symposiums, and documentaries. There are unauthorized biographies and of course DVD collections of his films, boxed sets, and all other form of remembrance. Turner Classic Movies host Robert Osborne constantly tells "John Wayne stories" before and after showing Duke's movies: the politics behind a shoot, troubles, director problems, weather difficulties, "nuclear fallout," location difficulties, and many other bits of trivia. WTBS and TNT have created cottage industries of Wayne films, his "movies for guys who like movies" a staple, as well as AMC's regular showing of Duke fare. Wayne "marathons" are common, and in Texas *The Alamo* gets played the way *It's a Wonderful Life* does every Christmas.

Despite all of this, few know anything about the complete flow of events of the 1966 USC–Texas football weekend. There is little if any mention in any of the books or articles about his weekend in Austin other than cursory side notes (like the Travelall he drove). There is a letter of thanks he wrote coach John McKay found on the USC sports information website but little beyond this. Yet the crazy, wild shenanigans, steeped in drunken Texas revelry with a touch of drama, a heavy dose of tragedy, and an extra heaping of hubris mixed with jingoism and anticommunist rhetoric matching the most dedicated Red-baiter, marks the event. Any filmmaker would chomp at the opportunity to make a movie about this singular event in the life of America's all-time most famous movie figure. Any actor worth his salt would consider portraying Duke in the events of this weekend the role of a lifetime.

In researching this book, I was stunned to discover that this weekend and the numerous assassination attempts on his life by Joseph Stalin, homegrown communists, and Chairman Mao Tse-tung's sniper between the early 1950s and 1966 were unknown to USC film professors Richard Jewell and Andrew Casper, university archivists Steve Hanson and Claude Zachary, and the Wayne Collection's director Elizabeth Daley. Wayne's good friend and Academy Award–winning producer Ronald Schwary, an eyewitness to events of the Austin weekend, knew *some* details of the night in question but nothing about Duke versus either Stalin or Mao. Steve Bisheff and Loel Schrader devoted a chapter to USC's Hollywood connections in *Fight On!* That shed a certain amount of light—but only a certain amount. The infamous Clara Bow "gangbang" rumor? Sure, that was, not surprisingly I suppose, well circulated, but communist plots, foreign or domestic, were not. It seemed in a strange way a correlation with McCarthyism and the Blacklist, papered over by history and told to schoolchildren it was just a right-wing "witch hunt" when in fact it was very real and insidious.

Numerous others who should have known did not. The assassination attempts were in Munn's 2003 book, but he lives in England (oddly even in the age of the Internet divided by water from America), and when repeated even to Wayne's confidantes, they sounded like urban legends. Nobody pieced the Austin events together in totality at all.

For me, it began in 1982 with enrollment at USC, where I purchased Ken Rappoport's *The Trojans: A Story of Southern California Football.* Perhaps the best chapter in that great work was the one on Wayne's USC football connections. Several former Trojans who played with or were close to Wayne were interviewed in that book, mainly Nick Pappas. He described the essential events of the 1966 Texas game, namely, Wayne speaking to the team the day of the game. The craziness of the night before is unmentioned. What happened that night had the ring of his earlier, wilder USC-related road-trip shenanigans with Ward Bond, although Bond was six years deceased by then.

In 2012–2013, Pappas was ninety-six or ninety-seven years old. His former son-in-law, Chuck Arrobio (a member of the 1966 Trojans), and his son Geoffrey Arrobio, who cared for his grandfather, said the elderly gentleman was unable to communicate or recall events in a meaningful way, so a trip to Pasadena to speak to him was canceled for this reason. Neither Chuck nor Geoffrey could re-call Nick providing the details inspiring this book.

I first found out the "story" (or what I at first believed the story to be) when in 2005 I researched the book *One Night, Two Teams: Alabama vs. USC and the Game That Changed a Nation*, the tale of the 1970 Trojans–Crimson Tide game, which had the effect of ending segregation in college football, which, oddly, the 1966 Trojans–Longhorns game—a very similar dynamic—did not.

That story came from Jeff Prugh, a mentor and superb sports-writer for the *Los Angeles Times*. While I at first took Jeff's details of the Austin weekend as fact, I have since discovered he was not there to see it in person and was giving me secondhand information that may have been exaggerated by his own sense of proportion when it came to Wayne and the Vietnam War. Unfortunately, he passed away before I started delving into this. A strange, unusual number of eyewitnesses are dead, most of them ranging from way too young to die to not all that old when they left this mortal coil, evoking the eerie demise of many who were exposed to atomic testing while filming in the Utah desert with Wayne in the 1950s. Among those I have known, who were there (often eyewitnesses), and whom I per-sonally interviewed for other projects but are gone and could not be interviewed for this book are Prugh, Craig Fertig, Marv Goux, John McKay, Bud Furillo, and Loel Schrader.

I told the story Prugh told me, which is woefully incomplete, in my previous books: *The USC Trojans: College Football's All-Time Greatest Dynasty* (2006), *One Night, Two Teams: Alabama vs. USC and the Game That Changed a Nation* (2007), *Trojans Essential: Everything You Need to Know to Be a Real Fan!* (2008), and *What It Means to Be a Trojan: Southern Cal's Greatest Players Talk about Trojans Football* (2009). Steve Bisheff pointed out that the story of Wayne's "fight" with a Los An-geles sportswriter, which was all I really had to go on until I asked him about it, was found in some detail in his great book *Fight On! The Colorful Story of USC Football* (2006), coauthored by the late, great Loel Schrader.

So, in telling the full tale herein, I find myself walking a well-worn path in that I exposed a myth and a legend as untrue in *One Night, Two Teams: Alabama vs. USC and the Game That Changed a Na-*

tion when I discovered, after interviewing some forty eyewitnesses and participants in the 1970 USC–Alabama game, including key players, coaches, and media *in the Crimson Tide dressing room after the game,* that coach Paul "Bear" Bryant *did not* put Trojans black running back Sam "Bam" Cunningham on a stool before his beaten team and announce, "Gentlemen, this here's what a football player looks like."

Good journalism sometimes means deflating the bubbles others have blown up and ridden for decades. John McKay, Marv Goux, Craig Fertig, and Tom Kelly told that story to USC boosters and luncheon groups for years. None of them were actually in the room and saw or heard it.

Schrader claimed to have seen it and stuck to the original story. While I spoke to him only once and did not really know him, others say he was a "great guy," so I take their word that he was, but the things he said and wrote to me after I exposed the story as false were borderline despicable. I was a personal friend of Craig Fertig, but he admitted he was too busy hobnobbing with alumni and media to witness what happened. My interviews with McKay and Goux were before I wrote my book, and they were not in the Alabama dressing room, anyway.

I do know Sam Cunningham very well. His words: "I don't want to be the one who says it didn't happen, but it didn't happen." In truth, what likely happened in piecing the event together and interviewing many who were actually there is that Bryant took Cunningham into the hallway between the two teams' dressing rooms; the door to the Alabama dressing room was open, and some players could see and hear what was going on; a player or two came out to shake Sam's hand, and Bryant probably said, more to assembled writers and reactionary alumni, "This here's what a football player looks like," than to his beaten team assembled at the feet of the conquering black running back, shirtless, in hip pads, glistening with sweat, as if at a "slave auction," as writer Allen Barra surmised.

As for the story of John Wayne in Austin, it remained, before now at least, largely unknown, about to be revealed like the virgin territories of the great American West that Wayne loved so much to those hardy first arrivers looking for the promised land.

"What happened was the day before, myself and three other players were standing outside the hotel, leaning against a wall, at the intersection of streets, when a big limo pulled up," recalled Ron Yary, a junior all-American prospect for the USC Trojans, of the limo in which John Wayne arrived at the Stephen F. Austin Hotel. "It was a black limo with tinted windows, so you couldn't see who was inside. He did go against traffic. He told the limo driver to go against traffic. John Wayne saw us and directed the limo to drive in front of where we were standing.

"It stops, and goes through a red light in the opposite direction in the road, although there was no traffic. It stops at the curb and John Wayne and a couple other actors jump out and Wayne introduces himself to some of the Sigma Chis. He was very imposing and we did not know what to say to John Wayne. We could not talk, we were all of eighteen- or nineteen-year-old kids.

"Maybe it was Dick Allman who gave him the Sigma Chi secret handshake. He was an imposing person, very engaging, yet humble. It was a nice thing for him to do."

Thus does our weekend story begin, the protagonist being none other than John "Duke" Wayne, the larger-than-life movie hero of countless westerns and war dramas, a swashbuckling, ruggedly macho idol of America, the very embodiment of what the United States had become: the new Rome, the most powerful military, political, and cultural empire in the annals of mankind. Wayne, like the nation itself, stood astride the world in colossus style, talking tough, taking no prisoners. Now he arrived in Austin to watch his team do battle with the Texas Longhorns: two collegiate football powerhouses, recent winners of the national championship with hopes to do it again.

The following is a compilation of early descriptions that come from Jeff Prugh, Tom Kelly, another USC announcer named Mike Walden, and assistant football coach Craig Fertig, who only two years earlier was the star quarterback who beat Notre Dame and, after being drafted by the Pittsburgh Steelers of the National Football League, was on McKay's staff. These were mainly offhand remarks made during the 2005 interview research for the book about the

1970 USC–Alabama game. Some of these memories are based on secondhand accounts, some from "witnesses" who are unidentified by these men. The following is the original way I heard the story, unfettered by later fact checking:

> The one-time pulling guard for coach Howard Jones was there
> . . . *with spurs on,* dressed in a black three-piece suit, white nine-gallon cowboy hat, and snakeskin boots. Whether he immediately repaired to the hotel bar is speculation.
>
> He had a full entourage who hung on his every word as if uttered from the Burning Bush. So it was when the Duke ordered his first whiskey. The bartender, shaking, poured the house blend. The Duke pushed it back at him.
>
> "I said *whiskey!*" he bellowed.
>
> Thus did the Duke get his special brand, which he began to knock back in the same style moviegoers had seen in countless film images. Surrounded by sycophants, John Wayne bellowed opinions, bromides, and pronouncements.
>
> "The Trojans er gonna smoke these here Texicans," he announced, making sure every native Texan got full wind of him. He seemingly dared one of them to challenge him. None did.
>
> "Texas is filled with two things: steers and queers," he shouted to raucous laughter. Still no answer from the gallery.
>
> Off to the side sat a sportswriter for one of the Los Angeles newspapers. He was liberal. The Duke was an archconservative. According to Prugh, *possibly* he liked UCLA, not USC. He was, Prugh speculated, adamantly opposed to the Vietnam War. He was normally not a heavy drinker, but when in Rome . . .
>
> Prugh was also not in that room, so his memories are just embellishments, urban legend. But very colorful, indeed.
>
> "You know what our boys er gonna do to those Commie bastards?" Wayne supposedly announced. "We're gonna use their guts to grease the treads of our tanks."
>
> The sportswriter listened to the Duke brag about how U.S. forces would "mop the floor" with the "pissant" Vietcong.
>
> "I got no respect for those little yellow pricks," Wayne stated. "They live in caves, fer crissakes."
>
> The writer drank and drank. "Another shot," the writer may have slurred to the bartender. Wayne went on and on and on.

Thus was the setup that Friday night. USC alumni and fans mixed with Texas people amid great revelry. Wayne's appearance lent great imprimatur to the event, what they called in Austin "Smokers," a combination of alcohol and barbecue.

The Duke truly loved to drink. He felt it was a manly, even an American thing to do. To drink and express his opinions in this great and free country was his God-given right. To cross swords with the Duke was to court trouble.

"Lousy Communist bastards er takin' over in Hollywood," Duke shouted for all to hear, or, at least according to legend, fueled by alcohol, fogged by time, or infused by legend, he *may* have said it. "Same criminals who've taken over at Berzerkley and Columbia. Low rent pissants flying North Vietnamese flags. Makin' all these movies about faggots and cowards who won't fight."

The Los Angeles writer, having sat a few yards away, listening and fuming. He looked at a man who had played many soldiers in many movies but in truth had not suited up in World War II or Korea. Now he espoused the virtues of American involvement in Vietnam, another war he was not personally fighting. Always somebody else's son, brother, or friend.

"I say bomb 'em back into the Stone Age," Wayne may have bellowed. "I'm gonna make a movie about the Green Berets. Tell it like it is. Let these Left-wing bastards know what-for."

"Make that a double," said the writer.

"You tell 'em, Duke."

"Right as rain, Duke."

The actor's sycophantic "friends" were in lockstep with everything he had to say.

On and on it went, until finally the writer had enough. He got up, uneasily, staggering toward the Duke. He got closer and closer, until Wayne and his crew began to eye him suspiciously. He rose to make his move, approaching John Wayne, ten pairs of eyes glaring at him suspiciously.

The confrontation was about to take place, and a wild weekend in Austin was about to be kicked off with fireworks and fury.

"They tell me they call you . . . *the Duke* . . ." the writer slurred, this "description" coming from Prugh, who was not actually there.

"Waal, what of it?" replied Wayne.

"Waal . . . *Duke . . . you ain's——t!*"

Wayne looked askance at the writer for about a second, then, according to the Prugh version, let fly with a right hook. It was speculated that Nick Pappas pulled Wayne back just enough so that his punch missed the writer by an inch, and that inch most probably saved John Wayne $1 million in legal fees and tortious damages. Pappas's grandson, Geoffrey Arrobio, and ex-son-in-law Chuck Arrobio (who was probably at a movie with the rest of the team at the time) do not recall Nick telling the story, and the old man was too frail to try and conjure up any memories by 2012–2013.

The writer was pulled away and so was Wayne.

"Lemme at 'im," Wayne is rumored to have shouted.

"Right-wing war monger," the writer might have shouted back at him.

"Fuzzy hippy prick. Go back to Hanoi."

"You tell 'im, Duke. . . . Get the hell outta here. . . . Go live with Castro. . . . Love it or leave it."

The writer was spirited out of the bar, ostensibly for his own protection as well as penance for having *John Wayne take a swing at him.*

"Bastard's lucky I missed," Wayne boasted.

"You'd a killed him, Duke, but it would a cost ya."

"Yeah, I guess yer right."

It was a shot of testosterone, as if any more of that was needed.

"Hey barkeep, another round on me."

Much of this comes from Jeff Prugh, the *Los Angeles Times* beat writer for USC football in the 1960s and 1970s. Here is his exact quote as it appears in *One Night, Two Teams*:

Well, there was this one L.A. sportswriter writer whose name shall remain anonymous. Everyone is gathered at the bar, and John Wayne's holding court. This old writer is off in the corner getting drunker and drunker. He's liberal and Wayne's an outspoken conservative Republican. Finally, this old writer has had enough, and he approaches Wayne, interrupts him in mid-sentence with all Wayne's pals staring at him.

"So . . ." the old drunk writer says, "they tell me, uh . . . they call ya . . . *the Duke!*"

"'Yeah, what of it?" says Wayne.

This writer just gathers himself.

"Waal . . . *Duke.* . . . you ain' *s–t!*"

Prugh and I were good friends, and he read that book thoroughly. We appeared on a panel at USC's Annenberg School for Communication in a class taught by Professor Daniel Durbin, "Sports, Culture and Society" (Professor Durbin has since created a sports media division within the communications major). Prugh never disputed the description. While such a scene simply demands literary license, if Prugh's general premise holds up, the color attributed to this tale is not so far out-of-bounds.

In 2009, I received a phone call from the editors at Potomac Books, who have published two of my works, *A Tale of Three Cities: The 1962 Baseball Season in New York, Los Angeles, and San Francisco* (2009) and *The Poet: The Life and* Los Angeles Times *of Jim Murray* (2013). Prugh was working on a manuscript for them but had missed his deadline, and they asked me if I knew where he was. Some investigation eventually revealed his obituary at age sixty-nine. Had he lived, I could have asked him who told him this story and pursued that thread. Alas, no, my friend, a storyteller for the ages, was gone.

The story, by now as much hyperbole as factual recitation, goes further along. This is extrapolated from Prugh, but Mike Walden, Tom Kelly, and Craig Fertig all referenced this event. Fertig was with the Trojans team at a movie, but they all came back around nine or so. Some coaches, maybe some accompanying media, sauntered in, where the following story, as well as boozy references to the "confrontation with the writer," was probably passed along in haphazard manner, often exaggerated by drink and the hyped-up presence of John Wayne in their midst:

Off to the side was a colorfully dressed man, out of place in this place. His sexuality was . . . in question, but he was a talented make-up artist. He was John Wayne's make-up artist. The Duke had spent years pounding whiskey, his skin exposed to the hot sun. Hiding that was this man's forte. The make-up artist was not a heavy drinker and generally avoided Duke's alcohol parties, but he was somewhat captive to his bosses' whims. He sauntered up to the bar.

"You with Mr. Wayne?" asked the bartender.

"I'm his make-up artist," he replied.

The bartender looked at him kind of funny.

None of this is verified, but it continues to be colorful.

"Suit yourself," he said. "What'll it be?"

"Uh, whiskey," the man replied.

The whiskey was produced and the make-up man downed it.

"Whew," he exclaimed. "Uh, gee whiz, give me . . . make it tequila."

It went on like that all night; the make-up artist mixing drinks: whiskey, tequila, vodka.

This is where literary license ends and reporting begins, at least regarding the events of the party. By no means does the "story" or the literary license end here, but the events of Friday night must be accounted for before moving on to unverified further hyperbole, less dramatic perhaps but not without tragedy and the sort of hype Wayne elicited, on Saturday.

I started with some people I knew who I figured had contact with John Wayne. One was a good friend named Bob Case, the best friend of former USC baseball coach Rod Dedeaux's son Justin. He assured me there was a connection and plenty of contact between John Wayne, Casey Stengel, and Rod Dedeaux, which made sense. Wayne, like Case, was from Glendale, where both Dedeaux and Stengel lived. Case told me he knew that ex-Trojans star Russ Saunders, who was involved on the set of *The Shootist*, and another player named Bob de Laure, who was in *Jim Thorpe: All-American*, spent "a lot of time" around Wayne (in the company of Stengel and Dedeaux) and that he "couldn't be a nicer guy." He did not have any specific information about the 1966 USC–Texas weekend.

Allan Graf starred on the 1972 Trojans, considered to be the greatest team in college football history. He became a stuntman and in that capacity met Wayne.

"I was an extra on *The Shootist*," he said. "I told him I was a for-mer SC player but there was not much dialogue. This was the 1970s. Ron Howard was on that film." He discussed a possible lead, Dick Cook, who, according to Graf, "played baseball for Dedeaux." A check of USC's baseball media guide does not list a Dick or Richard Cook among lettermen. Cook was a USC graduate who became the chairman of Walt Disney and then took over at Legendary Pictures, producers of *41*, the 2013 film about Jackie Robinson. I was curious to follow this lead, as Kerry McCluggage, a producer with Craftsman Films who was developing my book *One Night, Two Teams: Alabama vs. USC and the Game That Changed a Nation*, was at the time pitching the idea to Cook (who I was told was "waiting for financing"). Let-ters to Cook and Ron Howard, however, went unanswered.

Next came Sam Tsagalakis, a placekicker for the Trojans in the 1950s. I asked him about Wayne.

"He would come out to practice every once in a while with Ward Bond," he recalled. "We had a function at the Sports Arena and Wayne narrated from his record *America, Why I Love Her*. It was some record he had made. I was a spotter for Chick Hearn. I did it with Tom Kelly. I was at the Isthmus at Catalina when Wayne came in with his wife and kids, and I recall he talked about how nice it was to be a Boy Scout. I was twelve. I was in Skull and Dagger the same time as John Wayne. So was Leonard Firestone and Andy Devine." Beyond that, Tsagalakis was unable to provide details of the 1966 USC–Texas game.

Brian Downes was a young man when he interviewed Wayne in the 1970s. This led to his eventually becoming the executive director of the John Wayne Birthplace in Winterset, Iowa. He told me that Dave Grayson, author of *Duke: The Life and Times of John Wayne* (1985), had died. I was unable to track down the other two coauthors of that biography, Richard Slatzer and Donald Sheperd. Downes offered that Ward Bond died in Dallas in 1960 when he was in town for a football game (according to legend, singer Johnny Horton died that weekend in a car crash on his way to see Bond about a role in *Wagon Train*; apparently, however, the two men's deaths were unrelated).

"Thank you, Steve," he e-mailed. "This looks interesting but I'm not sure what sort of input you'd like from the John Wayne Birthplace. If I knew, I might be better able to direct you." Beyond that, he had no details related to my story.

From here, we try and piece together the events of the weekend. Nick Pappas granted his interview to Ken Rappoport for *The Trojans: A Story of Southern California Football* over thirty years ago. My Prugh and Craig Fertig interviews were for different books on different subjects, conducted in 2005 and 2008, and they were now gone. But I could retrace my steps with Walden and talk to Tom Kelly to try to piece together the events of the evening and the events of the game. I still did not know who the "make-up man" or "the liberal writer" were.

So, I called Mike Walden, one of the men who first mentioned details of John Wayne's appearance at Austin when I interviewed him about the 1970 USC–Alabama game in 2005.

"My first year announcing USC football was 1966," said Walden. "My first game was on the road versus Texas. There'd be a press gathering in Austin, what they called 'smokers' down there, where everybody got together. Well, Wayne was down there making *The War Wagon* in nearby Mexico, and he shows up with Bruce Cabot.

"'I'm gonna have some whiskey,' Wayne says to the bartender, who pours it, and Wayne just looks at it, shoved it back, and said, '*I said WHISKEY!*'"

When contacted again in 2012, Walden said he had no knowledge of a fight between Wayne and a "liberal writer." I had mistakenly believed he told me a similar story to the one Prugh told me. He said Texas had a sports information director named Jones Ramsey, but he passed away years ago. Queries of the UT sports information office revealed little beyond reference to a website with the 1966 Texas football roster. I was told "the man to speak to" was Bill Little, a keeper of the Texas flame. E-mails and a phone call to Little were met by zero response. The UT football media guide offered absolutely no help whatsoever. It is filled with photos and hype about modern-day Longhorns glory, but the one I possess offers very little about their history for reasons I cannot fathom since that history is fabulous. The USC media guide, on the other hand, is a paean to Trojans tradition offered in a very ordered, easy-to-find way.

I called Steve Bisheff, one of the most respected sportswriters in southern California. He was a longtime scribe covering USC, the Angels, and other sports for the *Orange County Register* and author of a number of fine books, including a Pete Carroll biography and of course *Fight On!*, a comprehensive history of Trojans football (with Schrader). It seems there are people in the profession of journalism who take a perverse delight in putting the screws to other writers. Then there are those like Bisheff who seem to delight in openly helping others, even going beyond the call of duty to do so. Bisheff certainly did that in helping me research my book on Jim Murray, but in tracking down the mysterious "liberal writer" of Austin, he had long before done all he could for me.

"In our book *Fight On!*, Loel wrote about the incident on pages 90–93," he said. "He was there and he captures the whole thing. The writer in question was Harley Tinkham of the *Herald-Examiner*. Tinkham was a great beat writer but also a big time drinker. Anyway, it's all there. I don't see how the incident could possibly be the subject of an entire book, but good luck with it.

"Tinkham was the beat writer for the *Herald-Examiner* at the time. He moved to the *Times* in 1968 and covered track and field, then took over the Morning Briefing column that became very popular but didn't have his byline. I have no information about his family, etc.

"I was covering college football for the *Santa Monica Outlook* in '66 and covered UCLA and USC home games. The paper didn't have the budget to let us travel, so I wasn't at the Texas game.

"The *Times* offered me a job as a glorified copy boy covering preps." Finally, Bisheff advised that I "speak to John Hall," a legendary *Times* staffer of the era.

Indeed, I had read Bisheffs and Schrader's book in 2006 and considered it perhaps the most complete USC history written (the original draft of my subsequent book, *The USC Trojans: College Football's All-Time Greatest Dynasty*, might be more comprehensive, but the editor forced its reduction from a 1,500-page document to a mere 236 pages, with some of the best stories about the Trojans ever told deleted) but missed the essentials somehow. There it was, the events—at least some of them—of the Stephen F. Austin Hotel in 1966. The first part of the mystery, at least, was solved. The so-called liberal writer was Harley "Ace" Tinkham, who as Bisheff stated created the Morning Briefing, a popular, longtime feature of the *Los Angeles Times* sports section. He was also nicknamed "Ace" because he tended to call other people by that moniker, not unlike the way Rod Dedeaux called most everybody "Tiger."

I knew who Tinkham was. Sam Tsagalakis spoke of his friendship with him in my book *What It Means to Be a Trojan.*

"He gave me that name, 'Sad Sam,'" Tsagalakis recalled. "I was a Kappa Alpha fraternity. I was a walk-on kicker, which is not exactly 'the man' at USC. There were not that many of us; me and a kicker from Iowa State. There were no specialists, no soccer-style kickers. Harley took a liking to me."

Tinkham was something of an institution in Los Angeles sports media in the 1950s and 1960s. A former Trojans track star, it was said that his knowledge of facts and sports trivia was exceeded by nobody. When he passed away in 1990, the headline in the *Los Angeles Times* read "Tinkham Made Special Contribution to Life."

"Twenty years ago, I had the privilege of working with Harley Tinkham at the *Times*," Jerry Sofer wrote. "Tinkham, who died last week, made an impression I won't ever forget

"I wanted to write as well as Tinkham. I wanted to know as much as Tinkham. I wanted to have as much fun in sports and life as he did.

"People did not call Tinkham 'Ace' solely because of the way he addressed them. Tinkham was the Ace because he was a unique person, a genuine person. People recognized those qualities in Tinkham.

"Tinkham would use one of his favorite expressions, 'What's your lead?' to other track reporters. In reality, they wanted to know what his lead was because he always had the right angle to the story."

In a related obituary, "His Morning Briefings Just Won't Be the Same without Reading 'Ace,'" Tom Fitzgerald wrote,

> The sports writing profession is long on cynicism but short on wit. Chalk up another severe loss for wit as a result of the death this week of Harley (Ace) Tinkham, who wrote the Morning Briefing column in the *Times*.

> His succinct style and keen eye for humorous quotes and an-
> ecdotes guaranteed a chuckle or two every morning. I'd like to
> say the column I began writing a year ago for the *San Francisco
> Chronicle*, Top of the Sixth, was influenced by Tinkham's writ-
> ing. Direct steal, is more like it.

He was known for "anecdotes and knowledge of statistics," making
"offbeat observations and statistics, as well as sports trivia and colorful anecdotes," another obit read. In 1950, Tinkham joined the *Los
Angeles Mirror*, which was absorbed by the *Times* in 1962. He then
went to work at the *Los Angeles Herald-Examiner* but returned to the
Times in 1968.

"Although Harley Tinkham wrote the column for many years
and distinguished himself by making MB one of the most widely-
read articles in the sports section, the column was the creation of
the late sports editor Bill Shirley back in the 1970s," one former
Times sports staffer e-mailed after Tinkham's passing. "He assigned
it first to former *Times* sportswriter Dwight Chapin. Shirley told
Chapin he wanted MB to be 'light but not too light.'"

In 1966, Tinkham was not with the *Los Angeles Times*. He was
with the *Los Angeles Herald-Examiner*. This creates further sorrow over
lost voices and memories, for another of my great friends and mentors was Bud "the Steamer" Furillo, at the time the sports editor of
the *Herald-Examiner*. Furillo was the man most singularly responsible
for making Bo Belinsky the most talked-about sports celebrity in
America between 1962 and 1964. My first screenplay, *Once He Was
an Angel*, was based on a biography and *Sports Illustrated* article about
Bo, written by Maury Allen and Pat Jordan, respectively. I was a complete, utter unknown with no writing background at all, yet Furillo,
Allen, and to some extent Jordan all gave me total cooperation in
researching and developing the project. Furillo remained a good
friend until his 2006 passing, which, like Jeff Prugh, Marv Goux,
John McKay, and Craig Fertig, came much too soon.

I could not verify whether Furillo was at Austin that weekend,
but I know despite being the editor, he often traveled to big road
games, especially if the teams were the Trojans or the Dodgers.
Chances are he was there, but neither his son Andy, now at the *Sac-*

ramento Bee, or his remarkable ex-wife Cherie Kerr could verify or offer specifics about Tinkham or Wayne.

"As the writers entered the party area, a booming voice rose above the noise," wrote Bisheff/Schrader. It belonged to Duke Wayne.

"Hey, Ace, it's eight o'clock and you're still standing. What's wrong?"

"Up yours, Duke?"

This indicates that Wayne and Tinkham knew each other and may have been out drinking with each other in the past. They may well have partied together on the Trojan specials in the company of Ward Bond, and Wayne's remark about Tinkham "still standing" at eight o'clock was amplified by others who said he did not drink too much but rather did not handle the alcohol he did consume. A lightweight, the opposite of John Wayne.

"There was general laughter, and Duke was among those laughing loudest," it continued in *Fight On!* "But a little guy standing near Ace growled and advanced on him in a belligerent manner, asking, 'What did you say to the Duke?'"

"I told him where he could put it," Tinkham replied.

"'You can't talk to him like that,' said the little guy, whereupon he unleashed a punch that missed. He also fell. When the little guy arose, Ace swung, missed, and also fell. Within seconds, the huge movie actor had both combatants in his grip."

"Take them to their rooms," he announced—to somebody (apparently USC football manager Ronald Schwary). He identified the "little guy" as his hairdresser. This story evokes memory of another sports-related fight involving a member of the Los Angeles sports media.

In 1964, the Los Angeles Angels featured the colorful playboy southpaw Bo Belinsky. Braven Dyer, a crusty old sportswriter for the *Times* renowned for having built the Trojans football legend going back to the Howard Jones era, took exception to Belinsky's "new breed" approach. Drunk late at night at the Shoreham Hotel in Washington, D.C., Dyer pounded on Bo's door demanding an exclusive on a rumored story that the pitcher was retiring at the beginning of what was still a promising career. An argument ensued.

Bo said Dyer took a swing at him with a bathroom appliance and missed, and Bo then punched him out, leaving him unconscious. Belinsky was traded to Philadelphia and never again had big-league success on the mound. Dyer was soon put out to pasture while young stars like Jim Murray and John Hall provided new blood to the newspaper.

Once Tinkham's identity was revealed, this began to open doors. Tim Tessalone, USC's sports information director and a guy who has provided me countless favors over the years, was my next call. He had some knowledge of the incident.

"They all got pretty hammered the night before," he said. "Maybe Mal Florence was there. Tinkham said something like, 'F——k you, Duke.'" Add Florence to the list of witnesses since deceased. But Tim's greatest contribution was helping me locate Tinkham's daughter Amanda, a USC graduate in her own right. Tim knew she had been a writer herself. A little Internet work revealed an Amanda Tinkham Boltax and a Facebook page for a married woman who was about the right age, had some journalistic background, and was a USC alum. It was Harley's daughter. Not only that, she was a student on campus when I was there, but we did not know each other.

A message on Facebook followed, some e-mail correspondence, and then a phone conversation, followed by a set of photos of Harley Tinkham, the man himself. Her dad was a spry-looking fellow with a bright smile and short, white hair. One photo showed young Amanda, a pretty sorority girl on the day of her initiation, with her beaming mom and dad, the familiar tree-lined campus in the background.

"I'd not heard that story," said Amanda, which really surprised me. Her father had gotten into a big argument in front of many witnesses, mostly USC alumni and media, in the presence of John Wayne, yet this event had not been passed down to her as urban legend.

"Dad was best of friends with George Ambrose," she said. Ambrose was USC's sports information director at the time. "My dad never boasted a lot, or name dropped. George and Dad had known each other since their college days. Dad was an extra in the movies growing up in Hollywood. He covered everything, but was known for his track expertise.

"Dad was on the 1943 Trojan track team that won the NCAA championship. He was a high jumper and decathlete. He wrote for the *Times Mirror*, which then became the *Herald-Examiner*. He created the Morning Briefing. Scott Ostler would call him for permission to run items but eventually they stopped doing that. He had a very conservative upbringing."

This indicated that Harley was not, as first thought, a "liberal writer."

"I spoke with Rachel Ambrose, George's wife, a few days after we spoke," continued Amanda. "She recalled hearing about what a wild weekend it was, but had never heard anything about a fight with John Wayne. George was there, but she said he didn't recall 'who said what.' He's ninety and Rachel says he is hard of hearing and doesn't like to speak on the phone. I don't know if you saw the post she left on my wall but here it is if you didn't see it:

> George doesn't remember the particulars of who said what at that party. Steve Travers left a message here. George suggests to Steve that he get in touch with John Hall in San Juan Capistrano or Jim Perry in Pasadena. Both were at the party. George only remembers that Wayne was down there to film *War Wagon*.

Amanda went on to explain that Harley had been in the USC marching band as well as on the track team, coached by the legendary Dean Cromwell. The photos she sent me included Harley as a sportswriter in 1963, one with his brother-in-law Bob from 1978, the sorority initiation photo, and his Trojans track team.

"He was a decathlete, but I believe his specialty was pole vault," she added. "He also was a good high jumper. I believe it is from 1941 or 1942.

"I also spoke with my brother and we both heard a lot of stories about our dad, but never one about John Wayne taking a swing at him. As far as I could tell my dad liked John Wayne the actor. My mom was a huge fan and I recall watching John Wayne movies on

TV and my dad would sometimes sit and watch. He never said or did anything to indicate he didn't like him."

Amanda was also directed to the passage from *Fight On!*

"I also saw the excerpt from Bisheff's book on Amazon and the way he writes it was 'Ace' (my dad) and Wayne's hairdresser that exchanged swings that both missed," she e-mailed. "Bisheff writes that Wayne shouted a friendly barb at my dad about being surprised that my dad was still standing at eight o'clock and that Ace retorts with 'Up yours Duke,' and everyone laughs, including Wayne who laughed the loudest. To me this fits with what I know of my dad and his personality. He tended to drink way too much at parties and passing out wasn't uncommon, so I can understand Wayne ribbing him about that. The 'up yours Duke,' I can hear my dad saying, it would have been loud and with a big smile on his face. I don't think he was angry. My dad wasn't the type to get all worked up about things. He was very laid back.

"Anyway, I sent you an earlier email with some information from George Ambrose on who else was at the party and might remember the sequence of events.

"Hope this helps.

"Amanda."

Slowly but surely, the events of the weekend begin to come into focus, although many questions remained. The identity of the "liberal writer" as Harley "Ace" Tinkham shed further light in that his daughter, Amanda Tinkham Boltax, said he was fairly conservative, not liberal, and he was a USC graduate, a tremendous Trojan supporter. That would appear to dispel the insinuation from Jeff Prugh that he was motivated to argue with Duke over the Vietnam War in part because his sympathies lay with UCLA.

Amanda urged that I contact George Ambrose, still a close family friend. Ambrose was the sports information director at the time. His wife Rachel had informed Amanda that George did not recall "particulars" and provided names of several people who might be good leads. I managed to get hold of Ambrose by phone at his home in palatial Palos Verdes Estates, a peninsula enclave that is, like Newport Beach, home to many a Trojan alum.

"My memory is not what it used to be," he said, but with some urging it proved to be quite good indeed. He was apprised of the altercation between Tinkham and the hairdresser. "It was a verbal thing, not a physical thing," Ambrose recalled. "No blows were struck as I recall. It's possible somebody took a swing but missed and nothing happened.

"There was another party in another room. Harley was dancing with some of the women. There's a funny story Hall related. Wayne encountered him and asked his rating on individual players and teams. John said, 'I don't know,' and Wayne said, 'That's the right answer.'

"I was never really involved with Wayne. He was there making *The War Wagon*. I don't think he followed the Trojans that closely. Wayne was quite a character. Harley was my best friend and the best man at my wedding.

"Harley and I were in school. We met working on what was called the athletic news, which later became known as the sports information office. At the time we were undergraduates. We worked for Dick Nash, who handled sports news for USC. We'd have lunch over at the student union all the time. He was one of the most knowledgeable guys I've ever known, especially regarding track and field, which today does not get much attention from the press.

"Harley had great personal attributes. I have some wonderful memories of him. He was a big movie fan and could tell you all the character actors, not just the stars. If I didn't know who some guy was, he did. He was attracted by all the character actors.

"He had great knowledge of all sports and was the most knowledgeable guy I knew. If there was any argument, you asked Harley and that decided it.

"He was a high jumper when they used the 'western roll,' before the belly flop. His best was maybe 6-5 or 6-6. He followed track closely and had a great memory. He also played in the USC marching band, playing the drums. He was a versatile guy. He was a man for all seasons, and to some degree or another had good knowledge of all things. He had such a great sense of humor. One time we attended the Dean Cromwell funeral. He passed away five days before Stanford's old track coach, Dink Templeton. There were all these sportswriters there. Harley just looked at the casket and joked, 'Well, Cromwell beat Dink Templeton again.' We all laughed. He always made wry comments and just had a marvelous sense of humor.

"He was about six-one, 165 pounds. He was a slender guy, not real husky. He was always well dressed and in good shape. He was a good-looking man with dark hair. He was not Jewish. His mother was a pioneer of California. She was a remarkable lady. Once we took her to see *Some Like It Hot* and she fell asleep, but would wake up with a start and applaud. Harley's wife's name was Ena. She was Latina. He was married before 1966.

"Dwain Esper was closer to Harley. We went to the 1948 London Olympics. Esper came along and he was always riding you, being confrontational. He was moving ahead of us and we passed a restaurant, and there were people in the restaurant who saw us, the way he walked really fast swinging his arms, and they laughed and made fun of him, imitating him. Esper was a UCLA graduate but he was objective.

"They called Tinkham 'Ace' because he always referred to people as 'Ace,' and over time people started calling him Ace."

As a USC historian, I had been honored to speak to a very large number of legends associated with USC over the years, not only great players and coaches in all sports but also a number of writers and media people, some of whom were in the school's prestigious Hall of Fame, which inducts a class only every two years. One I had never met or spoken to was the great John Hall, who I grew up reading in the *Los Angeles Times*. I knew he was close to McKay, who spoke fondly of him in a 2000 interview I managed to get with the old coach. Every old-timer I ever spoke to about McKay holding court at Julie's included Hall in his memories. This evoked in me a sense of nostalgia that I had never experienced but had grown up reading about in such books as Maury Allen's *Bo: Pitching and Wooing* or Pat Jordan's *The Suitors of Spring*.

There was a time when writers like Bud Furillo were friends with players and coaches. Today, the economic disparity creates a huge gulf that is almost never crossed, but in the 1960s Bo Belinsky and "Hot Rod" Hundley of the Lakers drank with Furillo at a Crenshaw-area pub near Baldwin Hills in a place known as View Park, called Ernie's House of Serfas, where "Stocker, La Brea, Overhill, and good friends meet." According to Allen, the place even provided living quarters. Bo and Hundley reportedly stayed there, raising all kinds of hell.

Similarly, scribes like John Hall and Mal Florence, another legend who is no longer with us to share memories of these golden days, would drink long into the night with McKay, an Irishman who, like Wayne's Rooster Cogburn from *True Grit*, "liked to pull a cork" at Julie's. Tom Kelly, Marv Goux, Dave Levy, and many others would join in. Reportedly, young Craig Fertig often handled the duties of driving McKay home to West Covina, which is no short journey.

Now I finally was able to speak to Mr. Hall, whom I found living in "John Wayne country," the south Orange County city of San Clemente, where Richard Nixon's "Western White House" once had been host to Soviet premiers and heads of state.

Before getting into the nuts and bolts of the John Wayne story, Hall dispensed wisdom, wit, and memories from a lifetime on the Los Angeles sports scene.

"I was the first to call Cunningham Sam 'Bam' . . . I was the first to call Jerry Tarkanian 'Tark the Shark.' . . . It was such a great era. . . . I like Tom Lasorda, too. I'd drive to Fullerton where he lived, when I lived in Placentia. . . . I loved Bill Rigney. He entertained us in 1961 with stories of the Giants coming back to win the 1951 pennant. There were so many colorful guys on the Dodgers, too. I also loved Gary Beban. Don Drysdale was another guy I loved. I got to know him better later when he was the Angels' broadcaster. He always gave an honest account and had a sense of humor even about his own temper . . .

"Steve Garvey was easy to quote. Wally Moon was great, too. . . . I did not attend USC, but I'm in the USC Hall of Fame. I wrote a lot about Mike Garrett. I felt he was a very special player and young man."

This is John Hall, old schoolmaster. I tell him I wrote a biography of Jim Murray, and he is quite impressed.

"You really are quite the historian," he says. So now we get to the subject, first of all John McKay.

"One of my favorite memories was being part of McKay's inner circle at Julie's," Hall said. "McKay did not get along with Tommy Prothro. He said he took credit for being a 'great bridge player.' McKay said his wife was a great bridge player. He did not like John Ralston because he said he cheated in recruiting and told false stories about USC. He got along with most of the other coaches."

Finally, the 1966 weekend in Austin.

"I was there," Hall said. "I was traveling with the Angels. Paul Zimmerman asked me to come and help him. Zimmerman and I wrote for the *Times*. I flew in from Baltimore where I was with the Angels, and got in after nine at night. I remember Texas had 'Super Bill' Bradley.

"Wayne was holding court with students, alumni and the writers. The band was playing and it was a wild party. Jeff Prugh was not covering USC for the *Times*. Loel was there. Harley was in several Friday night brawls over the years. He was an all-time all-star. Bud Furillo and I did a lot of partying. Dwight Chapin was not there. I was close to Chapin.

"I got there at nine and got a drink at the other end of the room. There were about fifty students and alums surrounding Wayne, who was holding court like in a university seminar setting. I had this funny smile on my face and he looked up and saw me. He asked, 'Are you listening to what we're talking about?' Then he asked whether he could speak to me in private. We went off to the side of the ballroom, and Duke asks me, 'What do you think about the world?' I just told him, 'I'm just a dumb sportswriter and I don't know nothin' about the world.' Duke smiles and thinks about that and replies, 'That's the right answer.'

"What did I think of the world? He was talking to students about the importance of general education. I don't think he was talking about the Vietnam War; he was talking about education, and making the world better."

Hall may not have felt Wayne was talking about Vietnam, but by his own admission he did not arrive until nine. Ron Yary described Wayne's limousine pulling up, probably in the late afternoon before the team had their dinner and went to a movie as a group. Wayne very well might have started partying and pontificating much earlier. It was, as Mike Walden called it, a "smoker," with plenty of barbecued ribs, steak, chicken, and probably most every creature found on Noah's Ark spit fired to Texas perfection, all resplendent with beer, wine, tequila, whiskey ("*I said WHISKEY!*" Walden recalled the Duke ordering)—any kind of alcohol imaginable. This was *Texas* in all its 1960s politically incorrect glory, the biggest of the big putting on a show for the USC Trojans, the biggest, baddest team in college football come all the way from the West Coast. Unless one can truly understand not only the competitive nature of college football but also the cultural significance, the regional pride, and the bragging rights associated with the game, one cannot appreciate how elaborate a scene this was (Hall: "The band was playing and it was a wild party.").

Why would John Wayne single out John Hall for a private conversation and ask him, "What do you think about the world?" It seems logical to conceive that he was being challenged on Vietnam, as Jeff Prugh suggested in 2005. Despite no evidence that it was Harley or that it was Harley who came up to him and said, "Waal . . . *Duke . . .* you ain' *s—t!*" most of the witnesses admitted they came after nine, while Harley, and Nick Pappas, now too old to give details, were there all night.

Loel Schrader's description may have captured this confrontation or at least what he—drinking, partying, and socializing himself, definitely not observing everything with the practiced eye of a reporter—saw of it, which were aggressive words between John Wayne and Harley Tinkham, with Ace telling him, "Up yours, Duke." Just because Tinkham got into a physical confrontation with a hairdresser does not mean at some point he did not get into a confrontation of a physical nature with the Duke.

While Amanda Tinkham said he grew up in a conservative way, it does not mean that he was a supporter of the Vietnam War, certainly not the "bomb 'em to the Stone Age" brand of Curt LeMay jingoism Wayne was likely espousing. Wayne may well have had his sycophants hanging on every word, not challenging him, but as Hall described the scene by the time he got there, he was surrounded by students, who most definitely would not have been hanging on every word with reverence and support for the war, conservative school or no conservative school, Texas and the Alamo or no Texas and the Alamo. Besides, this was still Austin, just about the closest place to "liberal" in the Lone Star State.

So Duke very well might have found a middle-aged conservative man he knew was "safe" and singled him out for some political support, except that when he asked the very leading question,

"What do you think about the world?" Hall did not give him the answer he may have been seeking, something like, "Hell, Duke, there's too many hippies 'n' protestors and Commie-libs, in my opinion." Wayne, a smart man, may have realized he could not coax something out of Hall that the writer did not want to give and just backed off the premise.

"Wayne believed in a strong coach, and McKay was a strong coach," continued Hall. "He was tough. He could burn up a room but had a great sense of humor. He told great stories, but didn't cotton to any 'phony baloney.'

"McKay hated those student protest marches. 'You notice they never march in the rain,' he'd say of those protesters at Berkeley, who always stayed dry.

"All I know is that all those protests and problems happened at a helluva colorful time. I did not notice with all my time covering sports that it ever reduced the greatness of sports. I was aware, though, about what happened at Berkeley. I thought it was a disgrace. During those years there were so many things that were a disgrace.

"John Wayne was a great defender of America; an America that does not really exist any more. I can imagine Harley kidding Wayne, but there's no way Wayne would touch him."

John Hall spoke a mile a minute in a stream-of-consciousness manner.

"Bruce Cabot was a hero of mine from being with Fay Wray in *King Kong*. Maybe he grabbed Harley and said, 'Take it easy.' I just knew Cabot that one night. I think he was a headwaiter before he was in *King Kong*.

"The fight was not between Wayne and Tinkham; it was between Tinkham and Wayne's hairdresser. His hairdresser got in a fight with Harley. Maybe both were trying to dance with the same person, but Wayne sure wasn't in any fight. It was the hairdresser who got in the mix-up.

"Tinkham was an outstanding reporter. He was with the *Times* and the *Mirror*. He was outstanding. The day of the NFL merger he was covering the L.A. Open for the *Mirror*. Later he created the Morning Briefing. He was an excellent, reliable, outstanding reporter and a good writer. He would travel with the teams and party on Friday nights before the games. Sometimes he had too much to drink and got in several brawls over the years.

"No, he did not have a real drinking problem. He would get a little high on just a couple drinks. He'd get a little goofy, so I'd say it was not that he drank a lot, but that he got high on just a couple drinks. But he was a great sportswriter. He knew every stat.

"I wouldn't say he looked handsome. I would say Harley was good looking. He wore glasses and was old enough to pick up the tab one or two times. He was never too busy to do a little drinkin'. He wore open shirts. We all did in those days, open shirts with a sport coat, a jacket. On Friday nights on the road we'd wear a tie."

One writer who chose anonymity did say that he *heard*, possibly thirdhand and years later, that Wayne grabbed him by the tie.

Wayne grabbed him by the tie.

This account is "confirmed" by Dwight Chapin, who covered Trojans and Bruins football and basketball. Chapin at first indicated that he did not have "direct" knowledge but added "I did hear a great story involving him. Not sure if it's suitable for your book, or how it might be verified. But . . .

"Harley Tinkham, the late L.A. journalist, track and field guru and super USC supporter, supposedly was at a party where the Duke was in attendance one night. Tinkham had had more than several drinks and decided to meet Wayne. So he walks up to him and says, 'So, they call you the Duke, huh?' Wayne nods, and Tinkham promptly adds, 'Well, f——k you, Duke!' At which point, Wayne supposedly grabs Tinkham by the knot in his tie and begins shaking him and lifting him up and down off the floor, until he drops Tinkham in a heap at his feet.

"That's a story I heard several times in my L.A. days, I'm sure at least once from Mal Florence."

Florence is, like many others, mysteriously not around to tell this tale in its entirety. Another is Jeff Prugh, who like Chapin was not there but told me the story, only his description was more vivid, involving Wayne's Vietnam diatribe and of course a full swing at Tinkham, possibly not landing because Pappas may have pulled him back. Prugh probably heard it from Florence, too. But at least the description from the anonymous media person and Chapin lends some credence to Prugh's tale. It seems that *something* happened beyond just Harley and a hairdresser getting into a squabble, possibly over a woman they wanted to dance with.

Assistant Trojan football coach Dave Levy was there that night, too.

"Wayne went to the alumni cocktail party and brought twenty or thirty alumni with him," he recalled. "We took the team to a movie but I know they're there. Harley was a great drinker. He usually could be found passed out in a couch before we got back from the movie. In those years writers were prone to drinking a lot. I knew him from his beat writer days, taking trips with the team. He was a non-descript guy. Harley was just Harley. He was not a big guy. So he was drinking. Harley was a very friendly guy.

"Wayne was with Bruce Cabot. Oh my, I guess I saw them in the bar and thought, 'Well, they're still here.' They'd started before we left and were still there after the movie."

"Duke was an invited guest when USC played Texas," announcer Tom Kelly said. "I did not know he and Harley got into a fight. Harley Tinkham was the most lovable guy who covered the Trojans. He was irascible and irreverent. Everybody *loved* him. I don't know anybody in the media then who did not like him. Harley was a sweetheart.

"I don't know that I agreed with Wayne politically but how could you not *love* the Duke?

"It was a press relationship. There were thirteen different guys covering the daily papers; the *Times*, the Hearst papers, the valley, Orange County . . . I can't tell you who the TV people were, it was all press, newspaper guys. If you had an up close relationship with McKay, you were a newspaperman. Ambrose was the first SID."

"I'm not sure too many guys liked this sportswriter," said Ron Yary, who did recall Tinkham's name but offered a differing view, likely the player's perspective. "He seemed the kind of person who was always complaining about somebody else's opinion like his was the only one that mattered."

"I didn't join the *Times* until 1968 but I knew Harley Tinkham fairly well," said the great baseball writer Ross Newhan. "He was an authority on track and field, which was a major sport in those years, and pretty much a statistical encyclopedia on other sports, as well as a fine writer. I had no dealings with John Wayne."

"Indeed, most are deceased," recalled Art Spander, who moved from the *Santa Monica Evening Outlook* to the *San Francisco Examiner*. "I never heard about a fight—I had moved to the Bay Area in 1965—and I doubt it was any of the three you mentioned. Maybe Dwight Chapin was at the *Times* (he's now living in Marin), then perhaps Steve Bisheff, who came to the *Outlook* in '65 when I left and came north, knew/knows what happened. Mike Waldner is another. I sat next to Waldner and two seats from Bisheff at the ND-SC game Saturday. Also, Joe Jares, the SC grad who went from UPI (where he and I were together briefly) to *SI* to the *Times*, could be a good source."

Jares did not return a phone call.

"I have a great photo of Wayne at Dedeaux Field," said Justin Dedeaux. "Both Dad and Wayne were members of Lakeside Golf Club. We lived in Glendale. They would kid each other about Dad's appearance in *Death on the Diamond* as an extra in a baseball movie. Tinkham and Dad knew each other, but he was better friends with Murray, John Hall and Braven Dyer. Have not heard of the Tinkham story. Dad was probably there. I was a student in 1966. Garrett won the Heisman in 1965 and did not play baseball in the spring of 1966. I did not know the film crowd except for Ron Schwary."

In questioning eyewitnesses, I discovered that while Tinkham's "fight" was apparently not with Wayne but with the makeup artist, the memory of the late Jeff Prugh (the anonymous media member), Dwight Chapin's story from the deceased Mal Florence, Nick Pappas's inability to answer questions, and the fact that most of those I found arrived around nine and may have missed events from earlier allow for some possibility that indeed Wayne was pontificating on Vietnam, that possibly Tinkham argued with him about it, and that a physical confrontation (if not a missed punch, apparently Wayne grabbing the writer by the necktie) could have happened.

The first insinuation that the hairdresser was gay is also inaccurate, as several witnesses said the altercation with Tinkham came not because he popped off to Duke but because they were vying for the attention of a girl both of them danced with at the party. While not impossible, it also seems unlikely that Wayne would employ and travel with a gay makeup artist.

So who was the makeup man, Wayne's "little buddy"? Some Google searches indicated it probably was Larry Butterworth, but I could not find specifics about his passing away in Austin the night before the game. Ed Asner recalled Butterworth was Wayne's makeup man on *El Dorado*, but among those confirming his identity was Ronald Schwary.

Schwary, a native of Portland, Oregon, decided to study film at USC and became the football team's student manager.

"Robert Kardashian was the student manager before me," said Schwary. Schwary was close friends with a number of players and so integral to Coach McKay's operation that he was given a fifth-year scholarship to stay on as the team's manager in the national championship season of 1967. Schwary was at the party, apparently arriving late with McKay, Fertig, Goux, and some writers after the team returned from a movie.

When Wayne "ordered" both Butterworth and Tinkham to be taken to their rooms, Schwary was given the task of seeing Butterworth to his.

"I took Butterworth to his room," Schwary said. "Wayne asked me, 'Would you do me a favor? Take him upstairs, take off his shoes and put him to bed?'"

Butterworth had been mixing drinks all night, Craig Fertig said, and was very intoxicated. Fertig was the "low man on the totem pole" on USC's coaching staff. One of his jobs was to "escort" Trojan VIPs—former stars, political figures, or one of their many Hollywood luminaries—when they attended USC games.

According to his descriptions recounted in both *One Night, Two Teams* and *What It Means to Be a Trojan*, his phone rang, and it was McKay telling him to take care of John Wayne. However, Fertig's recollections must be considered in the light of several factors. He described in several different interviews how he drove McKay to Los Angeles International Airport to discuss scheduling of the 1970 USC game at Birmingham with Bear Bryant without any apparent contradiction, but he cannot be counted as a witness to Bryant's "this here's what a football player looks like" speech after the game. While he was tasked with "escorting" Sam Cunningham, he admitted that he was distracted by well-wishers and left Cunningham and Bryant to their own devices. This was, however, after years of alumni banquets in which he promoted the story.

By the mid-2000s, Fertig, whose nephew was Todd Marinovich, a one-time star USC quarterback who fell on very hard times before finding sobriety and a happy marriage in large measure because of his great artistic ability, experienced personal tragedy himself. He was drinking heavily at the time he was giving interviews about both the 1966 and the 1970 USC trips to Austin and Birmingham, respectively, and in 2008 passed away—like many of the others, far too young.

"Craiger, John Wayne's gonna speak to the team," McKay is said to have told him. "I want you to make sure he gets everything he needs."

"Sure, Coach."

Fertig headed off to the movie star's room. He knocked on the door, and there, larger than life, was John Wayne in his underwear.

"Mr. Wayne, I'm Craig Fertig."

"How the hell are ya Craig? And call me Duke. I'm a big fan, Craig, I saw ya beat the Irish two years ago."

Fertig entered the room.

"Craig, I need ya to help me get dressed. God——n makeup man's never here when ya need 'im. Whaddaya think, how should I dress?"

"Gee, Duke, we're in Texas. Everybody thinks of ya as a cowboy, dress like that."

Fertig helped Duke into a new three-piece suit, again dolled up with a nine-gallon cowboy hat and cowboy boots.

Obviously, Wayne was unaware of anything seriously wrong with Butterworth at that point.

"Ron Schwary, my equipment manager put him to bed," said Chuck Arrobio, a standout USC player (1962–1966) who played for the Minnesota Vikings of the NFL and currently has a dental practice in the Pasadena area. "I remember something like that. Schwary did it all for McKay. He put the hairdresser to bed that night."

During filming of *Wake of the Red Witch*, Wayne labored in the high altitude of the Mexican Sierras, 6,200 feet above sea level. Apparently, he, like other members of the crew, had trouble dealing with the altitude. The Internet Movie Database does not list Butterworth as the makeup man or hairstylist on that shoot, but he probably was, like Duke, affected by the altitude.

His job was to prepare Duke Wayne in the morning. The sequence of events is confusing, as there are accounts indicating it was not until the wee hours of the morning that Wayne's plan to address the Trojans was set, while Loel Schrader's account has Wayne asking for and being granted the chance at the party, which might have happened before Butterworth was put to bed.

After repeated calls to the makeup artist's room went unanswered in the morning, some of Duke's entourage came to knock on his door. Eventually, concerned about him after he had done far too much drinking, mixing alcohol all night long, the security staff was directed to open his room. There they found him: dead from a heart attack.

"At 6:30 or seven A.M. Duke asked me, 'Did Larry say anything to you?'" recalled Schwary.

"The most amazing thing about that night was the hairdresser who died," recalled Steve Bisheff. An Internet search for "John Wayne's hairdresser" under 1966 *Los Angeles Times* obituaries did not reveal anything.

"His make-up man died over night, but I do not know his name," said Tom Kelly.

Shortly after eight the next morning, a writer entered the lobby and noticed Wayne and Cabot standing near a door to the street.

"Anything wrong?" he asked.

"My little buddy [Butterworth] died in his sleep last night," Wayne replied. "Heart attack, I guess. We found his body this morning. We're waiting for a hearse now."

Then two men came pushing a gurney. "We're here to pick up a body," one of them said.

"What's the gurney for?" Wayne asked.

"We have to pick up the body," repeated the man.

"Not my buddy. Wait here, I'll get him." Wayne carried his body. "I'll take him to the hearse."

Then, the Schrader/Bisheff book details, Pappas arrived and escorted them not to the stadium but to the hotel dining room, where the team was having their pregame meal.

"At breakfast he did not say much," Schwary said.

"Wayne said the hairdresser had a heart problem the next day," recalled Hall. "Bruce Cabot was also traveling to San Antonio."

"What a way to go; drinkin' and brawlin' right to the last breath," Wayne said.

The wild events of that weekend are interspersed with each other. Happening roughly at the same time that Tinkham and Butterworth got into it, which may or may not have contributed to Butterworth's heart attack (mixing drinks did not help), was the invitation to speak to the Trojans and the actual speech.

Nick Pappas was a Trojans football star in his own right. He was Pat O'Brien's double for the football scenes in the 1940 classic *Knute Rockne: All-American* (starring Ronald Reagan). Pappas developed a very close relationship with Wayne and used Duke many times in his role as director of Trojans' Athletic Support Groups. His interview with Ken Rappoport for the book *The Trojans: A Story of Southern California Football* took place prior to Wayne's 1979 passing.

"Nick Pappas was everywhere," recalled Bisheff.

"I have very fond memories of Nick," recalled Lloyd Robinson, a 1964 USC graduate who also came through their law school and became a Hollywood talent agent. "In the '70s and '80s we had two support memberships, Cardinal and Gold and Women of Troy, and as a result had nine USC football tickets for our family. Each membership included a preferred parking pass but with nine people we used three cars. Each year before the start of the football season I would go to Nick's office. We would start by talking football, then I would come to the purpose of the visit, that I needed one additional season parking pass. He kept a large fishbowl on his desk which always had money in it. I would start by putting in $50 and then he would go back to talking football. I would add $20 but still football talk. Then when I put in $30 more, having reached that year's magic number, suddenly from within his desk would come a preferred season parking pass. Without missing a beat he would continue talking football. No words about the money or the resulting pass were ever uttered during the process. Incidentally all of the money collected went to help football players with incidental expenses."

Robinson recalled that "Nick passed away" but was mistaken.

"He's a fraternity brother of mine, and the night before a big game with Texas in 1966 we were having cocktails together," Pappas told Rappoport. "This is in Austin, see, and he had come in just for the game. We drank until about four in the morning—Wayne's drinking scotch and soda all this time. All the guys at the party had gone to dinner and come back and then gone to bed, and we're still in there drinking.

"In the course of our conversation, he says, 'Pap, I want to talk to the kids at breakfast tomorrow.'

"I told him, 'You're in, Duke,' without thinking. I hadn't asked anyone whether it would be all right for Wayne to talk to our football team on the morning of the game. It was a big one, a season opener with Texas ranked number one and us number two."

Pappas was incorrect about the rankings.

"But I remembered that coach John McKay loved John Wayne movies. He used to talk about his big evening—sitting home with a peanut butter sandwich and a glass of chocolate milk and watching a John Wayne movie. And he never met him. I also remembered that McKay would awaken early on the day of games, he was always up by six o'clock, and read the papers. Have breakfast, and go over his diagrams. He was constantly working on football.

"So I call McKay and tell him I had a problem. 'Look, John,' I said. 'I was with John Wayne last night. He asked me if he could talk to the kids, and I said, yeah.' And before I could finish, McKay says, 'Geez, great . . . bring him down.'"

Pappas's account to Rappoport said the meeting was at 10:00 at the stadium, but most significantly he described a private conversation in the wee hours of the morning in his hotel room, not apparently at the party as described in *Fight On!*

"We've been invited by the Texas student body, but we're also on our way to Mexico to film *The War Wagon*," *Fight On!* quotes

Wayne telling those around him in the hotel's ballroom during the party. Actor Bruce Cabot, the "bad guy" in *The War Wagon*, was a big football fan and in some ways Ward Bond's replacement as his side-kick. He was with him.

Wayne sipped tequila, according to *Fight On!*, then turned and said to Pappas, "Nick, you know what I'd like to do? I'd like to talk to the team before tomorrow's game. Do you think John McKay would let me do that?"

"Well, why don't I find out? I'll go call Coach now."

The book says he returned shortly.

"Coach would love to have you. Nine A.M., Duke. I'll meet you in the lobby at five to nine," Schrader/Bisheff quoted Pappas as saying.

"The kids are all assembled in the locker room at ten in the morning, and in walks Wayne," was Rappoport's version.

According to most others, it was not the "locker room" but a pregame breakfast at the hotel.

"Damn, he was fantastic. He walks in with this white 20,000-gallon cowboy hat and black suit—he looked just beautiful," said Pappas. "The kids look up, and their eyeballs pop. Here's the REAL John Wayne. And Wayne walks over to the coach and gives him a big hello and squeezes him—you'd think he and McKay were long lost buddies. They had never met before."

"John Wayne and my dad were friendly if not friends," said John K. "J.K." McKay. "I may have seen Wayne a few times in dark bars, maybe in Julie's. There is some Wayne memorabilia from 1966 in the new McKay Center. I met him once or twice. My dad watched a ridiculous amount of John Wayne Westerns. He was a junkie for John Wayne movies. I probably saw Wayne on the sidelines a few times."

"Duke was on his way to Mexico to make a film, so we knew he'd be in Austin," said Dave Levy. "McKay loved John Wayne movies. On Friday nights Marv Goux arranged for the team to see a movie, that was his deal, and we always went to see if Wayne was playing anywhere. If so we saw that over any 'double-oh seven' movie, or *Easy Rider*.

"Coach McKay regularly rented vacation homes over the years in Newport and would see Wayne down there. The only other times I saw John Wayne was, a couple of his kids went to SC. Pilar was best friends of my brother-in-law's wife. I saw them at a cocktail party in Newport. His son was a big guy."

"It was beautiful," continued Pappas. "A former player and all, Wayne gives one of the greatest fight talks you've ever heard—and the kids got all fired up."

The Trojans gathered in a banquet room next to the hotel's main lobby. They had already eaten breakfast and been taped up. They were only told they now had a "special surprise" in store. Once gathered, the door opened, and in walked John "Duke" Wayne. If Pappas's story is accurate, he had hardly slept and may have still been inebriated, having never stopped drinking, either, but thanks to the "artistry" of Craig Fertig, he looked, if Fertig was accurate, like a million bucks in his suit, hat, and boots.

The players immediately recognized the icon and began whooping it up like crazy. After the din died down, McKay introduced the actor. For ten minutes Duke spoke. Nobody has any memory of his slurring his words. He was a professional actor who knew how to keep it together.

"He spoke to the team the next day," recalled Dave Levy. "Wayne spoke to the team at breakfast. He was charming. His language was upbeat and positive; very appropriate. He loved the university and Coach Jones. Wayne talked about Coach Jones with reverence. He talked like an undergrad, he was very reverent, talking about playing in big games. He was wearing a sport coat, slacks, and a shirt with no tie."

This differs with Fertig's recollection that he "dressed" the movie star "into a new three-piece suit, again dolled up with a nine-gallon cowboy hat and cowboy boots."

"We had heard he'd speak at breakfast, the pre-game meal," recalled Ron Yary. "We were all waiting for McKay, who was late. We had heard his long time publicist or hairdresser had died but the party never slowed down. Anyway he came into the room, Wayne walked in before McKay, but I can't remember what he said. He was dressed in casual business attire, I think a sport coat, and he had boots on. He had boots when he came up. He was very down to earth and straightforward, and had nothing bad to say about Texas.

. . . He was respectable but not loud, he was not yelling, but the whole time John Wayne treated us as equals."

"He came to the morning breakfast, the pre-game meal," recalled running back Steve Grady. "I don't remember much. Obviously it was a big thrill to see John Wayne in the morning. Having Wayne was Hollywood at its finest. As I remember it was not earth shaking. He spoke to us as a former SC player in enemy country. There was no fire or brimstone. I don't recall jokes. He was funny but modest, not into himself even though he was big time at SC. My impression of him was positive and favorable."

"Steve Grady out of Loyola was between Garrett and Simpson, which became an old tired gag in 1966," recalled Tom Kelly, of the fact that Grady, along with Don McCall, had the difficult historical role of being Trojans tailbacks in between Heisman Trophy winners Mike Garrett and O.J. Simpson.

"No I forget," said the appropriately named six-foot, one inch, 175-pound safety Mike Battle, a sophomore that year. "I remember he spoke for quite a while."

"I wish I could be of some help to you in your new project, but it was a long time ago and I was probably too nervous about the game to remember John Wayne's speech," said quarterback Steve Sogge. "I do remember him being there and how impressed all of the players were to meet a 'great man and a great Trojan.' Sorry I can't be of more help. Good luck with your book!"

"McKay introduced Wayne to the team, which sat spellbound as the Duke launched his pep talk, mentioning first his USC coach, Howard Jones," wrote Schrader and Bisheff.

"The Head Man always told us that each of us should get the best of the man opposite us," Wayne told the team. "He said that if we did that, we would be sure to win. And, if you do that today, you will win, too."

"There wasn't a sound," their book continued. "It was doubtful any players were breathing, so taken with the message Wayne delivered."

This description—and other descriptions by players who heard Wayne—differs with some other wild descriptions I have heard for years. Based upon corroboration of players interviewed for this book, *Fight On!* appears to be the accurate version, while the rumors I heard years ago are probably less accurate. However, considering Wayne's conversation with Nikita Khrushchev in 1958, it raises some questions about Hollywood and literary license.

I majored in communications at USC but took several classes in the acclaimed film school, including one or two taught by the legendary Dr. Andrew Casper. I maintained communication with elements of the USC School of Cinematic Arts and later, when I was a Hollywood screenwriter between 1994 and 2001, had quite a bit of association in various capacities with my alma mater. During that time, I heard a rumor that George C. Scott's speech to the troops, outlined against a giant American flag at the beginning of *Patton* (1970), was based on Duke Wayne's incendiary speech to the USC football team at Austin in 1966.

Wayne was said to have used phrases like "go through them like s———t through a goose . . . we're gonna murder 'em . . . ," and other violent terminology. While this has not been verified, what can be verified is that Marv Goux regularly mimicked the *Patton* speech in fiery oratory to the Trojans before most games, particularly big ones on the road when he would speak of "conquest being going into another man's house and taking what another man holds dear," of "robbing him of his pride," of "stealing his confidence," and of "taking what's yours without asking." The marching band and song girls, all crowded into a small room in the old USC football building, before the erection of Heritage Hall in the early 1970s, accompanied Goux's legendary addresses. Goux's father had fought and died during the Battle of the Bulge, where Patton's army relieved the "Screaming Eagles" of the 101st Airborne Division holding off a Nazi onslaught at Bastogne. His speeches, laced with Pattonesque terminology, began *before* the film was released in 1970.

The whole nexus of Hollywood, Trojan football, John Wayne, Marv Goux, and the USC film students of the 1960s adds to the theory that perhaps the "Patton speech" was based on Wayne at Austin. Goux was one of many USC and UCLA football players portraying gladiators in Stanley Kubrick's *Spartacus* (1960). Francis Ford Coppola attended the UCLA film school but was closely aligned with

1960s USC film students George Lucas, John Milius, and Walter Murch (plus Steven Spielberg). Milius, a right-wing devotee of John Wayne's who watched *The Searchers* "hundreds of times," was a student at USC in 1966. It would not be at all unreasonable to conceive that he knew players or spoke to somebody who told him or possibly exaggerated to him what the Duke said to the team that Saturday morning. Milius, filled with hubris and literary license, may well have relayed this to Coppola—the man who wrote the screenplay for *Patton*.

Letters written to Lucas and Coppola posing this very question for this book were not responded to. An inquiry of Milius was met by the very sad news that he is, as of the time of this writing, in ill health and unable to handle any interview requests. Perhaps the publication of this book will spur some debate that might draw the likes of Lucas and Coppola into addressing the question, but it does not end there.

John Wayne's conversation with Nikita Khrushchev in 1958, recounted in Michael Munn's biography of him, sounds eerily similar to George C. Scott's Patton telling the Russian interpreter that he does not desire to have a drink with the Russian general or "any other Russian son of a bitch." In the Wayne–Khrushchev imbroglio, the Duke got his back up when the Russian dictator reiterated that communism would win in the end, at which time Wayne told the interpreter he wanted to knock the diminutive Soviet off his barstool. The interpreter, as with the interpreter in *Patton*, told Wayne he could not repeat such a line to Khrushchev, that he needed to maintain diplomatic relations.

Again, the connection continues. Wayne was up for the lead in *Patton*, which was also offered to Rod Steiger (who turned it down because of anti-Vietnam pacifism), before landing with Scott. Even if Wayne did not make an incendiary speech to the Trojans in 1966, while up for the lead, he may have researched and spoken to somebody about Patton, a conversation that reasonably would have been related to the screenwriter researching the man, Coppola. A *very interested party*, Milius, was at Wayne's alma mater, where the connection was very strong. In speaking about Patton and his anticommunism expressed at the end of the film, Wayne could easily have told *somebody near Coppola and Milius* about his tête-à-tête with Nikita Khrushchev.

During my screenwriting career, as mentioned, I heard, to quote Milius from his classic *Apocalypse Now*, "rumors and random intelligence" that Wayne said to the Trojans what Scott says at the beginning of *Patton*. I can recall hearing people at the USC film school talking about this on several occasions, which include an airing of *The Right Stuff* on campus when I was an undergraduate in 1983, in conversation with a number of film students when I was at the school looking at their bulletin boards in hopes of finding work, at a 1998 Academy Awards party I attended at the Beverly Hills Hotel, and again at the on-campus premiere of the Julia Roberts film *Erin Brockovich.*

Considering the descriptions in *Fight On!* and the players interviewed for this book, it is reasonable to believe that Wayne did not talk like George C. Scott in *Patton* when addressing the 1966 Trojans.

"When you put your hand in some blood next to you, and it's your best friend, your teammate, you'll know what to do . . . we're gonna go through those Texas bastards like s——t through a goose. . . . I actually feel sorry for those Longhorn bastards, 'cause we're not just gonna kill 'em, we're not just gonna murder 'em, we're gonna use their guts to grease our cleats."

This fictional "talk," liberally interspersing football language with descriptions of what Wayne believed the American army no doubt was doing to the "pissant communists" in Vietnam, apparently did not occur, although to quote Alabama quarterback Scott Hunter, who said Bear Bryant "did not lord Sam Cunningham over us and say, 'This here's what a football player looks like' . . . but he should have. It's too good a story not to be true."

The same might be said of John Wayne. The prospect of the Duke standing ten feet tall before the Trojans and making the speech that made George Scott's career is too delicious to at least not *want it to be true,* which leads to John Milius. This was a film student who loved John Wayne, totally backed the Vietnam War, and was by his own accounts almost filled with bloodlust over his desire to wipe out communism. Hollywood is filled from floor to rafter with wild stories (think the Clara Bow legend) that, while untrue, end up portrayed on screen. Consider his biography, *Patton: Ordeal and Triumph* (1963) by Ladislas Farago, a book I read in high school that, along with *The Rise and Fall of the Third Reich* by William Shirer, formed my political philosophy with the simple belief that there is a thin red line between good and evil and that in this world—at least until recently—this thin red line is the United States of America.

I recall in reading Farago's book that it did not contain Patton's flowery language attributable to the movie. I did read someplace that the *Patton* speech was based on his address to his troops before a major battle, although I have heard different battles described. He could have made a "standard speech" that carried throughout the war, as Patton led men into battle in North Africa, Sicily, France, and Belgium and eventually into the heart of the Third Reich. A search inside the Amazon.com toolbar using the famous phrases "no bastard ever won a war by dying for his country" and "we're gonna go through the Hun like s——t through a goose" reveals nothing. General Omar Bradley, who wrote his own autobiography, was an adviser on the film, directed by Franklin Schaffner, who served in North Africa with Patton. Bradley's bland personality was the anti-Patton, and he never would have come up with or suggested the kind of diatribe Scott gives in the opening scene.

In *Making Patton*, author Nicholas Sarantakes wrote, "*Patton* helped shape the screenplay of *Apocalypse Now* (1979)," noting that Milius liked Patton's screed about war: "I love it. God help me I do love it so. I love it more than my life." Coppola wrote *Patton* as a huge antiwar script. These lines are perhaps his most blatant attempt to paint George Patton as a crazed warmonger, a picture of why America needed to get out of Vietnam, of My Lai, and of the immorality he viewed it to be. But these words were favorites of the prowar Milius, a conundrum.

This leads to one last, intriguing question. Coppola wrote *Patton* as an antiwar diatribe, the general portrayed in his hoped-for view as unhinged, violently extreme. Could Duke Wayne have been Coppola's model for Patton, a strange twist of life imitating art imitating life? If Francis Ford Coppola would have deigned to answer this question posed in the letter I wrote him, the answer might appear in these pages. We can only hope to hear more later.

Patton's reputation as a great war movie comes from Scott's charisma and the fact that Schaffner ultimately was not going to downgrade the man he served under, which leads to the theory that Coppola's model for Patton *might have been Milius*. If Milius heard exaggerated stories about John Wayne or just used his own imagination to channel Duke's on-screen war persona, then expressed this *to his well-known good friend and collaborator* Coppola, all at the time Coppola *was writing Patton*, it becomes a little easier to try to connect the dots. Coppola had a cavalier attitude about writing *Patton* anyway. No sooner did he finish it than he headed to San Francisco to make documentaries and indies, saying "good riddance" to Hollywood. So uncaring was he that it was only when called back to Twentieth Century Fox to fix an editing machine he had invented did he discover the movie he wrote was already in postproduction.

Most of the players were still for the war in 1966, but a few were starting to turn against it, worried that, as their college careers were ending, they would be subject to the draft. If Duke's grandiose predictions of victory had come true, it likely would have led to the war's end before their numbers were called. Regardless, Wayne finished, McKay thanked him, and the Trojans headed off to Memorial Stadium.

An added twist to the so-called six degrees of separation between *Patton*, John Wayne, and USC comes from former sports information director Jim Perry.

"I co-wrote *McKay: A Coach's Story*," he recalled. "John McKay wanted to call it *1st and 25*. McKay was a unique personality. McKay was Catholic, but I'm not sure how religious he was. His favorites were old John Wayne movies, but he was also highly influenced by *Patton*, starring George C. Scott. He used to lecture me. I'm over at UCLA and he's lecturing me, why am I writing about that crap? He said, 'You should see *Patton*.' I'm 21 and anti-war and just snorted, but he just said, 'I know how you feel, but you should see it. It's revealing.' When his assistants saw that movie, they felt that McKay *was Patton*, an absolute dictator who cared about his men but was tougher than hell. You knew who the boss was. That was McKay. *McKay* felt he was *Patton*."

The next phase of the story was at Austin's Memorial Stadium, and the best description comes from the colorful Craig Fertig. Craig's father was Henry Fertig, chief of police for the Huntington Park Police Department. Huntington Park is a suburb of Los Angeles (at least suburban when Fertig grew up there in the late 1950s). Today, it is part of the urban sprawl, completely Latino with few whites left. Known simply as Chief, Henry Fertig began taking extension classes at USC when his son enrolled there. He enjoyed partying just like Craig.

"Hey, son, let's go to the Nine-Oh."

"I got a criminal justice class Dad."

"Aw, heck, Craig, I been fixing his tickets for years. That's an A. Let's get a beer."

Chief Fertig had become USC's unofficial "security chief." According to Craig, Chief Fertig was recruited by his son to handle the "John Wayne detail" at Memorial Stadium. The Duke, wearing a nine-gallon cowboy hat, sat in the back of a golf cart driven by Chief Fertig. To Duke's gratification, Chief produced a bottle of whiskey in a paper bag and a Dixie cup.

"I gotcha covered, Duke."

"God bless ya, Chief."

Chief poured whiskey into Duke's paper cup, and the star gulped it down.

"Drive on, Chief."

Craig believed that, having "dressed" Wayne early that morning, Wayne had never really slept or stopped drinking from the night before, a feat most men could not handle, but John Wayne was said to have a prodigious ability to consume alcohol. His family and coworkers often described Wayne carousing late into the night, only to be the first one on the set, ready to go in the morning.

The cart began to wheel around the sidelines of Memorial Stadium.

"Ladies and gentlemen, give a BIG TEXAS WELCOME to an American hero: John Wayne."

The Longhorn partisans rose as one to whoop and holler for the Duke. Few of them had the slightest idea that he had once played football *for USC!* Wayne raised his right arm and gave the fans the "hook 'em 'Horns" sign. Meanwhile, the man who referred to the people he was now appearing before as "Texicans" on screen told Chief Fertig, "F——k the 'Horns."

"I love the John Wayne story, flipping off the Texas fans with his Longhorn finger," said Tom Kelly. "He paraded around the stadium lifting his index finger, his little finger in the 'hook 'em 'Horns' salute but was all the while saying, 'F——k you, Texas.'"

"My only remembrance during the game was that he was near our bench, which was relatively close to the fans, and he was walking up and down behind the bench," said Levy. "He may have come over once or twice to grab a Coke. He'd give 'em that 'hook 'em 'Horns' sign but under his breath he was saying, 'F——k the 'Horns.'"

"I don't remember Wayne in a golf cart before the game, but I heard him cheering, but I was in a game time mindset, and I'd not break it the day of the game," recalled Ron Yary. "I was not wavering and there was no room for extemporaneous stuff. The game takes that much obsession, an unbreakable concentration."

During the game, Wayne and Cabot were in front of the UT student section. "Let's go down and see what's going on," one writer said to another in *Fight On!* They went with field passes, taking the press box elevator to field level.

"Wayne had the students aroused," Schrader/Bisheff wrote. "He had his index and little fingers shaped into the 'hook 'em 'Horns' salute Longhorn fans employ. But as he raised his right arm toward the sky, he wasn't saying 'hook 'em 'Horns.' He was telling the Texans where they could deposit their team."

"He led yells at halftime," said Hall.

"At halftime, Duke was leading cheers before the fans, giving 'em the 'hook 'em 'Horns' sign, but giving 'em the finger with his hands," said Schwary.

"I don't remember the game or Wayne's appearance," said UT professor Dave Edwards, who was a young man in 1966, already involved in the opposition to the Vietnam War. "I have a vague recollection but don't remember well enough, so I can't say anything. I don't even remember anything in the *Daily Texan.*

"My general impression of John Wayne in 1966 was that he was a kind of Western actor, not a particularly good one, but an interesting public figure; a real presence with an emphasis on the war thing, or as a tough guy. I don't believe he was particularly prominent among students, and they would not have been interested in him other than the fact he was a prominent Hollywood figure.

"I remember him as Right-wing, kind of an unquestioning sort of patriotic speaker, but always from the Right-wing. I don't remember him in the role as an anti-Communist rooting them out."

Fellow UT professor David Prindle e-mailed, "Sounds like an interesting topic. Wish I could help. But I know nothing about John Wayne and Texans. I have never heard or read anything about Texas's reaction to the 1960 movie *The Alamo*, although I can tell you that Texans did not like the film *Giant*."

13

BATTLE ROYAL

THEN THEY PLAYED THE GAME. THE GAME? THE GAME WAS BORING. USC won, 10–6. There is really not much to add beyond that.

In 2008, I had the honor of going to dinner at El Cholo's, a famed and favorite USC hangout on Western Avenue, a few miles from the campus, with Trojan legends Ron Yary, C. R. Roberts, and Jeff Bregel; memorabilia collector Bob Case; and two of my best USC pals, ex-Trojan pitcher Phil Smith and Heath Seltzer. Yary was asked whether he felt the presence of the C. R. Roberts game from a decade earlier.

"Nobody dwelt in our past," he replied. "If you are a good team you won't look past today, no farther than tomorrow; so no, there was no part of the Texas relationship that entered into our thinking. If anybody says that, don't believe it.

"We did not give consideration to the fact McKay and Royal were very big, successful young coaches. There was a clear separation between the coaches and players. We did not talk to coaches. It was old time football. I was left out of ninety percent of all that went on.

"The only thing I cared about was how I played. It was the only thing I could control. I would gather myself, to get ready to go back out there, and evaluate myself. It's one of the smartest things you can ever do in sports.

"I don't remember the weather in Texas. I don't remember if it was hot but it did not make a difference to me if it was hot or cold. I didn't care. A good team does not care how hot or cold it gets."

For the record, it was seventy degrees (eighty-eight with humidity) at the 1:30 kickoff, with a ten-mile-per-hour wind from the northeast, cloudy to partly cloudy, and scattered showers. In a real sign of the times, only 42,000 fans were at the opening game of the season featuring two marquee teams led by superstar coaches, four and three years removed, respectively, from national championships, with more to come in the following seasons for both. The Trojans had won the previous year's Heisman and would win another in 1968. It was the middle of what unquestionably remains the greatest decade in Texas football history and was in the middle of a golden age not only for Trojan football but for all USC sports as well, perhaps the most dominant athletic department ever under A. D. Jess Hill. It was the height of California sports and cultural dominance (movies, music, politics, business, and growth), and the arrival of a team from the Golden State carried enormous panache. Despite all of that, it was far from a sellout. Today, a game between these two schools in Austin would be sold out within hours of tickets going on sale, with scalpers selling for upwards of $1,000.

Texas won the coin toss. David Conway of Texas kicked off, and USC's Earl McCullough downed the ball in the end zone. USC was held and punted. Texas sophomore quarterback Bill Bradley, making his collegiate debut, returned Rich Leon's forty-six-yard punt six yards to the twenty-one. On his first play, Bradley ran for a ten-yard first down, stopped by Mike Battle, but from there the Trojans held.

USC mounted a seventy-four-yard, fifteen-play drive late in the first quarter, capped by a twenty-three-yard field goal by linebacker Tim Rossovich, who did double duty as a placekicker. USC held a 3–0 lead.

In the second quarter, USC quarterback Troy Winslow's pass was almost intercepted. A bad snap on a punt attempt forced Leon to try to run it out, but he was swarmed. Texas drove to the USC thirty-seven, but Conway's field goal missed.

Winslow led a ball control drive beginning on his own twenty, but on fourth and eight at the UT eleven, McKay decided against a field goal. Winslow's pass to Leon was ruled out of bounds, giving UT the ball back.

"Troy Winslow was our first string quarterback in 1965 and 1966," McKay wrote in *A Coach's Story* with Jim Perry. "Some of his passes floated so slowly I could have autographed them in the air. But we worked and worked and worked with him."

After a three-and-out, Bradley had to punt a forty-six-yarder out of bounds, giving USC good field position on their own forty-five. Fifty-five yards and seven plays later, Winslow ran it in from the nine with 2:36 to play in the first half. USC led, 10–0.

Bradley's ill-advised pitchout ended one possession at the USC eleven. Andy White replaced Bradley at quarterback, but with Bradley split out as a receiver, an attempted pass to him failed, and the Longhorns had to give the ball up after another three-and-out. After an exchange of possession, Texas missed a field goal from the thirty-nine. The teams went into halftime with the score still 10–0.

The third quarter was a scoreless stalemate, but in the fourth quarter, the great sophomore running back Chris Gilbert of Texas began to churn up yardage. With Bradley back behind center, Texas drove ninety-one yards for a touchdown. Bradley tried to run a two-point conversion in but failed. USC led 10–6. Bradley led two long second-half drives.

With 8:20 left, Bradley punted forty-eight yards, pinning USC on their own two. From there, McKay made brilliant decisions. He did not have his usual tools at his disposal. There was no Mike Garrett, and O. J. Simpson was still at City College of San Francisco. But utilizing ball control offense, Winslow was able to avoid mistakes in a series of running plays and safe, short passes, eventually running out the clock for the 10–6 victory.

"You don't perform much on fifteen plays," Darrell Royal said of Bradley after the game. "He spent most of the afternoon with me [on the sidelines]."

Steve Grady rushed fifteen times for sixty-four yards. Don Mc-Call gained twenty-four yards. Gilbert launched his Hall of Fame career with fourteen rushes for 103 yards. Bradley, known for his running ability, gained forty-three yards.

Winslow was fifteen of twenty-eight for 177 yards with one interception. In the 1960s, Royal truly disdained the forward pass, and "Super Bill" completed only three for forty-two yards. One was intercepted. Rod Sherman caught three passes for thirty-five yards, his longest a twelve-yard gain. Bob Klein had three catches.

Bradley punted three times for a 46.3-yard average. Rossovich, Young, and Battle were all on their way to legend status, making twelve tackles between them.

"Texas had a quarterback they called 'Super Bill' Bradley who was supposed to be outstanding, but SC just controlled the ball and won, 10–6," said Mike Walden.

"We win the ballgame 10–6, and back in the locker room after the game, McKay says, 'Hey, guys, how about it? Let's give the game ball to John Wayne,'" recalled Nick Pappas.

"For a moment Wayne stands there—nonplussed. It was probably the first time in his life that he couldn't think of anything to say. Then he looks at the ball for a minute and pumps it like a quarterback. Then he puts the ball under his arm, and the kids break into a cheer, 'Hooray, Hooray.' All the guys joined in. He's still a Trojan."

"Wayne was enjoying himself to the fullest and was even happier when the Trojans hung on for a 10–6 victory," wrote Schrader and Bisheff in *Fight On!*

"He and Cabot headed for the USC locker room. . . . As both parties entered the locker room, McKay, who had been given the game ball for his brilliant play-calling in the final minutes, spotted Wayne."

He tossed him the ball, twenty-five feet away.

"To the greatest Trojan of them all," said McKay.

Wayne was "genuinely touched," raising the ball over his head and leading the team in a "rousing rendition of 'Bless 'em All.'

"Oh, the place was rocking. As Wayne headed for the door with Cabot, he turned around and said, 'Gentlemen, I'm highly honored.'"

"Afterwards, [assistant coach Marv] Goux came in and said wasn't it great, we didn't get anybody 'chipped off,'" recalled Walden. "Well, Wayne and Cabot were somewhere, and someone got in an argument the next morning and their make-up artist was dead of a heart attack. It was confusing, I don't know for sure what all happened. Wayne and all of 'em were out drinking all night and came in at seven in the morning, maybe it was too much for this guy, but this make-up artist died."

"Well," Cabot said, "*we* got somebody 'chipped off.'"

"He talked to the team in the dressing room before and after the game," said Hall. "After the game Duke was in the locker room. He made a little speech. He congratulated the Trojans. At halftime he led yells on the field. He was leading cheers, chanting, 'Hold that line' when Texas mounted a drive. He impressed me completely."

After the game, Wayne and Cabot left for Mexico.

"That night before I left for San Antonio, we were supposed to get together at the Balboa Bay Club, but he never called, it never happened," recalled Hall.

"The only thing I remember anybody saying about that game was that Texas were a bunch of good losers," said John K. McKay, who was in the eighth grade.

After the game, UT had to prepare for rival Texas Tech, while McKay's team was looking at the Wisconsin Badgers in a rematch of the crazy 1963 Rose Bowl. On Monday, the Trojans moved up to fifth in the Associated Press poll.

"We left after the game," said Schwary. "I delivered the game ball to him at Bayshore." Schwary wanted to break into the movie business and asked Wayne if he could help him get a Screen Actors Guild card, which he did.

"He paid the $218 for me to take the assistant director's trainee test. I took the test a year later." From there, Schwary worked his way up until he became one of the most successful producers in Hollywood. He produced the Oscar-winning films *Ordinary People* and *Tootsie* in addition to *Absence of Malice* and *A Soldier's Story* and is currently producing the television show *Medium*.

"I never saw Wayne again," said Ron Yary, who made the 1966 all-American team and in 1967 was a consensus all-American offensive tackle, winner of the Outland Trophy, and the number one pick of the 1968 NFL draft by the Minnesota Vikings. He played fifteen years in the NFL.

"Bud Grant of the Vikings never let us have heaters," he stated.

Yary played in four Super Bowls, was a perennial all-pro and Pro-Bowler, and after his career became a member of both the College and the Pro Football Halls of Fame.

"The decision for me came when Coach John McKay showed me his 1962 national championship ring, and he said what he says to everybody: 'Do you want one of these?' or something like that," recalled linebacker Tim Rossovich.

"Where do I sign?" Rossovich told McKay, like most who heard that line.

After an all-American career at USC, where he roomed with actor Tom Selleck, Rossovich played seven seasons for the Philadelphia Eagles, San Diego Chargers, and Houston Oilers. He became a stuntman-actor, appearing in a number of movies and television shows. He was also considered borderline "crazy," once featured in *Sports Illustrated* eating glass and setting himself on fire. In a story told by author Jim Gigliotti in *Stadium Stories: USC Trojans,* Rossovich swallowed goldfish and drove his sports car onto his fraternity house steps.

"I look back sometimes and think maybe it would have been better to stay on the straight and narrow. But remember, this was the '60s and '70s, and I don't think I ever did anything that was really a problem or embarrassment to the university. It was just hijinks."

Someone had a goldfish, and he ate it. "I thought, 'Okay, that was kind of gross,' but then I drank the water. And then I ate the bowl. It was just one step more to be better. I was just searching for excellence, I guess."

As wild as Rossovich was, Mike Battle might have outdone him.

"Mike Battle was . . . the baddest, toughest dude and nobody was going to be his master," he said. "Marv Goux loved him."

Battle and Rossovich roomed together and would go on trips to the Colorado River and Lake Tahoe, where a fraternity brother owned a cabin and "the kids came from wealthy families," said Battle. "Tim's family had a little money. I didn't have a pot to piss in, but I'd go along for the ride . . .

"I don't know, they had Bill Bradley, Darrell Royal," he said of the 1966 Texas game. "They had a pretty good team. We beat 'em 10–6."

Battle was a sophomore in 1966. After his senior year (1968), he played for the New York Jets.

"I was in Joe Namath's movie and he was shooting a cowboy movie in Tucson, and I went up to him and I shot the s——t with him," he recalled. "I said I was an SC grad and we talked a little bit."

Former Los Angeles Rams star Fred Dryer, Battle's high school teammate in south Los Angeles County, once said he heard Battle was "institutionalized," but as of 2008 and again in 2012, he seemed to be okay.

"Well, Fred has a sense of humor," John McKay replied when told of Dryer's comment in 2000. "I heard Battle was married, but I don't know. I don't really know what was up with Rossovich.

"Once I was called to his dorm because he had 'mooned' some girl, but then I found out the girl mooned him first. Neither one was ever arrested, and they were both fine players."

Linebacker Adrian Young had no "specific memory of a story to relate that may have an interest to readers" regarding John Wayne's involvement that weekend but was deeply affected by his USC experience.

"As a kid from a poor background, you learned so much at USC," he said. "Across the hall from you might be the son of a famous Hollywood entrepreneur, but we were all in it together, we all belonged. It was USC. Sometimes, only people who have been through it can relate to it.

"At USC, you are comfortable around wealth, and you are in an arena where expectations are tremendous. People you live with expect big things from you. You have peers who went through this experience with you, and they all have high expectations . . .

"Marv would give a pep talk, and he'd say that we'll rape, pillage, take no prisoners, steal their confidence, don't let them in our territory."

Young's description of Goux's incendiary pregame speeches, given before *Patton* (1970), again conjure up the notion that John Milius heard of them or maybe even snuck into the room with the band and song girls to hear them personally. He may have influenced Francis Ford Coppola to have George Patton say similar things as Goux, Milius, or John Wayne.

"A lot of USC guys were with Nixon, and many of them went down with Watergate," Young added. "McKay was with you but he kept his distance. He had his reasons. He hired Goux to get involved with guys . . .

"What I liked about McKay was that he did not just think that hard work all week would get us in, but he was sensitive to the team's emotions."

In 1967, Young intercepted four passes in a 24–7 USC victory at South Bend, the first Trojans win at Notre Dame since 1939. He received added headlines because he was actually born in Dublin, Ireland, before coming to Los Angeles at a young age with his family. He played at Bishop Amat High School, where Pat Haden, John K. McKay, John Sciarra, and USC all-American quarterback Paul McDonald also played. After his NFL career ended, he went into investment banking, where he has a thriving business with his sons in the Inland Empire.

"They were rated pretty high and we upset them," said Steve Grady. "They had a quarterback named 'Super Bill' Bradley, and were coached by Darrell Royal, that whole shot. We had a solid ground game and got out of there with a victory.

"Donnie McCall and I were there that year. McCall started against Texas but after the first quarter I went in and played decent, so I started the second half.

"McKay when he wrote his book mentioned my name. He said his system could provide an ordinary tailback with a chance to succeed in the 'student body right.'"

Grady became a schoolteacher in Los Angeles. McCall finished as USC's rushing leader with 560 yards.

"I was lucky to play for two outstanding coaches, Rod Dedeaux and John McKay," said Steve Sogge, also a star catcher on the baseball team. "I learned different things from both of them, and these are life-long lessons on self-worth, my ethic, my confidence."

Other Trojan stars of that era included all-American defensive back Nate Shaw, who played in the Hula Bowl, then two years for the Los Angeles Rams. Tight end Bob Klein went on to stardom with the Rams and Chargers from 1969 to 1979 and is now a top administrator at Saint John's Hospital in Santa Monica, California.

After the game, USC appeared to be in a good position to challenge for the national championship. The next week, they dismantled Wisconsin, 38–3, at the Coliseum. "We were 6–0 until the Miami game, ranked number one," recalled Yary (his memory was faulty; they were number five, the same ranking they held the Monday after beating Texas). "I heard the night before some of us snuck out and goofed around, and we did not play well. We had played Wyoming and their coach said he thought USC was arrogant, and that Miami would beat us."

Some of the Trojans apparently succumbed to the pleasures of South Beach the night before, losing to the Hurricanes, 10–7, at the Orange Bowl. On November 19, they lost to crosstown rival UCLA for the second straight year, 14–7, despite the Bruins playing without their star quarterback, Gary Beban.

"Take the UCLA game," said John K. McKay. "That's a big game, we all want to win it, it's for bragging rights, but in my family, at least for a number of years, that game meant my dad's job, literally. We had to beat them or we'd have to move."

McKay also had this interesting observation, which might be considered anecdotal on the subject of "global warming": "The air quality when I was in school was so bad there were days one side of the Coliseum could hardly see the other. Not anymore. The air is unbelievably cleaner now than it was then. The neighborhood is cleaner and safer. It's a real revitalization."

His father's job was never in jeopardy (after surviving his first two seasons), but in a fifteen-year Hall of Fame career, what happened in the last regular game of the 1966 season remains the worst moment in Coach McKay's football life. Throughout the season, unbeaten, untied Notre Dame, Michigan State, and Alabama vied for the top spot, with the Fighting Irish—probably Coach Ara Parseghian's greatest team—holding on to number one. But Notre Dame tied Michigan State in the famed "Game of the Century" at East Lansing, 10–10. Neither the Irish nor the Spartans were bowl bound because of restrictions, both self-imposed (Notre Dame) and Big Ten–imposed (Michigan State). Alabama, on the other hand, was headed to the Sugar Bowl. Parseghian knew he needed a big win over USC at the Coliseum in the last game of the season to convince voters his team deserved to be national champions.

The Irish destroyed USC, 51–0, the worst loss of McKay's career. Late in the game, the Trojans continued to pass, trying to score instead of just playing out the clock, keeping the score more respectable.

"McKay never admitted his team lost," said Adrian Young, who compared the "lost cause" defeat to the Mel Gibson film *Braveheart.*

McKay respected Notre Dame, the team he rooted for in his Catholic youth, but felt mostly animosity toward UCLA and coach Tommy Prothro. "Ara Parseghian and my dad had more in common," John K. McKay said. "They were good friends." This relationship probably made the loss sting even harder.

"He and Ara Parseghian liked each other, although he got upset when he lost to Notre Dame, 51–0, in 1966," said John Hall. "He said that would never happen again, and it never did."

"When we lost to Notre Dame, 51–0, I told the team to take their showers, that a billion Chinese don't care if we win or lose," McKay said in a 2000 StreetZebra.com article.

"McKay was a real *Dr. Jekyll and Mr. Hyde* personality, but I always respected him after the 1966 Notre Dame game," said Mike Walden. "He lost 51–0. Notre Dame had an All-American named George Goeddeke. He played only one or two games that year; he'd been injured but had earned All-American the previous year. On the last play of the game, Notre Dame sent him in and McKay told players not to block him, to see to it he didn't reinjure himself. After the game, and remember this was the first year of the Cultural Revolution, McKay told the writers that 'a billion Chinese don't give a damn whether we won this game or not' to put it into perspective."

"The next day I got two wires from China asking for the score," joked McKay. "I told the press we'd never lose, 51–0, again, but over time it was changed to 'We'll never lose to Notre Dame again.' We almost never did."

In fact, USC beat the Irish, 24–7, at South Bend en route to McKay's second national championship in 1967. In 1972, USC running back Anthony "A.D." Davis scored six touchdowns as the "greatest team of all time" Trojans beat Notre Dame, 45–23, on their way to his third national championship. In 1974, Davis did it again, earning the moniker "Notre Dame killer" by scoring four touchdowns to lead USC from a 24–0 deficit to a stirring 55–24 win that probably ranks as the greatest moment in Trojan annals. That spurred McKay's fourth title.

McKay left for the NFL after the 1975 season, having lost to Notre Dome only once after the 1966 debacle. In 1978, USC won another national title under coach John Robinson, when Frank Jordan's field goal gave Ronnie Lott and the Trojans a 27–25 win over Joe Montana's Irish. Between 1967 and 1982, USC lost only two games to Notre Dame (both years, the Irish won the national title).

USC played hard in the 1967 Rose Bowl. Unlike Ara Parseghian, who had lain down and "tied one for the Gipper" to preserve his ranking in the 1966 "Game of the Century," USC scored at the end to make it 14–13 in favor of Bob Griese and Purdue. McKay chose to go for two instead of a tie. USC failed, but that's *What It Means to Be a Trojan*, the title of the 2009 book in which "Southern Cal's greatest players talk about Trojans football."

A recruit from City College of San Francisco named Orenthal James Simpson, about to enroll at USC, was at the Rose Bowl and in the dressing room after the game. O.J. told his disappointed future teammates not to worry, that when he arrived they would win the Rose Bowl. USC finished eighteenth in the final United Press International poll.

McKay's tenure at USC is part of a two-decade run (1962–1982) that likely ranks as the greatest dynasty (not to mention overall athletic department dominance) in collegiate football history. Certainly, the early years were propelled in large measure by the opportunities McKay provided for black athletes. His influence would spread throughout the nation and played a major role in changing the land-scape of the game.

Under McKay and Robinson (1976–1982), the Trojans cap-tured five national championships (all legitimately earned with Rose Bowl victories), established dominance against Notre Dame, UCLA, and both Woody Hayes (Ohio State) and Bo Schembechler (Michi-gan) in Pasadena while winning four Heisman Trophies. Told that the USC dynasty was greater than Knute Rockne and Notre Dame (1920s), Howard Jones and USC's Thundering Herd (1930s), Bud Wilkinson and Oklahoma (1950s), Miami (1980s), or Bobby Bowden at Florida State (1990s), McKay simply said, "Well, I guess that's true or close to being true. At least we never had a player go to jail. We did have very good players."

In 1967, a still all-white Texas squad traveled to Los Angeles for a rematch. O.J. established himself as a star while leading USC to a 17–13 win. USC captured the national title that season, and O.J. won the 1968 Heisman Trophy.

When Texas traveled to the Rose Bowl to play Pete Carroll and USC for the 2005 BCS national championship, they were 0–4 all-time versus USC but behind quarterback Vince Young rallied to defeat USC, 41–38, for the title in what most believe was the best college football game ever played.

"Memories of that day in Austin in 1966 came cascading back on January 4, 2006, when the Trojans met Texas at the Rose Bowl with a national championship at stake," wrote Loel Schrader and Steve Bisheff in *Fight On!* "Maybe if the Duke had been there to give the Trojans the Head Man speech . . . well, who knows?"

In 1969, Texas defeated Arkansas, 15–14, in another "Game of the Century." Trailing 14–0 entering the fourth quarter at Fayetteville, Texas scored a touchdown, and Royal—like McKay but unlike Par-seghian—went for two points. Royal needed a win, not a tie, since unbeaten Penn State could have moved into the number one posi-tion with their eventual Orange Bowl win over Missouri. He also had precedent, having failed on a two-point try, also against Arkansas, in a

14–13 loss in 1964 that likely cost his team a repeat national title, giving coach Frank Broyles's Razorbacks the legitimate national championship when Alabama lost to the Longhorns in the Orange Bowl.

In 1969, it worked, making the score 14–8 and setting up a famed fourth-quarter pass from Street to wide receiver Randy Peschel, leading to the winning score in a stirring 15–14 triumph. After the game, President Richard Nixon, who was in attendance, presented the team with a "national championship trophy," to the consternation of unbeaten Penn State Coach Joe Paterno. Vietnam War protestors paraded outside the stadium. Also part of the Nixon entourage that day was J. William Fulbright, a Democratic antiwar senator from Arkansas, and Congressman George H. W. Bush of Texas.

After rallying to defeat Joe Theismann and Notre Dame in the Cotton Bowl, Darrell Royal had his second national championship. The 1969 Longhorns were the last all-white national champions in college football.

Julius Whittier, a freshman ineligible for varsity play that season, became their first African American player in 1970. He played three years, ushering in a new era that included star players like Roosevelt Leaks and Earl Campbell.

"The athletic department became sensitized in dealing with black athletes," said Whittier. "They discovered some of the range of personality, humor, etiquette, social protocol that you see among blacks. [Royal] didn't know everything, but he set the tone about how we were treated."

As author Terry Frei wrote and as Professor Dave Edwards agreed, Royal was not a crusader but also not racist. The black rights organization known as BAD and Arkansas activist Hiram McBeth also won a victory in 1969 when their efforts dissuaded the University of Arkansas band from playing "Dixie" during the "Big Shootout," as the game with Texas was called.

UT football never returned to the full glory of the Royal era until Mack Brown's tenure. The stadium was renamed Darrel K. Royal Texas Memorial Stadium in 1996. Royal passed away a few years ago, his tombstone reading, "He meant well." Both he and McKay are in the Hall of Fame.

On September 24, 1966, John Wayne wrote a letter to John McKay:

Mexico Courts
Durango, Mexico
September 24, 1966

Mr. John McKay
University of Southern California
University Park
Los Angeles, Calif.

Dear John:

I want to thank you and your staff and your whole squad for the wonderful manner in which you made me feel a part of the group.

I shall treasure the football and start using it to train my four-and-a-half year old kid.

I think the Texas bunch were good losers, but tell the squad we don't care whether their opponents are good losers or bad losers as long as they lose.

Good luck for the rest of the season. There'll be two fellows in Mexico rooting all way—Cabot and Wayne.

Fond regards,
John Wayne

POSTSCRIPT

JOHN "DUKE" WAYNE MADE *THE GREEN BERETS* (1968), WHICH UTTERLY infuriated the left. Perhaps just as infuriating was its box office success at the time and continued popularity on television to this day. It was a jingoistic depiction of the Vietnam War, told entirely through Wayne's prism. It was not realistic but in truth was no less realistic than much reporting of the war, which, for instance, used the image of a naked peasant girl as an example of American aggression when in fact she was escaping a communist invasion, perpetuated the fiction that the My Lai massacre was typical of the American experience in Vietnam, and through movies further emphasized that this was as common as Secretary of State John Kerry incorrectly said it was in the early 1970s.

The 2004 presidential election appeared to be a direct refutation of Kerry's Winter Soldier testimony, yet the 2008 Obama election served the opposite effect, seemingly America's "admitting" that its past was indeed sinful and immoral. Now she was begging the black man to forgive her by electing one.

In 1969, just as Hollywood appeared to have turned its back on Wayne's traditional values, he received raves for his Oscar-winning performance in *True Grit*. A parade of adoring liberals like

Barbra Streisand and Jane Fonda genuflected before him as they awarded the Best Actor award to Wayne.

Certainly, Barack Obama would not likely look upon John Wayne as "great," not in the adoring manner of so many other Americans. There is little doubt that if Duke could travel in a time machine, he would be unimpressed with President Obama. This is the great chasm of American culture and politics, the world dominated by Duke Wayne versus Obamanation.

There was a time when no candidate could be elected president unless he either believed or convinced the electorate of his belief in the greatness of Duke Wayne. That time has come and gone. Obama no doubt looks upon the image of Wayne with a certain amount of disdain. Wayne's movie world was Manifest Destiny, great men forging a great country in the American West. Obama would see only genocide against Indians, an extension of the colonialism that his father was raised in and that many argue drives his politics of revenge. In public schools and throughout academia, in popular culture, this view is the overwhelming template today. Only an increasingly silent *minority* (?) holds on to the image of Wayne as a heroic figure.

Above all other cultural divisions in this nation, none so starkly separates the John Wayne fans from his detractors, Barack Obama's liberalism from Ronald Reagan's conservatism, than the Vietnam War. Wayne supported the Vietnam War all the way. He believed it was a test of American honor to stand up to and defeat Godless communism. *America, Why I Love Her* was his response to that chorus of unrelenting voices he viewed as unpatriotic. He believed in their right to dissent, that it had been fought for and won with blood, and expressed such sentiments along with a series of highly patriotic, emotional, and loving tributes to all aspects of traditional Americana, some militaristic.

The Barack Obama wing of America, indeed world politics, would view *America, Why I Love Her* not merely as an anachronism but also as a racist screed glorifying all they consider immoral, unjust, and illegitimate. By extension, if Wayne and his views can be discredited, then the moral authority of the founding fathers and the U.S. Constitution and even the powerful place the United States ascended to by winning two world wars and the Cold War can be discredited. This effort has long been the goal of the left. The real question, to still be resolved over the next century, is which view will prevail.

John Wayne, "God's lonely man," was called by the "Man Upstairs," as Duke called Him, in 1979. Facing death, while his good friend Ronald Reagan was gearing up for what would be a successful 1980 presidential campaign, he gave a last interview.

"I have deep faith that there is a Supreme Being," he said. "There has to be. . . . The fact that He's let me stick around a little longer, certainly goes great with me, and I want to hang around as long as I'm healthy and not in anybody's way." Of death he added, "I don't look forward to it, because, maybe He won't be as nice to me as I think He will, but I think He will."

When his interviewer, Barbara Walters, was pilloried by Gilda Radner on *Saturday Night Live*, Wayne sent her a telegram: "Don't let the bastards get you down." He appeared at the Dorothy Chandler Pavilion for the 1979 Oscar ceremonies, receiving a warm ovation that was really good-bye.

Wayne maintained a strong association with USC until the end, attending celebrity softball games at Dedeaux Field. His biggest guilt was avoiding military service and getting divorced.

"The greatest mistake I ever made was leaving Josie and those kids," he told Mary St. John.

All his children were products of parochial educations. Michael, Patrick, Toni, and Melinda attended Loyola Marymount University. At the encouragement of his kids, he allowed a Catholic priest to administer comfort to him and passed away on June 11, 1979, a Catholic.

"After the death of Grant Withers and Ward Bond . . . though believing in Jesus Christ and God, my father never once went with my mother and me to our Catholic Church, and was skeptical as a rule toward organized religion," recalled Aissa Wayne. "When asked, he used to refer to himself with a grin as a 'Presby-god—neterian.'"

Michael Wayne said his father was a "deeply religious man" with "no formal religion."

A Japanese newspaper greeted Wayne's passing with this headline: "Mr. America passes on." Orange County renamed its airport after John Wayne. Barry Goldwater proposed a special gold medal for Duke. It was approved.

"John Wayne is not just an actor," Maureen O'Hara said. "John Wayne *is* the United States of America."

"No man's lifetime of work has better expressed the land of the free and the home of the brave," said one-time foe-turned-friend Frank Sinatra.

"John Wayne was bigger than life . . . he was more than just a hero."

"It was because of what John Wayne said about what we are and what we can be that his great and deep love of America was returned in full measure," said President Jimmy Carter.

"John Wayne was a unique, magnificent person who met every challenge in his own life and responded to the nation's problems with courage, wisdom and conviction," said former President Gerald Ford.

President Reagan expressed the wish that Wayne could have lived long enough to serve in his cabinet.

Wayne was larger than life. He lived by his words: "A man's got to have a code, a creed to live by, no matter his job."

JOHN WAYNE'S
FILMOGRAPHY

The Shootist (1976), J. B. Books

Rooster Cogburn (1975), Rooster Cogburn

Brannigan (1975), Lieutenant Brannigan

McQ (1974), McQ

Cahill U.S. Marshal (1973), J. D. Cahill

The Train Robbers (1973), Lane

The Cowboys (1972), Wil Andersen

Big Jake (1971), Jacob McCandles

Rio Lobo (1970), Colonel Cord McNally

Chisum (1970), John Chisum

The Undefeated (1969), Colonel John Henry Thomas

True Grit (1969), Rooster Cogburn

Hellfighters (1968), Chance Buckman

The Green Berets (1968), Colonel Mike Kirby

The War Wagon (1967), Taw Jackson

El Dorado (1966), Cole Thornton

Magic Mansion, television series (1966), John Wayne, "Ride 'em Cowboy"

Cast a Giant Shadow (1966), General Mike Randolph

The Sons of Katie Elder (1965), John Elder

In Harm's Way (1965), Captain Rockwell "Rock" Torrey

The Greatest Story Ever Told (1965), centurion at crucifixion

Circus World (1964), Matt Masters

McLintock! (1963), George Washington McLintock

Donovan's Reef (1963), Michael Patrick "Guns" Donovan

How the West Was Won (1962), General William Tecumseh Sherman

Alcoa Premiere, television series (1962), sergeant-umpire in Korea, "Flashing Spikes"

The Longest Day (1962), Lieutenant Colonel Benjamin Vandervoort

Hatari (1962), Sean Mercer

The Man Who Shot Liberty Valance (1962), Tom Doniphon

The Comancheros (1961), Ranger Captain Jake Cutter

Wagon Train, television series (1960), General William Tecumseh Sherman, "The Colter Craven Story"

North to Alaska (1960), Sam McCord

The Alamo (1960), Colonel Davy Crockett

The Horse Soldiers (1959), Colonel John Marlowe

Rio Bravo (1959), Sheriff John T. Chance

The Barbarian and the Geisha (1958), Townsend Harris

I Married a Woman (1958), Leonard (uncredited), John Wayne (uncredited)

Legend of the Lost (1957), Joe January

Jet Pilot (1957), Colonel Jim Shannon

The Wings of Eagles (1957), Frank W. "Spig" Wead

The Searchers (1956), Ethan Edwards

The Conqueror (1956), Temujin, later Genghis Khan

Screen Directors Playhouse, television series (1955), Mike Cronin, "Rookie of the Year"

Blood Alley (1955), Captain Tom Wilder

The Sea Chase (1955), Captain Karl Ehrlich

The High and the Mighty (1954), Dan Roman

Hondo (1953), Hondo Lane

Island in the Sky (1953), Captain Dooley

Trouble along the Way (1953), Steve Aloysius Williams

Three Lives, short (1953), commentator

Big Jim McLain (1952), Jim McLain

The Quiet Man (1952), Sean Thornton

Miracle in Motion, short (1952), narrator

Flying Leathernecks (1951), Major Daniel Xavier Kirby

Operation Pacific (1951), Lieutenant Commander Duke E. Gifford

Rio Grande (1950), Lieutenant Colonel Kirby Yorke

Sands of Iwo Jima (1949), Sergeant John M. Stryker

She Wore a Yellow Ribbon (1949), Captain Nathan Cutting Brittles

The Fighting Kentuckian (1949), John Breen

Wake of the Red Witch (1948), Captain Ralls

3 Godfathers (1948), Robert Marmaduke Hightower

Red River (1948), Thomas Dunson

Fort Apache (1948), Captain Kirby York

Tycoon (1947), Johnny

Angel and the Badman (1947), Quirt Evans

Without Reservations (1946), Rusty

They Were Expendable (1945), Lieutenant (J. G.) "Rusty" Ryan

Dakota (1945), John Devlin

Back to Bataan (1945), Colonel Joseph Madden

Flame of Barbary Coast (1945), Duke Fergus

Tall in the Saddle (1944), Rocklin

The Fighting Seabees (1944), Lieutenant Commander Wedge Donovan

In Old Oklahoma (1943), Daniel F. Somers

A Lady Takes a Chance (1943), Duke Hudkins

Reunion in France (1942), Pat Talbot

Pittsburgh (1942), Pittsburgh Markham

Flying Tigers (1942), Captain Jim Gordon

In Old California (1942), Tom Craig

The Spoilers (1942), Roy Glennister

Reap the Wild Wind (1942), Captain Jack Stuart

Lady for a Night (1942), Jackson Morgan

The Shepherd of the Hills (1941), Young Matt

Lady from Louisiana (1941), John Reynolds

A Man Betrayed (1941), Lynn Hollister

Seven Sinners (1940), Dan

The Long Voyage Home (1940), Olsen

Three Faces West (1940), John Phillips

Dark Command (1940), Bob Seton

Allegheny Uprising (1939), Jim Smith

New Frontier (1939), Stony Brooke

Wyoming Outlaw (1939), Stony Brooke

Three Texas Steers (1939), Stony Brooke

The Night Riders (1939), Stony Brooke

Stagecoach (1939), Ringo Kid

Red River Range (1938), Stony Brooke

Santa Fe Stampede (1938), Stony Brooke

Overland Stage Raiders (1938), Stony Brooke

Pals of the Saddle (1938), Stony Brooke

Born to the West (1937), Dare Rudd

Adventure's End (1937), Duke Slade

Idol of the Crowds (1937), Johnny Hanson

I Cover the War (1937), Bob Adams

California Straight Ahead! (1937), Biff Smith

Conflict (1936), Pat Glendon

Sea Spoilers (1936), Bob Randall

Winds of the Wasteland (1936), John Blair

The Lonely Trail (1936), Captain John Ashley

King of the Pecos (1936), John Clayborn

The Lawless Nineties (1936), John Tipton

The Oregon Trail (1936), Captain John Delmont

Lawless Range (1935), John Middleton

The New Frontier (1935), John Dawson

Westward Ho (1935), John Wyatt

Paradise Canyon (1935), John Wyatt/John Rogers

The Dawn Rider (1935), John Mason

The Desert Trail (1935), John Scott/John Jones

Rainbow Valley (1935), John Martin

Texas Terror (1935), John Higgins

'Neath the Arizona Skies (1934), Chris Morrell

The Lawless Frontier (1934), John Tobin

The Trail Beyond (1934), Rod Drew

The Star Packer (1934), John Travers

Randy Rides Alone (1934), Randy Bowers

The Man from Utah (1934), John Weston

Blue Steel (1934), John Carruthers

West of the Divide (1934), Ted Hayden, aka Gat Ganns

The Lucky Texan (1934), Jerry Mason

Sagebrush Trail (1933), John Brant

College Coach (1933), student greeting Phil (uncredited)

Riders of Destiny (1933), Singin' Sandy Saunders

The Man from Monterey (1933), Captain John Holmes

Baby Face (1933), Jimmy McCoy Jr.

His Private Secretary (1933), Dick Wallace

The Life of Jimmy Dolan (1933), Smith

Somewhere in Sonora (1933), John Bishop

Central Airport (1933), copilot in wreck (uncredited)

The Three Musketeers (1933), Lieutenant Tom Wayne

The Telegraph Trail (1933), John Trent

Haunted Gold (1932), John Mason

The Big Stampede (1932), Deputy Sheriff John Steele

That's My Boy (1932), football player (uncredited)

Ride Him, Cowboy (1932), John Drury

The Hurricane Express (1932), the air pilot

Lady and Gent (1932), Buzz Kinney

Two-Fisted Law (1932), Duke

Texas Cyclone (1932), Steve Pickett

The Shadow of the Eagle (1932), Craig McCoy

Maker of Men (1931), Dusty Rhodes

The Range Feud (1931), Clint Turner

The Deceiver (1931), Richard Thorpe as a corpse

Arizona (1931), Lieutenant Bob Denton

Three Girls Lost (1931), Gordon Wales

Girls Demand Excitement (1931), Peter Brooks

The Big Trail (1930), Breck Coleman

Cheer Up and Smile (1930), Roy (uncredited)

Rough Romance (1930), lumberjack (uncredited)

Born Reckless (1930), extra (uncredited)

Men Without Women (1930), radioman on surface (uncredited)

The Forward Pass (1929), extra (uncredited)

Salute (1929), Midshipman Bill (uncredited)

Words and Music (1929), Pete Donahue (as Duke Morrison)

The Black Watch (1929), 42nd Highlander (uncredited)

Speakeasy (1929), extra (uncredited)

Noah's Ark (1928), flood extra (uncredited)

Hangman's House (1928), horse race spectator (uncredited)/
condemned man in flashback (uncredited)

Four Sons (1928), officer (uncredited)

Mother Machree (1928), extra (uncredited)

The Drop Kick (1927), football player (uncredited)/extra in stands
(uncredited)

Annie Laurie (1927), extra (uncredited)

The Great K & A Train Robbery (1926), extra (uncredited)

Bardelys the Magnificent (1926), guard (uncredited)

Brown of Harvard (1926), Yale football player (uncredited)

BIBLIOGRAPHY

2000 University of Texas Baseball College World Series Baseball Guide. Austin: University of Texas Press, 2000.

2006 Texas Football Media Guide. Austin: University of Texas Press, 2006.

2006 USC Football Media Guide. Los Angeles: University of Southern California Press, 2006.

2009 USC Baseball Media Guide. Los Angeles: University of Southern California Press, 2009.

Alabama Media Guide 2006. Tuscaloosa: University of Alabama Press, 2006.

Acuña, Rodolfo. *Occupied America: A History of Chicanos.* New York: Harper & Row, 1981.

———. *A Community under Siege: A Chronicle of Chicanos East of the Los Angeles River, 1945–1975.* Los Angeles: Chicano Studies Research Center, Publications, University of California, Los Angeles, 1984.

Avila, Eric. *Popular Culture in the Age of White Flight: Fear and Fantasy in Suburban Los Angeles.* Berkeley: University of California Press, 2004.

Barra, Allen. *The Last Coach: A Life of Paul "Bear" Bryant.* New York: Norton, 2005.

Best American Sports Writing of the Century, The. Edited by David Halberstam. Boston: Houghton Mifflin, 1999.

Bisheff, Steve, and Loel Schrader. *Fight On! The Colorful Story of USC Football.* Nashville, TN: Cumberland House, 2006.

Biskind, Peter. *Easy Riders, Raging Bulls: How the Sex-Drugs-and-Rock 'n' Roll Generation Saved Hollywood.* New York: Simon & Schuster, 1998.

Bottles, Scott L. *Los Angeles and the Automobile: The Making of the Modern City.* Berkeley: University of California Press, 1987.

Boyles, Bob, and Paul Guido. *Fifty Years of College Football.* Wilmington, DE: Sideline Communications, 2005.

Chupp, Charles. *The Nth Reader: Neglected Texas History.* Dallas: University of Texas Press, 2003.

Clary, Jack. *College Football's Great Dynasties: USC.* Popular Culture Ink, 1991.

Collier, Gene. "Mitchell's tale still twisting." *Pittsburgh Post-Gazette,* September 2, 2004.

Dalton, Dennis. *Power over People: Classical and Modern Political Theory.* Recorded course from Barnard College at Columbia University, New York. Available at www.teach12.com.

Dettlinger, Chet, and Jeff Prugh. *The List.* Atlanta: Philmay Enterprises, 1984.

Diaz, David R. *Barrio Urbanism: Chicanos, Planning, and American Cities.* New York: Routledge, 2005.

Dunnavant, Keith. *Coach: The Life of Paul "Bear" Bryant.* New York: Simon & Schuster, 1996.

————. *The Missing Ring.* New York: St. Martin's Press, 2006.

Echoes of Notre Dame Football. Edited by John Heisler. Chicago: Triumph Books, 2006.

ESPN College Football Encyclopedia. Edited by Michael MacCambridge. New York: ESPN Books, 2005.

Eyles, Allen. *John Wayne*. Cranbury, NJ: A. S. Barnes, 1976.

Fighting Irish: The Might, the Magic, the Mystique of Notre Dame Football. St. Louis, MO: The Sporting News, 2003.

Florence, Mal. *The Heritage of Troy*. JCP Corp., 1980.

Frei, Terry. *Horns, Hogs, & Nixon Coming: Texas vs. Arkansas in Dixie's Last Stand*. New York: Simon & Schuster, 2002.

Friedman, Kinky. *God Bless John Wayne*. New York: Simon & Schuster, 1995.

Front Page: A Collection of Historical Headlines from the Los Angeles Times *1881–1987*. New York: Harry N. Abrams, 1987.

Katz, Fred. *The Glory of Notre Dame*. Bartholomey House.

Gallagher, John Andrew. *Film Directors on Directing*. Westport, CT: Praeger, 1989.

Game Day: Notre Dame Football. Foreword by Mike Golic. Chicago: Triumph Books, 2006.

Game Day: Southern California Football. Foreword by Manfred Moore. Chicago: Triumph Books, 2006.

Game Day: Texas Football. Foreword by James Street. Chicago: Triumph Books, 2005.

Gigliotti, Jim. *Stadium Stories: USC Trojans*. Guilford, CT: The Globe Pequot Press, 2005.

Gildea, William, and Christopher Jennison. *The Fighting Irish*. Englewood Cliffs, NJ: Prentice Hall, 1976.

Gottlieb, Robert. *The Next Los Angeles: The Struggle for a Livable City*. Berkeley: University of California Press, 2005.

Gottlieb, Robert, and Irene Wolf. *Thinking Big: The Story of the* Los Angeles Times*, Its Publishers, and Their Influence on Southern California*. New York: G. P. Putnam's Sons, 1977.

Groom, Winston. *The Crimson Tide: An Illustrated History of Football at the University of Alabama*. Tuscaloosa: University of Alabama Press, 2000.

Halberstam, David. *The Powers That Be*. New York: Alfred A. Knopf, 1979.

Hickenlooper, George. *Reel Conversations: Candid Interviews with Film's Foremost Directors and Critics.* New York: Citadel Press, 1991.

Hines, Thomas S. "Housing, Baseball, and Creeping Socialism: The Battle of Chavez Ravine, Los Angeles 1949–1959." *Journal of Urban History*, 1982.

Images of Our Times: Sixty Years of Photography from the Los Angeles Times. New York: Harry N. Abrams, 1987.

Jares, Joe, and John Robinson. *Conquest.*

Kahn, Roger. *The Boys of Summer.* New York: Perennial Library, 1987.

Keisser, Bob. "Bam's impact not forgotten." *Long Beach Press-Telegram*, September 12, 2005.

Kline, Sally, ed. *George Lucas.* Jackson: University Press of Mississippi, 1999.

Little, Bill, and Jenna McEachern, eds. *What It Means to Be a Longhorn: Darrell Royal and Mack Brown and Many of Texas' Greatest Players.* Chicago: Triumph Books, 2007.

LeBrock, Barry. *The Trojan Ten.* New York: New American Library, 2006.

Leach, Robert. *Never Make the Same Mistake Once.* Los Angeles: Figueroa Press, 2003.

López, Ronald William. "The Battle for Chavez Ravine: Public Policy and Chicano Community Resistance in Post-war Los Angeles, 1945–1962." PhD diss., University of California, Berkeley, 1999.

Lumpkin, Bill. "USC back wasn't the real key to integration." *Birmingham Post-Herald.*

McBride, Joseph. *Steven Spielberg: A Biography.* New York: Simon & Schuster, 1997.

McCluggage, Matt. *The Construction of Dodger Stadium and the Battle for Chavez Ravine.* PhD diss., Chapman University, 2010.

McCoy-Murray, Linda. *Quotable Jim Murray.* Nashville, TN: Towle-House Publishing, 2003.

McCready, Neal. "Cunningham had impact on 'Bama football." *Mobile Press-Register*, August 2003.

McDougal, Dennis. *Privileged Son. Otis Chandler and the Rise and Fall of the* L.A. Times *Dynasty.* Cambridge, MA: Perseus, 2001.

McKay, John, with Jim Perry. *McKay: A Coach's Story.* New York: Atheneum, 1974.

Mueller, Carol Lea. *The Quotable John Wayne: The Grit and Wisdom of an American Icon.* Lanham, MD: Taylor Trade, 2007.

Munn, Michael. *John Wayne: The Man behind the Myth.* New York: New American Library, 2003.

Murray, Jim. *The Best of Jim Murray.* Garden City, NY: Doubleday, 1965.

———. *The Sporting World of Jim Murray.* Garden City, NY: Doubleday, 1968.

———. "Hatred shut out as Alabama finally joins the Union." *Los Angeles Times,* September 13, 1970.

———. "If You're Expecting One-Liners, Wait, a Column." *Los Angeles Times,* July 1, 1979.

———. *The Jim Murray Collection.* Dallas: Taylor Publishing, 1988.

———. *Jim Murray: An Autobiography.* New York: Macmillan, 1993.

———. *The Last of the Best.* Los Angeles: Los Angeles Times Books, 1998.

———. *The Great Ones.* Los Angeles: Los Angeles Times Books, 1999.

Negrete-White, Charlotte Rebecca. "Power vs. the People of Chávez Ravine: A Study of Their Determination and Fortitude." PhD diss., Claremont Graduate University, 2008.

Nelson, Kevin. *The Golden Game: The Story of California Baseball.* San Francisco: California Historical Society, 2004.

Nyiri, Alan. *The Heritage of USC.* Los Angeles: University of Southern California Press, 1999.

Ordona, Michael. "Director goes for action 40 years into his career." *San Francisco Chronicle,* January 20, 2013.

Paglia, Camille. *Glittering Images: A Journey through Art from Egypt to Star Wars.* New York: Pantheon, 2012.

Pantsov, Alexander, with Stephen I. Levin. *Mao: The Real Story*. New York: Simon & Schuster, 2012.

Parseghian, Ara. *What It Means to Be Fighting Irish*. Chicago: Triumph Books, 2004.

Parson, Donald Craig. *Making a Better World: Public Housing, the Red Scare, and the Direction of Modern Los Angeles*. Minneapolis: University of Minnesota Press, 2005.

Patterson, James T. *The Eve of Destruction*. New York: Basic Books, 2012.

Perry, Jim. "Alabama goes black 'n' white." *Los Angeles Herald-Examiner*, September 11, 1971.

———. "USC loses one of its legends with the death of McKay." *Trojan Tail*, 2001.

Pierson, Don. *The Trojans: Southern California Football*. Chicago: Henry Regnery, 1974.

Prince, Carl E. *Brooklyn's Dodgers: The Bums, the Borough, and the Best of Baseball, 1947–1957*. New York: Oxford University Press, 1997.

Prugh, Jeff. "Trojans fall on Alabama . . ." *Los Angeles Times*, September 13, 1970.

———. "Two black students had enrolled before Wallace showdown." *Los Angeles Times*, June 11, 1978.

———. *The Herschel Walker Story*. New York: Fawcett, 1983.

———. "George Wallace was America's merchant of venom." *Marin Independent Journal*, September 15, 1998.

———. "Anger boiled within Gerald Ford before this football game." *Marin Independent Journal*, August 12, 1999.

Rappoport, Ken. *The Trojans: A Story of Southern California Football*. Huntsville, AL: Strode Publishers, 1974.

Ricci, Mark, Boris Zmijewsky, and Steve Zmijewsky. *The Complete Films of John Wayne*. Seacaucus, NJ: Carol Publishing Group, 1995.

Roberts, Randy, and James S. Olson. *John Wayne: American*. New York: Free Press, 1995.

Salewicz, Chris. *George Lucas Close Up: The Making of His Movies*. New York: Thunder's Mouth Press, 1999.

Sánchez, George J. *Becoming Mexican American: Ethnicity, Culture, and Identity in Chicano Los Angeles, 1900–1945.* New York: Oxford University Press, 1995.

Sarantakes, Nicholas Evan. *Making* Patton*: A Classic War Film's Epic Journey to the Silver Screen.* Lawrence: University Press of Kansas, 2012.

Shapiro, Michael. *The Last Good Season: Brooklyn, the Dodgers, and Their Final Pennant Race Together.* New York: Doubleday, 2003.

Sitton, Tom. *Los Angeles Transformed: Fletcher Bowron's Urban Reform Revival, 1938–1953.* Albuquerque: University of New Mexico Press, 2005.

Smith, Curt. *Pull Up a Chair: The Vin Scully Story.* Dulles, VA: Potomac Books, 2009.

Springer, Steve, and Michael Arkush. *60 Years of USC-UCLA Football.* Stamford, CT: Longmeadow Press, 1991.

Starr, Kevin. *Golden Dreams: California in an Age of Abundance, 1950–1963.* Oxford: Oxford University Press, 2009.

Steele, Michael R. *Knute Rockne: A Portrait of a Notre Dame Legend.* Champaign, IL: Sports Publishing, 1998.

Steinmark, Freddie. *I Play to Win.* Boston: Little, Brown, 1971.

Sullivan, Neil J. *The Dodgers Move West.* New York: Oxford University Press, 1987.

Taylor, Phil. "The Tide gets rolled." *Sports Illustrated,* September 27, 2004.

Travers, Steven. "The tradition of Troy." Unpublished book proposal, 1995.

———. "When legends played." www.streetzebra.com, September 1999.

———. "Legend: A conversation with John McKay." www.streetzebra .com, March 2000.

———. "Rich McKay." www.streetzebra.com, April 2000.

———. "The eternal Trojan." www.streetzebra.com, September 2000.

———. "Villa Park wins rivalry game." *Los Angeles Times,* September 25, 2000.

———. "It wasn't a football game, it was a sighting." www.streetzebra .com November 2000.

———. "He was a legend of the old school variety." Unpublished essay, 2001.

———. *Barry Bonds: Baseball's Superman*. Champaign, IL: Sports Publishing, 2002.

———. "God's country: A conservative, Christian worldview of how history formed the United States Empire and America's Manifest Destiny for the twenty-first century. Unpublished manuscript, 2003.

———. "Dynasty: The new centurions of Troy." Excerpted from *The USC Trojans: College Football's All-Time Greatest Dynasty*. Lanham, MD: Taylor Trade, 2006. (Based on "2005 USC Trojans: Greatest college football dynasty ever?," available at AmericanReporter.com, July 4, 2005.)

———. "Orange Countification: The true story of how the GOP helped the South rise again." Unpublished essay, 2005.

———. "The four horsemen of Southern California." Excerpted from *The USC Trojans: College Football's All-Time Greatest Dynasty*. Lanham, MD: Taylor Trade, 2006.

———. *The USC Trojans: College Football's All-Time Greatest Dynasty*. Lanham, MD: Taylor Trade, 2006.

———. *Angels Essential: Everything You Need to Know to Be a Real Fan!* Chicago: Triumph Books, 2007.

———. *Dodgers Essential: Everything You Need to Know to Be a Real Fan!* Chicago: Triumph Books, 2007.

———. *The Good, the Bad, & the Ugly Los Angeles Lakers: Heart-Pounding, Jaw-Dropping, and Gut-Wrenching Moments from Los Angeles Lakers History*. Chicago: Triumph Books, 2007.

———. *One Night, Two Teams: Alabama vs. USC and the Game That Changed a Nation*. Lanham, MD: Taylor Trade, 2007.

———. *The Good, the Bad, & the Ugly Oakland Raiders: Heart-Pounding, Jaw-Dropping, and Gut-Wrenching Moments from Oakland Raiders History*. Chicago: Triumph Books, 2008.

———. *Trojans Essential: Everything You Need to Know to Be a Real Fan!* Chicago: Triumph Books, 2008.

———. *The 1969 Miracle Mets: The Improbable Story of the World's Greatest Underdog Team.* Guilford, CT: Lyons Press, 2009.

———. *Dodgers Past & Present.* Minneapolis: MVP Books, 2009.

———. *Pigskin Warriors: 140 Years of College Football's Greatest Traditions, Games, and Stars.* Lanham, MD: Taylor Trade, 2009.

———. *A Tale of Three Cities: The 1962 Baseball Season in New York, Los Angeles, and San Francisco.* Washington, DC: Potomac Books, 2009.

———. *What It Means to Be a Trojan: Southern Cal's Greatest Players Talk about Trojans Football.* Chicago: Triumph Books, 2009.

———. *The Poet: The Life and* Los Angeles Times *of Jim Murray.* Washington, DC: Potomac Books, 2012.

Trojan Football Alumni Club Membership Directory. Los Angeles: Trojan Football Alumni Club, 2008.

Wayne, Aissa, with Steve Delsohn. *John Wayne: My Father.* Lanham, MD: Taylor Trade, 1998.

Wayne, Pilar, with Alex Thorleifson. *John Wayne: My Life with the Duke.* New York: McGraw-Hill, 1987.

White, Lonnie. *UCLA vs. USC: 75 Years of the Greatest Rivalry in Sports.* Los Angeles: Los Angeles Times Books, 2004.

Wojciechowski, Gene. "USC setting standard for football dominance." http://sports.espn.go.com/espn/columns/story?columnist= wojciechowski_gene&i%20d=2249925%3E%20&id=2249925, December 6, 2005.

Wonderful World of Sport, The. New York: Time Inc., 1967.

Yaeger, Don, Sam Cunningham, and John Papadakis. *Turning of the Tide.* New York: Center Street, 2006.

Yaeger, Don, and Douglas S. Looney. *Under the Tarnished Dome.* New York: Simon & Schuster, 1993.

Zakaria, Fareed. *The Future of Freedom: Illiberal Democracy at Home and Abroad.* New York: Norton, 2003.

Websites

alydar.com/murray.html

amazon.com/What-Means-Be-Longhorn-Greatest/dp/1572439513
/ref=sr_1_1?s=books&ie=UTF8&qid=1357946871&sr=1-1&key
words=what+it+means+to+be+a+longhorn

articles.latimes.com/keyword/harley-tinkham

articles.latimes.com/1990-07-07/sports/sp-125_1_morning-briefing
-column-tinkham-san-francisco-chronicle

articles.orlandosentinel.com/1990-07-06/news/9007060236_1
_tinkham-sports-trivia-harley

bizpacreview.com/2013/02/21/obama-delusional-in-explaining
-deficit-cuts-51719

blog.hemmings.com/index.php/2011/10/06/texas-rep-selling
-john-waynes-war-wagon-waynemobile-travelall-for-1-million/

blogtalkradio.com/thekneejerks/2010/09/20/the-knee-jerks--detroit
-sports-talk-with-eno-and-b

blogs.ocweekly.com/navelgazing/a-clockwork-orange/john-wayne
-vs-mark-sanchez/boltax.com

classicshowbiz.blogspot.com/2012/09/an-interview-with-ed-asner
.html

cnsnews.com/news/article/having-added-record-59t-debt-obama
-claims-he-s-cut-deficit-25t

cstv.com

dukewayne.com/

ebay.com/itm/RARE-1966-ORIGINAL-CANDID-JOHN-WAYNE
-PHOTOGRAPH-LOT-TEXAS-HEREFORD-ASSOCIATION

en.wikipedia.org/wiki/Bill_Bradley_(American_football)

en.wikipedia.org/wiki/Chris_Gilbert_(American_football)

en.wikipedia.org/wiki/John_Wayne

espn.go.com/college-football/story/_/id/8970293/segregation-led
-star-players-michigan-state-spartans-1960s-college-football

guardian.co.uk/world/2003/aug/01/film.russia

google.com/#hl=en&tbo=d&biw=1024&bih=1087&sclient=psy-ab&
    q=nick+pappas+usc+football&oq=nick+pappas+usc&gs_l=hp
    .1.1.0i30l2.1189.3817.0.6381.15.15.0.0.0.0.263.1827.8j5j2.15.0
    .les%3Bcqn%2Ccconf%3D1-2%2Cmin_length%3D2%2Crate_
    low%3D0-035%2Crate_high%3D0-035%2Csecond
    _pass%3Dfalse%2Cnum_suggestions%3D2%2Cignore_bad
    _origquery%3Dtrue%2Conetoken%3Dfalse..0.0...1c.1.oBatEFqe
    Sek&pbx=1&bav=on.2,or.r_gc.r_pw.r_qf.&fp=7a39aeae8d1a943
    4&bpcl=39580677

facebook.com/amanda.boltax?fref=ts

fanbase.com/photo/1118255

jimmurrayfoundation.com

johnwaynebirthplace.org/museum.html

ibloga.blogspot.com/2010/09/no-remorse-george-soros-worked-as
    -nazi.html

laobserved.com/archive/2008/10/nation_mourns_for_morning
    .php

laobserved.com/sports/2007/09/roadtripping_with_jim_murray
    .php

latimesblogs.latimes.com/thedailymirror/jim-murray/

latimesblogs.latimes.com/thedailymirror/2010/03/jim-murray
    -march-13-1980.html#more

mackbrown-texasfootball.com/sports/m-footbl/spec-rel/all-time
    -results.html

mackbrown-texasfootball.com/sports/m-footbl/spec-rel/080901
    aab.html

mackbrown-texasfootball.com/sports/m-footbl/spec-rel/roster-1966
    .html

news.bbc.co.uk/2/hi/americas/3114963.stm

redroom.com/member/steven-robert-travers/books/what-it-means
    -to-be-a-trojan-southern-cals-greatest-players-talkgoo

rolltide.com

route66news.com/2008/08/27/john-wayne-memorabilia-displayed
    -at-williams-museum/

snopes.com/movies/actors/clarabow.asp

sports.espn.go.com/los-angeles/news/story?id=5466960

sportsillustrated.cnn.com/vault/article/magazine/MAG1064748
    /1/index.htm

sportsjournalists.com/forum/index.php?topic=45896.35;wap2

tidesports.com/article/20100107/NEWS/100109720?p=6&tc=pg

trojanreport.com

usatoday30.usatoday.com/travel/destinations/2008-04-03-john
    -wayne-museum_N.htm

usc.247sports.com/

usc.edu/uscnews/stories/15465.html

uscfootball.blogspot.com

usctrojans.com

usctrojans.com/blog/2011/07/mr-trojan.html

usctrojans.com/blog/2010/09/the-duke.html

usctrojans.com/genrel/usc-specrel03.html

youtube.com/watch?v=VblzgPhGj-4

wearesc.com

DVDs

John Wayne: The Duke. Mill Creek Entertainment, 2010.

John Wayne: The Duke Collection. TUTM Entertainment, 2009.

INDEX